TO THE ACTOR

"Just practicing, even superficially, the first nine exercises in *To the Actor*, you can find a satisfaction – a living beauty in you . . . Chekhov reminds us what a great feast life can be."
Anthony Quinn

"You have to teach yourself to act but Michael Chekhov will give you the necessary tools – and for me, Psychological Gesture and Centers are extremely valuable . . . They work like a charm. I've used them all along and still do."
Clint Eastwood

"While my mother and sister were hiding in the dark and kind of watching me, ya know, hoping I was going to be in the movie business, I turned around and imagined I saw my director making fun of my newly acquired Psychological Gesture from Michael Chekhov."
Jack Nicholson, at the 1998 Golden Globe awards (speaking about his first job).

". . . There's this need to continue growth; to expand. For me, Chekhov's system is the most complete."
Robert Davi, interviewed on the set of his TV series, 'The Profiler'.

". . . with Michael Chekhov acting became more than a profession to me. It became a sort of religion."
Marilyn Monroe, from her book, *My Story*.

"I like to physicalize. I like to talk about Michael Chekhov – Psychological Gesture."
Sir Anthony Hopkins, from his 'Inside the Actor's Studio' interview, seen on the Bravo network.

TO THE ACTOR

Michael Chekhov

Routledge
Taylor & Francis Group

LONDON AND NEW YORK

First published in America 1953 by Harper & Row, New York

This edition first published 2002
by Routledge
2 Park Square, Milton Park, Abingdon, Oxon OX14 4RN

Simultaneously published in the USA and Canada
by Routledge
270 Madison Ave, New York, NY 10016

Reprinted 2003 (three times), 2004, 2005 (twice), 2006 (twice), 2007

Routledge is an imprint of the Taylor & Francis Group, an informa business

Typeset in Garamond by RefineCatch Limited, Bungay, Suffolk
Printed and bound in Great Britain by
TJ International Ltd, Padstow, Cornwall

British Library Cataloguing in Publication Data
A catalogue record for this book is available from the British Library

Library of Congress Cataloging in Publication Data
A catalog record for this book has been requested

ISBN10: 0–415–25875–8 Hbk
ISBN10: 0–415–25876–6 Pbk

ISBN13: 978–0–415–25875–3 Hbk
ISBN13: 978–0–415–25876–0 Pbk

20 04004 766

To George Shdanoff –
who shared with me the strenuous work, excitement and joys of the Chekhov Theater. His directorial ability and pedagogic experiments with the principles of the method I introduce in this book were stimulating influences.

This new publication of To the Actor
is dedicated to the memory of
Beatrice Straight (1918–2001)
With admiration and thanks for her all-important role in the original creation of this book.

CONTENTS

CONTRIBUTORS

Mala Powers, author of the article, *The Past, Present and Future of Michael Chekhov*, studied extensively with Chekhov during the last six years of his life and is the executrix of his literary estate. As an actress, she has starred on Broadway, in numerous television productions and in more than 26 films, including her memorable portayal of Roxanne in *Cyrano de Bergerac* opposite José Ferrer. She also teaches master classes in the Chekhov technique and produced, for Applause Theatre Books, the Audio-cassette-package, *Michael Chekhov: On Theatre and the Art of Acting*. A Walk of Fame honoree, she resides in North Hollywood, California.

Andrei Malaev-Babel, holds an MFA from the renowned Schukin School of the Vaktangov Theatre in Moscow. He co-founded Moscow Theatre Forms Theatre, one of Russia's first private repertory companies. He has served on the faculty of The Catholic University of America, and currently teaches and directs at the yearly *International Michael Chekhov Conference*. Mr Malaev-Babel is co-founder and producing artistic director of *The Stanislavsky Theater Studio*, an award winning repertory company and school in Washington DC. He is the recipient of the 2000 Helen Hayes Award Nomination for Outstanding Direction.

Mr. Malaev-Babel would like to acknowledge the following individuals for their invaluable help, advice and inspiration in creation of the Appendix: Mala Powers, Joanna Merlin, Pu-Mei Leng of *Neodesign*, Steven Eveland and Lisa Eveland Malaev.

Nicolai Remisoff (Illustrator – 1884, St. Petersburg – 1975, California), achieved fame in Russia, under the pseudonym "Re-my". He founded and served as principle contributor for the magazines, *Satiricon* and *Novy Satiricon*. After leaving Russia in the 1920s, Remisoff was set designer for Balieff's cabaret troupe *Chauve-Souris* (Paris/New York), set and costume designer for Max Reinhardt's American production of *Faust*, and Art Director and Production Designer for 31 movies, including *Of Mice and Men* (Hollywood, 1939). He also designed the set and costumes for Michael Chekhov's 1946 production of Gogol's *Inspector General* at *The Actor's Lab* in Los Angeles.

FOREWORD

At the beginning of the twenty-first century, we are in the throes of a crisis in theatre acting. It is clearly not a crisis in talent: actors are as eager, as gifted, as attractive as they have ever been – perhaps more so. The stars are younger, their bodies are in better condition, they apply themselves energetically to all the physical aspects of the job. But something isn't happening. Audiences feel it; actors feel it. Disappointment is in the air. The theatre isn't delivering. Audiences over a certain age start to rumble about the Golden Age when actors were really *actors*, while actors for their part start to complain about the declining quality of audiences. All sorts of other theatre experiences become more interesting than those which focus on acting: the musical theatre, for example, with its combination of spectacle, noise, rhythm, and sheer energy, which can, properly manipulated, whip an audience up into a state of frenetic excitement; or what is called physical theatre – as if theatre, in which the word is made flesh, could be anything other than physical! – which brings elements of dance, of acrobatics, of circus into play, taking the spotlight away from language and from character and into the realm of choreography. The search for new forms of theatre never ceases. What is curious is that no one ever discusses acting in this context.

The last time there was a full debate about acting in the British theatre was in the late 1950s and early 1960s of the last century, and it may be interesting to consider what came out of it. The debate was provoked by the revolution in playwriting at the Royal Court Theatre, which led to an urgent demand for new kinds of acting. The old guard of actors, whether suave exponents of drawing room comedy, or high priests and priestesses of the classics (often they were the same people), had dominated the post-war theatre and were now denounced as bourgeois, individualist, elitist, shallow, technical. Where were the new actors for the new plays? They were there, waiting in the wings, ready to swing into action, the generation famously trained by John Fernald at the RADA: working class, regional, feisty, real. For a while they and their mentors – the firebrand, mostly left-wing directors of the epoch – plunged into a heady exploration of the possibilities of acting. Sometimes from aesthetic, sometimes from political perspectives they investigated mask work, improvisation, theatre games; they embraced the theories of Bertolt Brecht. Occasionally they threw a loving glance sideways to the pioneering work of Joan Littlewood at Theatre Workshop in the East End of London. With her unique mix of theory and sheer bloody-mindedness, she had offered an approach both to new plays and to the classics which was almost medieval in its vitality and impudence and demanded of her actors a kind of magnificent rough poetry.

In the early 1960s, some of the results of this exploratory work passed into the mainstream of the theatre; both Olivier at the newly-created National Theatre at the Old Vic and Peter Hall at the Royal Shakespeare Company he had formed slightly earlier absorbed the work of these directors and actors. Every so often these companies would present a piece of truly experimental acting – like, for instance, Robert Stephen's electrifying performance of the Sun-God Attahualpa in Peter Shaffer's *The Royal Hunt of the Sun*, or Ian Richardson's Herald in *The Marat/Sade* – but the dust soon settled, and a consensus began to emerge, a sort of new realism: an unvarnished, unsentimental manner in which real life could be credibly presented, in plays both modern and classical. Above all, this approach eschewed theatricality. Any sense that actors were unusual or exceptional human beings was rejected. The job of actors was now to be as like their audience, or their hoped-for audience, as possible: the man on the stage was now the man on the street.

What the revolution had really achieved was the absolute

dominance of the director. Experiment became centred on design and *concept*, both under the control of the director. The actor's creative imagination – his fantasy, his instinct for gesture – was of no interest; all the creative imagining had already been done by the director and the designer. The best that an actor could do was to bring himself or herself to the stage and simply be. Actors, accepting the new rules, resigned themselves to serving the needs of the playwright as expressed by his representative on earth, the director. Of course they rebelled against this; they started to sneak amusing and charming and original elements into their work. But they had lost control of their own performances. And so they started to desert the theatre. The financial rewards could never compare with those of television or film; if there were to be no creative rewards, what was the point? It seemed like very hard work for very little return. Most of the celebrated actors of the recent revolutionary period disappeared into film. They came back again, from time to time, on a visit, but the theatre had ceased to be their natural habitat. It wasn't just a question of fame or money: the stage had become unexciting to them. They were simply not getting the response from their audiences. They were not satisfied by an activity which now had neither the grandeur, the glamour or the sense of heightened emotional power of the old school, which had engendered such intense energies in the auditorium, often taking the experience into the realm of the primal. Audiences felt this too. Despite the frequently challenging and inventive work of the dramatists, the designers and the directors, the contribution of the actors – what might be called the acting enterprise – was circumscribed. It was all very rational and objective and credible, but it was not markedly different from what was readily – and more cheaply – available in the cinema or on the television.

The older actors – that fabled generation of Evans and Ashcroft, Olivier, Gielgud, and Richardson, Redgrave, Guinness – never gave up, of course. They continued more or less unreformed, despite exposure – in the case of Olivier and Ashcroft – to the Royal Court during its fervent years; Gielgud and Richardson, in particular, became much loved as they ventured in extreme old age into plays by David Storey and Harold Pinter. But there was a clear shared sense that no one was going to replace these living national treasures: we were watching a gorgeous sunset without hope of a repeat. It was not the individuals that were dying, it was an entire view of acting and of actors. Above all what was disappearing was the idea that the actor was at the centre of the event; that his or her contribution was the core of the experience. Actors started to become embarrassed by their job; anyone who had the temerity to talk in public about the complex processes involved in acting, or to suggest that acting might be a great and important art, was remorselessly mocked. The phrase *luvvie* was invented by the British press to put actors in their place. Only those who claimed that there was no more to acting than learning the lines and avoiding the furniture were accorded any respect.

The roots of these developments are deep, and it is here that we need to mention the name of Konstantin Stanislavsky, a towering figure in the history of twentieth-century theatre, who – sometimes directly, sometimes more obliquely – has profoundly influenced attitudes towards acting. Stanislavsky's thinking about acting was a response firstly to the sloppy, lazy, formulaic work of much of the Russian theatre of the 1880s and 1890s, and secondly to what he perceived to be his own shortcomings as an actor, notably self-consciousness and narcissism. He sought to establish the job of acting as a properly structured activity in his work with his fellow amateurs, raising theatre standards to new heights. In time, with the playwright and director Vladimir Nemirovich-Danchenko, he founded a professional company, the Moscow Art Theatre, which consolidated the process. Stanislavsky was also deeply concerned to advance the art of acting itself, seeking to establish the conditions necessary for what he called creative acting. To do so, he studied the work of actors he admired and began to extrapolate theories from his observations. Little by little he formed a corpus of exercises and analysis which came to be known as the Stanislavsky system, the central tenets of which are brilliantly simple and convincing. In the theory of actions, he proposes that a play consists of a series of interlocking actions, or objectives, out of which the actor's path through the play is constructed; in the theory of emotional memory, he maintains that the actor finds the truth of the role by using his own experiences, thus achieving a life-like as opposed to a merely theatrical performance. These two ideas, most potently expressed in question form – What do I want? and Who am I? – formed a powerful tool for combating what Stanislavsky defined as the actor's worst pitfall: acting *in general*.

Stanislavsky had a naturally restless intellect and these simple formulations satisfied him for only a short time; striving to clarify, expand, diversify and enrich his system to accommodate his developing insights, he doggedly continued his quest for the key to acting until his dying day. Meanwhile, some of his earliest pupils, like Richard Boleslavsky and Maria Ouspenskaya, had left him at this formative stage, spreading the word in its most elementary form, particularly in America, where a technique rooted in emotional experience and deterministic action was eagerly received. The British theatre, too, though less susceptible, in its pragmatic way, to grand theories, quietly acknowledged that here was a way to reform the outmoded gestures and vocal mannerisms of the late Victorians and Edwardians, but also to counter the reliance on mere personality. The drama schools began to teach Stanislavskian precepts in simplified form, and this began to filter through to the theatre in general. From the 1920s, the Moscow Art Theatre, toured the West and astonished audiences with the detailed realism and emotional depth of its productions. The influence of Stanislavsky's ideas grew and grew. Like Freud's psychological theories, they swiftly established themselves as part of the common wisdom, passing into general currency among the population as much as among the profession, and they have since held sway in more or less diluted form in the theatre practice of the English-speaking world. All actors now aspire to give emotionally truthful, many-layered performances based on observation, utilising the raw material of their own lives; they aim above all for credibility. Whether they approach their roles from the inside out, or from the outside in, to use a familiar distinction, the desired end result is always the same: the recognisable truth. What else is there?

In Russia, the progress of Stanislavsky's ideas had taken a somewhat different path. Initially, his colleagues in the Moscow Art Theatre resisted the idea of his System, but bit by bit he wooed them – *bribed* them, in some cases, with the promise of this role or that – into accepting it. He never became popular with the established actors, nor with the ever-sceptical Nemirovich-Danchenko, who finally sidelined his partner into running the Studio Theatre and School. Out of this institution emerged an extraordinary group of young actor-theorists who swallowed Stanislavsky's ideas whole and then spat them out again in radically different form. Meyerhold and Vakhtangov rapidly evolved into radical directors, as different from each other as they were from Stanislavsky, while Mikhail Chekhov (nephew of the dramatist), who had come to the Moscow Art Theatre when he was already a well-known actor at the Maly Theatre in St Petersburg, gave a series of performances for the Studio of startling originality. Stanislavsky unreservedly acknowledged him as the most gifted actor with whom he had ever worked, although at a certain point he dismissed him from his classes on account of his "overheated imagination." Together they achieved an enormous success with Stanislavsky's production of *The Government Inspector*, in which Chekhov endowed the central character with mystical and bizarre elements, underlined by a design of grotesque menace. But despite this happy collaboration, it was clear that they had radically different views about acting. In a sense, Chekhov – intuitive, audacious, infinitely flexible, apparently able to transform himself into any shape he desired – was the actor the careful, cautious Stanislavsky had always dreamed of being. He was also terrifyingly volatile in his private life, alcoholic, paranoiac, wholly unpredictable. But he too was on a quest of his own quite as urgent as Stanislavsky's, first of all to discover meaning for himself in his own life, then to understand the source of his art.

Groping towards this meaning and that understanding, Chekhov immersed himself first in the study of yoga, then in the Anthroposophical works of Rudolf Steiner. He started to teach and to direct; in time he became the director of the Second Moscow Art Theatre School. His formulations were fundamentally different to Stanislavsky's. Their "idealistic" and "mystical" dimension caused violent opposition from some of his actors and from the state authorities; by now the first fine frenzy of the Russian Revolution, which had initially encouraged experiment and radicalism of every kind, had ossified bureaucracy which defined art in strictly political terms. Eventually, denounced as a "sick artist", Chekhov was driven from Russia and commenced the life-long odyssey during the course of which he sometimes seemed to be pursued, Orestes-like, by unrelenting Fates. From Riga to Berlin, from Paris to Dartington, from Connecticut to New York he moved. Time and again war, civil and global, forced him and his successive schools and companies into ever more distant hiding places, until he finally ended up in Hollywood, where he continued to teach, giving, before his early death, half-a-dozen charming cameo performances in various movies, among them *Spellbound*, for which he was nominated for an Academy Award.

Chekhov encapsulated his teaching in various publications over the years, culminating in the appearance of the present volume, *To the Actor*, which contains the essence of his working method. Another, more elaborate version of the same book has recently appeared under the title of *On the Technique of Acting*. The complex relationship of the two books to one another is described in Deirdre Du Hurst Prey's Introduction to the latter; both are indispensable handbooks, providing a detailed and practical guide to Chekhov's work. They were not, however, his first books. While he was still in Russia, he had described his early life and the development of his ideas in *The Path of the Actor*; and after he arrived in America he made another, even more visionary version of the same journey in *Life and Encounters*. These earlier works of spiritual and artistic autobiography convey the pressure out of which his ideas grew, vividly portraying Chekhov's frustration with what he perceived to be the unnecessary limitations and inhibitions which cramp and ultimately destroy actors' creativity. Many of these limitations and inhibitions seemed to Chekhov to stem directly from Stanislavsky's System.

Chekhov revered Stanislavsky, as anyone who cares about acting must, both as a man, and for his deeply sincere life-long quest to discover the laws of acting. But Chekhov's conception of acting was as different from the older man's as were their personalities. Stanislavsky's deep seriousness, his doggedness, his sense of personal guilt, his essentially partriarchal nature, his need for control, his suspicion of instinct, all found their expression in his System. At core, Stanislavsky did not trust actors or their impulses, believing that unless they were carefully monitored by themselves and by their teachers and directors, they would lapse into grotesque overacting or mere mechanical repetition. Chekhov believed, on the contrary, that the more actors trusted themselves and were trusted, the more extraordinary the work they would produce. For him, the child playing in front of his nanny, improvising wildly, generating emotions with easy spontaneity, changing shape according to the impulses of his fantasy, was the paradigm of the actor. Stanislavsky was unable to look back on his own childish efforts without embarrassment. Stanislavsky believed that the only acceptable truth in acting was to be found within the actor's own experience, whereas Chekhov was profoundly convinced that the imagination was the key to all art. Acting, he said, should never be autobiographical; constant recourse to one's own experience would lead, he said, to "degeneration of talent." The imagination, once engaged, never lost its freshness and power, but the limited pool of individual experience quickly stagnated. The actor's work on himself should focus on encouraging and liberating his imagination, by consciously inventing and fantasising, rather than by dredging the subconscious. For Chekhov, fairy tales were the ideal material for his teaching: all plays, in his view, aspired to the condition of fairy tales.

As far as the text was concerned, Chekhov had an almost mystical relationship to language, crystallised by his exposure to Steiner's Eurhythmy. He insisted on the vital importance of sound, of the vibrations which were released within the actor and within the audience by the consonants and vowels themselves. Stanislavsky had a very different approach. Interestingly, he was what we would now describe as severely dyslexic, and always sought the subtext, the emotional life behind the words, rather than engaging with the words themselves, which he was notoriously given to paraphrasing. As for character, Stanislavsky believed it had to be constructed painstakingly, detail by detail. This was anathema to Chekhov. "They call this work", he wrote in *The Path of the Actor*. "It is indeed work, it is tormenting and difficult – but unnecessary. The actor's work is to a significant extent a matter of waiting and being silent 'without working.'" To him the all-important prerequisite for acting was "a sense of the whole." In a parallel characteristically drawn from the natural world, he believed that a character was like a seed which contained the whole future life of the plant within it. If you grasped one phrase, one gesture, of the character you had access to all the rest; everything would fall harmoniously into place. Here was the origin of his famous "psychological gesture", the embodied essence of the character, a transforming and liberating principle of being which awakes the character into instant and complete life, and which then proliferates into a thousand details which spontaneously and harmoniously evolve. Stanislavsky believed that the actor must be wholly immersed in his character, who becomes a second "I." Chekhov, rather, believed that in a successful performance, the actor was always watching his character, moved by him, but never "violating his personal emotions." This *standing apart*, he said, "enabled me to approach that state whereby the artist purifies and ennobles the character he is playing, keeping him free from irrelevant aspects of his own personality."

Finally, and most significantly, Chekhov increasingly believed that the core of the theatrical event was to be found in the actor's relationship with his audience. For Stanislavsky, the audience was both intimidating and corrupting; he feared what he called "the black hole of the auditorium", but even worse he feared his own desire to pander to the audience. To solve this problem he erected the notorious imaginary Fourth Wall. Chekhov saw it differently. It was vital, he said, to engage with what he called "the will of the auditorium", to reach out to each member of the audience and share the creative act with him or her. "I understood that members of the audience have the right to influence the actor during a performance and that the actor should not prevent this." He spoke, mystically, of the actor *sacrificing* himself to the audience.

Stanislavsky's noble work has served its purpose; but it is Chekhov, it seems to me, who speaks to the crisis in our theatres. Audiences feel neglected. They are offered more or less naturalistic work which engages neither their imagination nor that of the actors. Prophetically, Chekhov wrote of naturalism: "The legacy that naturalism will leave behind it will be a coarsened and nervously disordered audience that has lost its artistic taste; and much time will be needed *to restore it to health*." He says that it breeds the necessity "of giving its audiences a series of 'powerful sensations' capable of arousing shock through a chain of pathological effects." Since actors no longer think of themselves as creative artists they have lost their self-respect. To be mere interpreters of the written word is not enough for them, or for their public, though it may be enough for some writers and directors. This is why the public increasingly turns to what is called "performance art", as if the theatre was not by absolute definition a performance art – as if the work of performance artists was expressive and imaginative, but that Marlowe, Ibsen, O'Casey, David Hare, required mere photographic realism. It is particularly absurd to attempt to perform the classics with a naturalistic technique, the very idea of which would have been inconceivable to a writer of the Elizabethan period: in the admirable epigram of the Shakespeare scholar Graham Holderness, "an actor playing naturalistically in an inn-yard is likely to be confused with a waiter."

Michael Chekhov was a highly individual artist, and it would be wholly inappropriate to hope for a generation of Michael Chekhovs. On the contrary, the central purpose of his teaching is to encourage the actor's respect for his or her own imagination and the freedom to create from it. It opens up the possibility of a full and reciprocal relationship with the audience, who can once again be introduced to the idea that actors provide them not with photographic facsimiles of life, but with works of art in which the actors' voices, their bodies and their souls are the medium for the production of unforgettable, heightened creations. In the past, when Ballet dancers originated roles, they would speak of them as "creations." "Every single performance that we give as actors should be of the same order," as Charles Laughton, an actor much after Michael Chekhov's own heart, said:

> Great acting is like painting. In the great masters of fine art one can see and recognise the small gesture of a finger, the turn of a

head, the vitriolic stare, the glazed eye, the pompous mouth, the back bending under a fearful load. In every swerve and stroke of a painter's brush, there is an abundance of life. Great artists reveal the god in man; and every character an actor plays must be this sort of creation. Not imitation – that is merely caricature – and any fool can be a mimic! But creation is a secret. The better – the truer – the creation, the more it will resemble a great painter's immortal work.

The possibilities are limitless, far beyond the demands of naturalism. Why should the art of the theatre be more restricted in genre than any other? In my first book, *Being an Actor*, I called for Cubist acting, Impressionistic acting, Secessionist acting (I said we perhaps had already had enough of Mannerist acting). Just as each of these painterly genres enriches truth's vocabulary, so might these different modes of acting.

All our lives in the theatre we have heard this maxim: LESS IS MORE. Most of the recent great explorations of acting – Brecht, Brook, Grotowski – have been directed towards this LESS: stripping back. But very often less is simply less, and more is actually MORE. We must overcome our fear of the theatre theatrical when it comes to acting. A theatre is where we are. The theatre is the place where extraordinary things happen, where you see people behaving, not as they do on the street, but as they might do in your dreams. Or your nightmares. When the shaman does his dance, nobody says: could you do a little less, please. When the great comedians, the great clowns walk on stage, we know we are in the presence of something else, something well-known to us but outside of our experience. At the very least an actor should, as the great Irish actor, Michaél macLiammoír used to say, "displace air." But he should also transform the energy in the auditorium; he should invade the collective unconscious of the audience and bring them up short. He should not merely quite interest them, or quite amuse them. He should brand himself on their souls, breaking down the prison walls of logic. This used to be the job of actors, and of clowns. As Michael Chekhov would say, it requires a certain openness to the great forces of the universe to attempt it.

This is not an impossible dream. We have seen this sort of work within our own lifetime, and on mainstream stages. When Ralph Richardson (another actor of whom Chekhov would warmly have approved) played John Gabriel Borkman at the National Theatre in the mid-1970s, in the visionary final scene when Borkman, nearing the end of his life, gazes down upon the docks, surveying the great world of capital to which he has sacrificed his soul, a noise escaped Richardson's lips that was like the hoot of an owl or the klaxon of some tiny tugboat negotiating the waters of Hades: *woo woo woo woo*. Nobody who heard it will ever forget it. It was unmistakably the sound of a soul escaping from the body. After the performance, I rushed home to find out what stage direction of Ibsen's had provoked this unearthly utterance, but there was nothing; nothing at all. I asked Peter Hall, who directed the play, whose idea it had been. "Ralph's." "And what did you say when he first did it in rehearsal?" "Nothing. We just knew that it was absolutely right." The supremely rational Hall, directing a play by the great realist, Ibsen, acknowledged that instinctive genius can fulfil the play's potential in a way that logical solutions are unable to supply.

Film and television will perfectly satisfy the demand for realism. It is only when the need for something which goes further is felt that people have recourse to the theatre, an inherently poetic medium. Actor-poets are what the theatre as a unique art form needs. Why else bother to go to the theatre? The profound importance of Chekhov's work – he would have hesitated to call it a system – is that its aim is to breed just such a race of actor-poets. The beauty of his approach is that he offers a direct route to the actor's creativity by the simplest of means. Stanislavsky's anxiety about his own lack of creativity, his insistence that what Chekhov called "inspired" acting was only available to the very few preternaturally gifted ones (of whom he did not consider himself one), and that only a cautious, logical method will pay dividends, is replaced by Chekhov's faith in the naturalness of the acting instinct, his conviction that if left untampered with, it will soar into the zones of human experience to which only the imagination has access. Using his work won't necessarily make you a great actor, but you will be approaching acting as an artist.

Simon Callow
October 2001

THE PAST, PRESENT AND FUTURE OF MICHAEL CHEKHOV

The basis for any true art is our ability to live consciously or unconsciously in the World of Imaginations.

The twentieth century was by no means lacking in geniuses. Most of the famous ones, particularly in the arts, were men and women who had their fingers on the pulse of their own immediate time. A few, however, had their fingers on the pulse of the future. Indeed, such a genius was Michael Chekhov.

Throughout his lifetime, Mischa, as he was called by friends and colleagues, was concerned with preparing for an *Ideal Theater of the Future*. He envisioned the time when Theater,[1] in addition to entertaining, would be the major influence of bringing positive, healing enlightenment to our entire world culture. *Chekhov believed that it is the actors who will determine what the Future Theater will be.*

Now, in this twenty-first century there is a burgeoning interest in applying the Theater Techniques originally given to us by Michael Chekhov. Recently, Academy Award-winning actors, Sir Anthony Hopkins, Clint Eastwood, Jack Nicholson, Helen Hunt, Anthony Quinn and Marisa Tomei spoke of choosing and using Centers or Psychological Gestures, two of Michael Chekhov's innovative Techniques for embodying the essence of a character.

James Lipton, the Producer Host of *Inside the Actors Studio* and Dean of The Actors Studio Drama School of New School University says,

> We have devoted ourselves to the exploration of all the tributaries that make up the influential stream called the Stanislavsky System. One of the most important of those tributaries is the work of Michael Chekhov. This new publication of *To the Actor*

should be welcomed by all of us with one of the most universal of Psychological Gestures – open arms.

Stella Adler, a brilliant actress, an original member of the Group Theater and Founder of the Stella Adler Conservatory of Acting, said that she considered Michael Chekhov the greatest actor of the twentieth century.

Harold Clurman, a seminal figure in the American Theater – Director, Author and Founder of the Group Theater – wrote of Michael Chekhov,

> Through him we learn once more that we have but to watch any moment of concentrated behavior to be fascinated. The smallest action thoroughly carried out seems to contain a kind of universal essence. This, in little, is the mystery of acting.

When interviewed for his book *On Acting*, Sanford Meisner, Director of New York's Neighborhood Playhouse said,

> . . . [it was] Michael Chekhov who made me realize that truth, as in naturalism, was far from the whole truth. In him I witnessed exciting theatrical form with no loss of inner content, and I knew I wanted this too.

When so many artists of this caliber find Chekhov's teachings so valuable, one may wonder why these Techniques are not an integral part of every actor's training. During the last twenty years of his life, Michael Chekhov lived first in England and then in the United States. Although the host of well-known actors and directors who attended his lectures and classes are too numerous to mention, Chekhov never had a knack for promoting himself or the Actor Training Techniques he developed. He never advertised nor traded on the names of those whom he coached or worked with; not even those who were Oscar, Emmy or Tony Award winners – among them, Gary Cooper, Gregory Peck, Patricia Neal, Yul Brynner, Beatrice Straight, Jack Palance, Jennifer Jones, Thomas Mitchell and Arthur Kennedy. All of them have either spoken glowingly about him or have written of their experiences with using the Chekhov Techniques.

In her book, *My Story*, Marilyn Monroe wrote,

> As Michael's pupil, I learned more than acting. . . . Every time he spoke, the world seemed to become bigger and more exciting. . . . Acting became . . . an art that increased your life and mind. I had always loved acting and tried hard to learn it. But with Michael Chekhov acting became more than a profession to me. It became a sort of religion.

Today, many young actors are finding that the training methods they have been exposed to do not fully prepare them for present stage and film requirements and conditions. Adequate rehearsal time is certainly the exception rather than the rule and the demand on the actor is not only to "feel it" but to "feel it" *right now!* Hi-tech special effects have invaded live theater as well as film. Computerized, revolving stages often transport us suddenly from the crest of one emotion to the peak of an entirely different emotion, calling on us for immediate feeling responses. For film, we are frequently required to work in front of a blue screen where the script gives us only a hint of what is around us. Only a strong connection with our own highly trained imagination can help us perform truthfully. Frequently our scene partners act with us only during the master shot and when it comes time for our close up, their lines may be read to us by the script supervisor or a non-actor – who has been known to do so while eating a lox and onion sandwich! *Moment to moment* goes out the window. However, if we have prepared so that we truly inhabit the body of our character, and have bonded with our character's Thinking, Feeling and Will impulses, the circumstances we *Imagine* will project to the audience.

Many of Michael Chekhov's techniques, *once mastered*, can be called upon instantly. The use of an Atmosphere, a Quality of Movement, a clearly Baptized Emotional Section; using your Character's Objective,[2] Imaging your Character's Psychological Gesture – any one of these will allow you to immediately call forth truthful, full-blown emotions, despite any technical hindrances.

During my studies with him, Michael Chekhov stressed that to move beyond the requirements of naturalism with all its banalities, and advance toward a *Theater of the Future*, actors would need to develop their Imaginations far beyond the actor training which was usual at that time. For one thing, he maintained that reliance upon an actor's personal life history and emotional experience is far too limiting.[3] Chekhov's approach to preparation for "inspired acting" emphasizes the use of Psycho-Physical exercises which provide the actor with simple and practical means for calling up energy and emotions while joining the actor's psychology, body and voice with the unique character he or she is bringing to life.

Chekhov always insisted that he did not create a method of acting. He said that he simply observed and studied himself and other creative artists during moments of inspiration. He asked what elements and qualities were present? Then he devised exercises that would train actors to develop those attributes with the least amount of floundering. Chekhov maintained that to truly be an artist, even in contemporary theater, the actor's body, voice and imagination must be so thoroughly trained that he can identify, work with, and radiate forth various kinds of energy. The audience can then receive not only an emotional impact, but a transforming impulse as well.

Although Konstantin Stanislavsky knew about the concrete reality of energy and thought, and used this knowledge to some degree in his work, he was prohibited from discussing or publicly working with unseen or spiritual energies by the Communist regime. Fortunately, Michael Chekhov, who fled from Russia in 1928, was able to develop his Actor Training Techniques free from those restrictions.

During the years when Chekhov taught, however, relatively few people, either students or audience, were open to accepting that imagination, thinking and many other unseen energies are realities. Much to his disappointment, his work was often labeled as mystical. His answer to this accusation was always, "Try the exercises and you will see that they are *not* mystical. Try them, and you will see that they are truly *practical*."

Since then, however, Quantum Physics, with its studies in the behavior of sub-atomic particles have made Michael Chekhov's ideas of *the Intangible creating the Tangible* much more understandable, current and acceptable. Sensitive and sophisticated machines are now measuring the human energy field and even how it is affected by the energy patterns emitted by others. The value of BioFeedback is currently recognized. We now talk quite openly about being "in the zone." *Visualization* is used in many of today's professions, from training athletes to improving health care. Corporate seminars are now commonplace that foster the development of right-brain thinking to engender more creativity in business executives. Many theories that once were labeled as insubstantial "will-o'-the-wisp" fantasies are now accepted as valid facts.

MICHAEL CHEKHOV'S FORMATIVE YEARS

Mikhail Alexandrovich Chekhov was born in 1891. His birthplace, St. Petersburg, was the most artistic and cosmopolitan city in Russia. Throughout his lifetime, Mischa recalled his "passionate love" for this city of his childhood in which painting, poetry, ballet and theater flourished. Its architecture, too, had enchanted and fired his youthful imagination. In his fantasies, the fire tower on Nevsky Prospect became a castle full of mystery, sheltering assemblies of strange imaginary creatures behind its red walls. And when they escaped, as they often did, spilling out of the very walls, they took little Mischa with them – out into the city, the country, the world!

Within the walls of his own home, even at a very early age, Mischa's imagination found expression through the use of his body. With his mother and nanny as audience, he would don a hat, a scarf, any available, odd piece of clothing and at once began to improvise. He became a different child, a new character – sometimes tragic, sometimes so humorous that his nanny would rock back and forth with laugher, until tears rolled down her cheeks.

Much of his childhood, however, was far from pleasant. His father, Alexander, brother of the famous playwright, Anton Chekhov, was an astonishingly brilliant man but an alcoholic, whose eccentricities bordered on the pathological. Michael Chekhov later wrote of his father, "I trembled before him, was amazed by him, and feared him – but I could never love him. To me every aspect of him was terrifying." Alexander's demands on the boy were so extreme that by the time Mischa was six or seven, he lived in a permanent state of anxiety.

Acting was Michael Chekhov's release, his joy and his passion. At sixteen he auditioned and was accepted into the Suvorin Theater School in St. Petersburg. According to Chekhov, his teachers there understood little about communicating the art of acting to their students. They were all great actors, however, and it was through studying their inspired performances on the stage of the Alexandrinsky Theater that Mischa probed their secrets and began to apply them to his own work. And, at the age of eighteen he was given the title role in Tolstoy's *Tsar Feodor* which he performed with his class at the Royal Palace before Tsar Nicholas II.

The following year, Chekhov was engaged by the Maly Suvorinsky Theater of St. Petersburg. Cast in roles that were extremely varied, he excelled in creating offbeat characterizations of much older men. He also toured the provinces with the Maly Theater Company and loved playing before so many different kinds of audiences.

At the time, the most consistently successful productions offered by the Moscow Art Theater (MAT) were *The Seagull*, *Uncle Vanya*, *The Cherry Orchard* and other plays by Mischa's uncle, Anton Chekhov. Although Anton Pavlovich Chekhov had died shortly before Mischa's thirteenth birthday in 1904, his wife, the famous MAT actress Olga Knipper-Chekhova, took a keen interest in the boy. When the MAT visited St. Petersburg in 1911, she arranged an audition for Michael Chekhov with Konstantin Stanislavsky.

"Well, well," said Stanislavsky, after Chekhov had finished giving Marmalodov's monologue from *Crime and Punishment* and a scene from *Tsar Feodor*, "Congratulations, you are now a member of the Art Theater." Although Stanislavsky personally supervised Mischa's artistic development, other MAT artists, especially Leopold Sulerzhitsky and Yevgeny Vakhtangov, were equally instrumental in his growth.

CHEKHOV COMES OF AGE

Shortly after joining the MAT, Chekhov began performing minor roles on stage. From the beginning he radiated energy so strongly and brought such originality to characters that audiences tended to focus their attention upon him, even during scenes with actors who were portraying more important roles. Very soon, he was cast in larger parts. One of these was "Caleb," the gentle, frightened toy-maker in *Cricket on the Hearth*. Stanislavsky was lavish with his praise for Chekhov's performance, calling it "absolutely brilliant." And much has been written about Chekhov's unique and compelling characterization of "Frazer" in *Deluge*.

Then came his memorable portrayal of Malvolio in *Twelfth Night*. A few years ago, I had a personal experience connected with this production which touched me deeply. While teaching a workshop in Moscow at an International Michael Chekhov Conference, I visited the theater which had been occupied by Chekhov during his four years as Artistic Director of the Second Moscow Art Theater.[4] It later became Moscow's Central Children's Theater and Anna Neckrasova, an elderly woman who was the Creative Director, greeted me. When she learned that I was the Executrix of Michael Chekhov's literary works, she began to tell of having seen him in the role of Malvolio when she herself was only eleven years old. She described scenes in which Chekhov's comic inventiveness had the audience convulsed with laughter and other scenes in which Chekhov revealed Malvolio's inner torment so affectingly that the audience wept. As she relived his performance, still so vivid in her memory, her own tears flowed once again.

During the sixteen years that Michael Chekhov performed with the Moscow Art Theater, he held his audiences spellbound. He had an amazing ability to show many levels of a character, often alternating humor and lightness with deeply troubled, pathological states.

In conversations, and in his various writings, Chekhov gave interesting clues about his interpretations of some of his most famous roles. For example, he wrote that he imagined Malvolio "caught in a swamp of horrifying eroticism." And when Yevgeny Vakhtangov directed him in the role of the half-mad King Erik in Strindberg's *Erik the XIVth*, Chekhov used the image of "an eagle with a broken wing." During his preparation for Klestakoff in Stanislavsky's production of *Inspector General*, he imagined that he had bedsprings tied to the bottom of his feet. After witnessing a performance of that play, one writer commented that "Chekhov was seemingly immune to gravity."

The noted artist and portrait painter, Margarita Woloschin, wrote of Chekhov's characterization of the tyrant, Pierre, in the Symbolist play, *Archangel Michael*, "His whole greatness as an actor appeared in the second act, where he simply stood there in silence, never uttering a single word. Yet he always remained the center, because the force going out from him fascinated the audience."

The "force" within him in his personal life, however, was raging out of control. The fighting in the streets of Moscow during the revolution affected his nervous system and the anxiety he had carried since childhood became acute. He drank heavily. And the more successful he became, the more lonely he became. He read during every spare moment; Schopenhauer, Nietzsche, Hartman . . . and spent hours arguing with them in his head. His sense of loneliness increased and he made a decision to marry. *After* he married Olga Knipper, the niece of his aunt, Olga Knipper-Chekhova, he fell passionately in love with her, which only added to his inner turmoil. She tried to help him but he continued to sink deeper into a chaos of thoughts and feelings. Obsessive images of something dire happening to his mother continually rose before him. He was afraid to leave the house and even stopped going to the theater. Stanislavsky sent psychiatrists to see him but Chekhov dismissed them. He did not act for more than a year.

One emotional blow after another struck him. His wife, Olga, left him and moved to Germany, taking their infant daughter, Ada, with her. His cousin Volodya, a friend since childhood, found Mischa's gun in a drawer and committed suicide. During Moscow's famine and typhoid epidemic, Chekhov's mother became gravely ill and was taken to a hospital where she died. When Mischa arrived there, her body had been taken away. Frantically he searched the morgue, through corpses lying on tables, on the floor, under benches in freakish poses – until at last he found her.

During the most difficult phase of his illness, Chekhov was persuaded to undergo several sessions of hypnosis. After the fifth session his obsessive visions and ideas disappeared and shortly thereafter he was able to return to the stage. However, he remained in a highly nervous state. At times depression clung to him like a black cloud and at others, bouts of inappropriate and uncontrollable laughter left him exhausted.

One day, he went to a bookshop in search of more books on Yoga. Even before his illness Mischa, like Stanislavsky, experimented with Yoga with the idea that its system of mind–body and energy control would also be useful for actors. In the window of the shop was a book entitled, *Knowledge of Higher Worlds and Its Attainment* by Rudolf Steiner, the Austrian philosopher and seer. He laughed at the time, thinking that if it were truly possible to achieve this knowledge, it would already have been achieved and there would be no need to write about it. Nevertheless, Chekhov bought the book.

Over the next few years this book and others by Rudolf Steiner influenced him enormously. Steiner's world conception answered many questions for Mischa. His entire outlook on life changed. His pessimism disappeared. Life took on new purpose and meaning. His health improved and he stopped drinking to excess.

His full return to the MAT, as actor, teacher and director, was welcomed enthusiastically. The Russian public loved him and when later, his autobiography *The Path of the Actor*[5] was published, it was an immediate success. It has been written that "Next to Chaliapin, the great opera singer, no artist of the Russian stage was ever so beloved, not to say adored. For the various ranks of Russian society, he seemed to be a source of spiritual comfort."

After Chekhov became Artistic Director of the Second MAT,[6] he conceived and produced a stylized production of *Hamlet*, in which he also appeared in the title role. He incorporated many of Rudolf Steiner's ideas of movement and speech, blending them with what he felt to be the best of Stanislavsky, then transforming them through his own unique artistry and technique. The result was a *Hamlet* unlike any that had ever been produced. It was a huge success. One remembrance of Chekhov's production and portrayal of Hamlet tells that "at the end of the tragedy everything changed into light, for he shed spiritual light upon the darkness, so that the spectators, grateful for the beauty he had given them, ran after his sleigh – as far as his house."

That very spiritual quality, which was so appreciated by many, was definitely unappreciated by the Communist Party. Soon party members told him that it would be a good idea for him to visit factories and "learn to like the machine." This would give him, they said, a new outlook on life and "help to divorce him from harmful mystical deviations."

One day he received a letter from the Commissariat of Education telling him that he must cease disseminating the ideas of Rudolf Steiner. He was asked to change the way in which he presented *Hamlet*. He refused. His activity as head of the Theater gradually drew to a halt. Contact with him became unsafe, even for members of his own company of actors. Shortly thereafter, a resolution was passed by the State Political Directorate concerning his arrest.

A high-ranking member of the Communist Party arranged for Chekhov and his second wife, Xenia, to be given passports for a vacation. Thirty-six hours later they left Russia, never to return. From then on, Chekhov became a "non-person" in Russia. All references to him at the Moscow Art Theater were eliminated and for more than fifty years his autobiography and records of his teachings were banned. Still, during all that time, an artistic underground perpetuated his work and those who were brave enough studied it. Today, once again, his pictures hang at the MAT and he is proudly described as their "acting genius of the century."

THE YEARS WITHOUT ROOTS

When he left Russia in the summer of 1928, Chekhov first went to Germany where he experienced both the upheaval of exile and the pain of not being able to perform in his native language. Max

Reinhardt, the famous German Impresario and Director, offered him the role of "Skid" the clown, in the play *Artisten*.[7] Mischa worked intensively with a German-language coach and opened in Vienna in February of 1929. He later wrote that that he had been absolutely terrified. Between the language difficulties and the unfamiliar acrobatic stunts he had to perform, he felt he was falling into an abyss. Quite suddenly, midway through the play on opening night, Chekhov experienced what he called an inspired *division of consciousness*. He felt himself in the audience, in his character whom he consciously directed, and in each of his partners – all at the same time. ". . . my entire being, and Skid's, were filled with a terrifying, almost unbearable force! And there were no barriers against it – it penetrated everything, and was capable of anything! I felt awestruck."[8]

This experience was for Chekhov the confirmation of what he had long held as an ideal for the actor as a truly creative artist – to be consciously connected to what Chekhov refers to as the Higher Ego. Henceforth he would organize and systematize the techniques he developed in order to lead the actor on the Path to Inspired Acting.

Mischa played Skid quite happily for a time, and continued working with Reinhardt while in Germany. He also appeared in several German films. One, *A Fool Through Love*, was directed by his first wife, Olga, who had become a popular film actress and was then living in Germany with their daughter, Ada. Chekhov also directed the Russian- and Hebrew-speaking actors of the Habima Theater in *Twelfth Night* and enjoyed the experience. When Stanislavsky visited Berlin, Chekhov introduced him to Max Reinhardt. Bringing together these two great men of the Theater, whom he loved and admired so much, was a deeply moving experience for him.

On the whole, however, he found the German Theater of that time superficial and longed to work again with Russian actors for Russian audiences. He decided to move to Paris, hoping the large

Russian colony that lived there would support him in establishing a new Theater.

He and Xenia arrived in Paris full of enthusiasm but the year he spent there was, in his own words, "disorderly, hectic and improbable. . . . I raced forward and stumbled over hard reality." Funding for the Russian Theater Abroad never materialized. Chekhov did, however, connect with an entrepreneurial and dedicated young producer, Georgette Boner. Unfortunately, the few productions they managed to mount on modest budgets at the Theatre de l'Avenue were dogged by ill luck and technical disasters. Nevertheless, Georgette's friendship and beneficial influence continued to help the Chekhovs long after their theater closed.

Fortunately, an invitation came from the Latvian State Theater and the Russian Drama Theater in Riga offering him permanent positions at both theaters, to direct as well as to act. When he performed, it was in Russian, while his partners spoke in Latvian. Audiences accepted this easily, as everyone in Riga also knew Russian. Next came an offer from the Lithuanian State Theater in Kaunas. Almost miraculously, Chekhov managed to direct at all three theaters at once.

Between the three theaters, during a period of two years, Chekhov performed and/or directed, *Inspector General* by Gogol, *The Death of Ivan the Terrible* by Tolstoy, *Hamlet, Eric the XIVth, The Deluge, Selo Stepanchikovo, Twelfth Night* and Mozart's opera *The Magic Flute*. This was one of the happiest and most artistic periods of his life.

Without warning, while directing the opera *Parsifal* in Riga, Mischa suffered a heart attack. And, before he could fully recover, a bloodless revolution took place in Latvia. This revolution was in favor of the fascists and once again, for political reasons, Chekhov was a *persona non grata*.

Mischa, Xenia and Georgette Boner then traveled to Italy. While Chekhov was recuperating, Georgette worked with him on the earliest formulation of this book. Back in Paris, after regaining his health, Chekhov and Boner formed the "Moscow Art Players" with Vera Soloviova,[9] Andrei Jilinsky[10] and other émigrés. In 1935, at the invitation of Sol Hurok, the renowned American Impresario, they brought the company to the United States. Chekhov played several different characters in *An Evening of Anton Chekhov Sketches*, in addition to his famous roles of Klestakoff in *Inspector General* and Frazer in *The Deluge*. Even though the entire company spoke in Russian, they received marvelous reviews and played to full houses in New York, Philadelphia and Boston. It was a personal triumph for Chekhov.

Members of the Group Theater came to see him and were enthusiastic in their praise. However, it was a talented young American actress, Beatrice Straight,[11] who next changed the course of Mischa's life. Enthralled by his performances, she persuaded him to create a Theater Center and School at her family's large estate in Devonshire, England. Beatrice Straight and her mother and stepfather, Dorothy and Leonard Elmhirst, were generous patrons and dedicated to the idea of creating a true center of arts in a rural area.

Chekhov learned to speak English in record time and in October of 1936, the Chekhov Theatre Studio at Dartington Hall began classes with twenty students from nine countries in residence. At last, for three satisfying years, Chekhov found a venue in which he could define his acting techniques in ideal surroundings. The daily curriculum of the Studio consisted of Psycho-Physical and Imagination exercises taught by Chekhov, speech and voice classes, art lessons featuring drawing and sculpture, and Eurythmy.[12] As an added bonus for Chekhov, Beatrice's devoted friend and secretary, Deirdre Hurst du Prey[13] transcribed his classes and gave him invaluable help in the preparation of the original English manuscript of this book.

Then, just as the Chekhov Studio *Professional Theatre* was preparing a production for the London stage, political upheaval once again intervened in Mischa's life and work. The threatening clouds of war with Germany hovered over the British Isles and could no longer be ignored. In January of 1939, the Elmhirsts and Beatrice Straight moved the Chekhov school from England to Ridgefield, Connecticut, in the United States.

THE NEW YORK AND HOLLYWOOD YEARS

Many of the students and teachers from Dartington were able to continue working together at Ridgefield, including Chekhov's assistant and close friend, George Shdanoff. Soon classes were running smoothly and the Chekhov Theater Studio Players began to mount productions in their small Ridgefield theater. Before long, Broadway luminaries were driving up to Connecticut to see them.

Chekhov and George Shdanoff also co-directed an adaptation of Dostoyevsky's *The Possessed* for Broadway. It was scripted by Shdanoff, with sets by the famous artist M. V. Dobuzhinski. Among others in the cast were Beatrice Straight and Hurd Hatfield.[14] The play opened on Broadway at the Lyceum Theater in October of 1939. It was too heavy and too ponderously Russian for the critics and closed after two weeks. It was a bitter disappointment for Chekhov and a financial disaster for the Studio and its backers.

In 1940, following the tradition in which Chekhov had been trained in Russia – bringing live theater to audiences who might otherwise never see it – the Chekhov Players traveled over 10,000 miles in New England and throughout the Southern States. At first, the company traveled in station wagons while Yul Brynner[15] drove the scenery and prop truck. Their productions of *Twelfth Night* and *Cricket on the Hearth* delighted audiences and local critics were lavish with their praise. The following year, a stylized production of *King Lear* was added with Ford Rainey[16] as Lear, Beatrice Straight as Goneril, Daphne Field and Mary Lou Taylor[17] alternating as Cordelia, Hurd Hatfield as Gloucester and Yul Brynner as Cornwall.

Chekhov also opened a studio in New York City and began teaching classes for well-established professional actors.[18] It was his fervent hope that through them a new, revitalized theater could be created. Many of the actors and directors who came to him had been a part of the recently disbanded Group Theater.

Under Chekhov and Shdanoff's co-direction, a production of *Twelfth Night* was mounted on Broadway. This time the reviews were enthusiastic. The timing, however, was disastrous. The play opened on the weekend of the Japanese attack on Pearl Harbor, December 7, 1941. The United States immediately went to war and the nation was in turmoil.

Once more, political upheaval brought a halt to Michael Chekhov's artistic plans. From January through March of 1942, the Chekhov Players were able to honor their previously booked tour of Southern and Mid-Western States. Sadly, however, their final performance on the road also heralded the demise of the Chekhov Theater School in Ridgefield. Too many of the actors had been drafted into military service and there were financial problems as well. Never again did destiny allow Mischa to work with a company of actors who had been thoroughly trained in the Chekhov Techniques.

After the Studio was disbanded, Mischa and Xenia moved to Hollywood where Chekhov was cast in the featured role of the village patriarch in the film, *Song of Russia*. He was immediately embraced by the Hollywood colony of Russian émigrés, who soon began to invite other actors, producers, directors and musicians to participate in a weekly evening with Chekhov, held at the home of Russian actor Akim Tamiroff.[19]

Those evenings were magical. Michael Chekhov talked about Theater, demonstrated his Acting Techniques and performed memorable sketches. In time, American actors joined in and Chekhov developed fascinating improvisations in which the actors often rose to heights of imagination and emotion hitherto unknown, even to themselves. On any one night you might find Anthony Quinn, Gary Cooper, Thomas Mitchell, Viveca Lindsfors, Patricia Neal, director Mark Robson, Joan Caulfield, and Iris Tree along with Feodor Chaliapin Jr., composer Sergei Rachmaninoff or violinist Vladimir Horowitz, gathered to join in or to witness the enchantment.

After *Song of Russia*, Michael Chekhov appeared in a succession of films: *In Our Time*, with Ida Lupino (1944), Ben Hecht's *Specter of the Rose* (1945), *Cross My Heart* (1946), *Abie's Irish Rose* (1946), *Texas, Brooklyn and Heaven* (1948), *Holiday For Sinners* (1952), *Invitation* (1952), *Rhapsody* (1954) and Hitchcock's *Spellbound* with Gregory Peck and Ingrid Bergman, for which Chekhov received an Academy Award Nomination.

Happily for me, he continued his weekly evenings at Akim Tamiroff's home. On a never-to-be-forgotten evening, which changed my life forever, I nervously knocked on the door of that house. It was opened by a small, kind, meticulously dressed, unassuming man with a strong Russian accent – Michael Chekhov. He welcomed me with a warmth that enveloped me and which I experienced as flowing right from his heart. Soon he began to demonstrate means for creating a character – and this rather frail, slender man grew to be a giant in front of us. Enthusiasm, humor, artistry and love of the Theater radiated from him and penetrated each of us while we watched and listened, spellbound.

In 1948 Chekhov was cast as the Gestapo agent in *Arch of Triumph*, starring Ingrid Bergman and Charles Boyer and directed by Louis Milestone. He had just begun filming when he suffered a second major heart attack and was unable to work for the better part of a year. Charles Laughton took over the role in the film.

Although Mischa never fully recovered his health, he was able to act and to teach again. For the first time since leaving Russia, he owned his own home, a small house in Beverly Hills, and he treasured the experience. He gave his private lessons there, and one evening each week he lectured in a rented studio just off the Sunset Strip for a group called the Drama Society,[20] headed by respected character actors John Dehner and John Abbott. Chekhov was also able to act in three more films, the last of which was *Rhapsody*, starring Elizabeth Taylor.

His great and most satisfying achievement in these final years was the completion, with the assistance of writer-producer Charles Leonard, of this book, *To the Actor* which was originally published in 1953 by Harper & Row. In order to satisfy the publisher there was much that had to be left out. This is particularly true of Michael Chekhov's most original contribution to "Creating a Character" – *Psychological Gesture*. As Executrix of Chekhov's literary properties, and as an actress, I am particularly grateful to Andrei Malaev-Babel for his excellent commentary and translation of Michael Chekhov's Russian-language chapter in which he was able to more fully explain his ideas about PG and give practical suggestions for its application.

Chekhov truly loved actors and empathized deeply with them as he watched them face the many challenges and demands of commercial Theater, Movies and Television in America. He deplored the fact that naturalism/realism had become the main criteria for opinions about good Theater and good performances, when, in truth, naturalism is only one style. *He understood, however, that in order to work in their chosen profession, actors must master that style.*

During the last two years of his life he devoted much time to finding additional techniques which would help actors prepare for their roles in the minimum amount of time, truthfully, and without resorting to banality and clichés. He presented these suggestions in a final series of Master Classes, many of which were pre-recorded in his home because he was too ill to attend his weekly class.[21] On September 30, 1955, while having dinner with his wife at their kitchen table, Michael Chekhov suffered a third and fatal heart attack. Fortunately, his unique ideas and techniques still live on.

THE FUTURE

Most of Michael Chekhov's life was occupied with discovering, demonstrating and writing about his vision of an *Ideal Theater of the Future* and the *Ideal Actor*. Ultimately, the future of Chekhov's life work is intimately bound up with you who read this book, for you are the creators of this Future Theater.

Much that Chekhov deplored about the Theater of his day, including commercialism, is even more prevalent now. He observed that we had lost the sense of both the beauty and the poetry around our art. "Our Theater has become a dry business," he said. "The Theater is not solving any problems. It is not interested in the future, in what *shall happen*." Chekhov maintained that in our Theater, too much is condensed to the present moment and that we must break this pattern of constantly condensing and trivializing language and human behavior until it is hardly alive. We must break out of this realm of "deadly theater" – to use the name which Peter Brook has so aptly given it.

Chekhov predicted that Future Theater will go the opposite way, the way of striving to enlarge everything – giving many points of view, many theatrical styles, many means of expression and innumerable themes for plays. And, he urged actors to work consciously to enlarge themselves and increase their abilities by the means of their profession – even to developing a different experience of space.

He also believed that those who create Theater must take responsibility for the impact their productions have upon their audience. They must be willing to ask if what is being presented to the spectators has any value for them as human beings. The more brilliant the artists, the more they must develop a certain *moral imagination* that will lead us into a more positive future.

For Chekhov, it was a given that all kinds of *Theater must be entertaining*. In addition, however, he brought ideas for a golden age of Theater which include words and phrases like "Inspiring" – "Healing" – "Nurturing" – "Strengthening" – "Elevating language to its rightful place as a creative force" – "Penetrating the mysteries of good and evil" – "Showing the nobility of the human being as well as his weaknesses" – "Portraying evil so that it has a positive transforming effect upon the spectator" – and more.

Above all, he urges each of us, as artists, to come to *our own* ideas of what we want Future Theater to be. As those ideas become clear for us, we can gather around us those who are of like mind. Never before in history, has the actor, the artist, the creator of entertainment had so much power to influence others. Strange as it may seem to us, a huge segment of the population will listen longer and more intently to what the actor has to say than to what our political leaders have to say.

Fortunately, many forces are at work today which attract artists to Michael Chekhov's work. An active Professional Theater in Madrid, one in Berlin, one in New York City and one in Upstate New York have created Ensemble Companies of Chekhov-trained actors for their productions.[22] In addition, there is a whole younger generation of actors and directors who teach the Technique – many of whom have studied personally with Chekhov's own students. There are Michael Chekhov Training Centers in various locales, including London, Los Angeles, New York and Portland, Maine,[23] as well as in Washington D.C., Berlin, Munich, Paris and also in Russia, the Netherlands, Australia, Lithuania, Israel and Japan, etc.[24]

All of us who have worked with the Techniques and Ideas which Michael Chekhov presents in this book, know how much they have expanded our awareness and changed us as artists and as human beings. Chekhov often said, "Do not toil over the exercises. Have fun with them. Let them nourish you and you will be surprised at how easily they will work."

I have endeavored to give you a glimpse of Chekhov's *Past*. His *Present* you hold in your hand in this book. And the *Future* of his vision? Only our individual and collective Power of Imagination can bring it to reality.

Mala Powers
September 2001

NOTES

1 In the context of this Biography, the word "*Theater*" with a capital 'T', as well as "Future *Theater*" and "Ideal *Theater* of the Future" etc., all include stage, motion pictures, television, and any medium in which the actor is called upon to perform.

2 The character's objective should work immediately provided you have carefully chosen a strong, "*actable*" *verb* which works directly upon your Will and your Feeling life. e.g. "I want to '*escape*' or "I need to '*convince*' him."

3 This technique of re-creating the actor's personal emotional memories for engendering truthful emotions in performance is usually referred to as "Affective Memory." Michael Chekhov always disagreed with its use, claiming that it limited actors to their own personal reactions and also made them more susceptible to hysteria and mental imbalances. The practice was originally developed by Stanislavsky in his early years and he later gave up advocating its use. It was brought to the United States during the 1930s and used by many members of the Group Theater. It is still taught by many teachers today.

4 As early as 1912, Stanislavsky created the more experimental *First Studio* under the auspices of the MAT. Later, Michael Chekhov differed with some of Stanislavsky's ideas about acting and theatrical style – as had Vakhtangov, Meyerhold and other brilliant MAT directors. In 1924 the *First Studio* was reorganized and renamed "*The Second Moscow Art Theater*" with Michael Chekhov as Artistic Director.

5 *The Path of the Actor* has not yet been published in English.

6 See note 4.

7 *Artisten* is the European version of the American play, *Burlesque*. It is based on the story of the opera *I Pagliacci*, by Leoncavallo.

8   This is a quote from *Life and Encounters*, a second autobiography written by Michael Chekhov in 1944, not yet published in English. For this translation, we are indebted to Professor Mel Gordon. His scholarship and his writings on Michael Chekhov are greatly appreciated. A special thanks for his helpful chronology of Chekhov's life which appeared in *The Drama Review* (MIT Press, Volume 27, Number 3 (T99), 1983.

9   Vera Soloviova had previously appeared with Chekhov in *Cricket on the Hearth* and was a leading lady in his company at the MAT II.

10 Andrei Jilinsky, as a leading actor of the MAT II, had previously appeared in Chekhov's productions of *Hamlet* and *Twelfth Night*.

11 Beatrice Straight (1918–2001). During her distinguished career she received Broadway's Antoinette Perry Award for Best Actress in *The Crucible* and the Academy Award for Best Supporting Actress in the film, *Network*.

12 Eurythmy, developed by Rudolf Steiner, is a form of movement which Steiner called the "science of visible speech." There is both Artistic Eurythmy and Curative Eurythmy. In 1922, Michael Chekhov traveled to Central Europe to see Steiner lecture on this subject, and to learn more about Anthroposophy (the name Steiner gave to his Spiritual Science and Path of Spiritual Training).

13 It is with deep gratitude that we acknowledge the work of Deirdre Hurst du Prey – for her two published books on Michael Chekhov, *Lessons for the Professional Actor* (Performing Arts Journal Publications, NY, 1985) and *Michael Chekhov: Lessons for Teachers of His Acting Technique* (Dovehouse Editions, Inc., Ottowa, Canada, 2000 by Deirdre Hurst du Prey) – and for her dedication in transcribing thousands of pages of Chekhov's lectures for Archives at Dartington Hall and elsewhere.

14 Hurd Hatfield's credits include scores of fine performances on Broadway and in movie and TV productions. He is best known for his starring role in the film of Oscar Wilde's *The Picture of Dorian Gray*.

15 Yul Brynner, who also wrote the original Preface for this book, appeared in more than 45 movies including *Anastasia, The Brothers Karamazov, The Madwoman of Chaillot*, and *Westworld*. His most famous role was the King of Siam in Rogers and Hammerstein's musical *The King and I*. He originated the role on Broadway and the later film version earned him The Academy Award for Best Actor.

16 Ford Rainey's career spans more than 6 decades. He has dozens of

stage plays and more than 100 notable television performances to his credit. His more than 60 feature movies, filmed in both the US and the UK, include his role opposite Colleen Dewhurst in *Bed & Breakfast* (1992).

17 Daphne Field and Mary Lou Taylor later founded the *High Valley Players*, in California, along with Hurd Hatfield, Iris Tree, Ford Rainey and three other members of the former Chekhov Players. They toured the West Coast with their productions. Both Field and Taylor teach the Chekhov Technique.

18 Participants included director Martin Ritt, Peter Frye, Paula Strasberg, Morris Carnovsky, Arthur Franz, Olive Deering, Michael Strong, John Berry and Jack Arnold.

19 Akim Tamiroff, (1899–1972), Russian character actor and veteran of more than 100 films, trained at the MAT. He immigrated to the US in 1923. In 1943 he was nominated for an Academy Award for his memorable performance as Pablo in *For Whom the Bell Tolls*.

20 Among those who attended Chekhov's classes with me during those years, two others are also prominent teachers of the Chekhov Technique, Jack Colvin on the West Coast and Joanna Merlin on the East Coast. Colvin has the distinction of having won the prestigious DramaLogue Awards in five separate categories: as actor, director, playwright, producer and production designer. Joanna Merlin made her debut into a long, distinguished acting career as Tzeitel in the original Broadway cast of *Fiddler on the Roof*.

21 This recorded series of Master Classes, *Michael Chekhov: On Theatre and the Art of Acting*, is available through Applause Theatre Book Publishers, 211 West 71st St. New York, NY 10023.

22 *Madrid* – Teatro de la Abadía – Director, José Luis Gómez – www. Teatroabadia.com; *Berlin* – Werkbühne Berlin–Directors, Jobst Langhans and Jörg Andreas – www.mtsb.de; *New York City* – Chekhov Theatre Ensemble (NY) – Director, Floyd Rumohr – www.chekhovtheatre.org; *Upstate NY* – The Actors Ensemble – Directors, Ted Pugh and Fern Sloan – ActorsEnsemble@hotmail.com

23 *London*: Michael Chekhov Centre UK – Director, Sarah Kane – www.pharo.com/Chekhov.shtml; *Hollywood*: Michael Chekhov Studio USA – Directors, Lisa Dalton and Jack Colvin – www.chekhov.net; *New York*: MiChA – Directors, Joanna Merlin and Jessica Cerullo – www.michaelchekhov.org; Chekhov Studio New York – Director, Lenard Petit – www.meglenium@earthlink.net; *Gorham, Maine:*

University of Southern Maine – Michael Chekhov Theatre Institute – Program Director, Wil Kilroy – Kilroy@usm.maine.edu

24   For information on locations and teachers contact www.Chekhov.net or info@Chekhov.net

PREFACE

ST. JAMES THEATRE
New York, July 23, 1952

Dear Mr. Chekhov, my dear Professor:

I believe the last time I had a chance to talk to you was close to ten years ago. I don't believe I ever told you, during the year or so that I had the privilege of working with you, the whole story of my pursuit of your theory of the art of acting.

It started in the late twenties when I saw you in a repertory of plays that you did in Paris: *Inspector General, Eric the Fourteenth, Twelfth Night, Hamlet*, etc. I came out with the deep conviction that through you and through you only I could find what I was working for – a concrete and tangible way to reach a mastery of the elusive thing that one calls the technique of acting.

This pursuit continued through the years and most of the time seemed unattainable. I tried to join your group when you first started the Chekhov Theater at Dartington Hall in England. Then I heard that you had moved to America with most of your group to continue your work in Connecticut, and it took me several years through all the world events to finally come to America with the sole purpose of at last working with you.

Now, holding the manuscript of *To the Actor* in my hands I have achieved my complete goal. In *To the Actor* I find the thing I was looking for and trying to find for myself; exactly what I have tried to apply to my work since the brief period when I had the privilege of working with you. For though visiting many schools and many very famous and very creative actors, directors and teachers I never found anything that taught one the most important part of the technique of acting. They knew well how to teach diction. They knew well how to teach you to pick up cues, but mostly they made you search for the vital and most important part of acting – yourself – with only vaguely stated "rules" that I found to be only terminology and of no concrete help.

When you are a pianist you have an outside instrument that you learn to master through finger work and arduous exercises and with it, you as a creative artist can perform and express your art. As an actor, you the artist have to perform on the most difficult instrument to master, that is, your own self – your physical being and your emotional being. That, I believe, is where all the confusion of the different schools of acting stems from, and that is why your manuscript, which I hold in front of me, is worth more than its weight in gold to every actor – in fact, I believe to every creative artist.

As I said before, everything I have learned from you I have applied through the years, in every medium in which I have worked, not only as an actor, but as a director, not only in the theater, but also in television, in camera work, scenery design, in co-ordination of the complex thing that is a live dramatic television production.

To my mind your book, *To the Actor*, is so far the best book of its kind that it can't even begin to be compared to anything that has ever appeared in the field. And, in my opinion, it reads as well as any good fiction I've ever come across.

At this point I can only express my thanks to you for having now made available, for me and for other artists, a valuable shortcut to mastering what you refer to as "creative process."

Yours,

YUL BRYNNER

FOREWORD

This book is the result of prying behind the curtain of the *Creative Process* – prying that began many years ago in Russia at the Moscow Art Theater, with which I was associated for sixteen years. During that time I worked with Stanislavsky, Nemirovich-Danchenko, Vachtangov and Sulerjitsky. In my capacity as actor, director, teacher and, finally, head of the Second Moscow Art Theater, I was able to develop my methods of acting and directing and formulate them into a definite technique, of which this book is an outgrowth.

After leaving Russia, I worked for many years in the theaters of Latvia, Lithuania, Austria, France, England, and with Max Reinhardt in Germany.

It has also been my good fortune and privilege to know and observe renowned actors and directors of all types and traditions, among them such memorable personalities as Chaliapin, Meyerhold, Moissi, Jouvet, Gielgud, and others.

I was further able to acquire much useful knowledge while directing *Twelfth Night* for the Hebrew "Habima" Theater in Europe, the opera, *Parsifal*, in Riga and the opera, *The Fair of Sorochinsk*, in New York. During my work with the latter, a series of discussions I had with the late Sergei Rachmaninoff inspired many additional contributions to this technique.

In 1936 Mr. and Mrs. L. K. Elmhirst and Miss Beatrice Straight opened a dramatic school at Dartington Hall, Devonshire, England, with the intention of creating the Chekhov Theater. As head of that school, I had the opportunity to make a great number of valuable experiments in connection with my technique. These experiments continued after the school was transferred to the United States on the brink of World War II and, beyond that, during the school's evolvement as a professional theater known as the Chekhov Players.

This theater might have continued to adventure in some new principles of dramatic art in the course of its tour as a classical repertory company; however, its activity was disrupted when most of its male members were called to arms. My experiments struggled on for a while longer with the aid of Broadway actors, but eventually had to be postponed indefinitely when many of this company's members also went into the armed services.

Now, after all these years of experimental testing and verifying, I feel that the time has come to commit the ideas to paper and offer them as my life's work for the judgment of my colleagues and readers at large.

In doing so I wish to express my first gratitude to Paul Marshall Allen for his generous help with the formative version; to Betty Raskin Appleton, Dr. Sergei Bertensson, Leonidas Dudarew-Ossetynski, Hurd Hatfield and, in particular, to Deirdre du Prey, my former pupil and qualified teacher of the method, for their respective contributions.

A special note of appreciation is reserved for Charles Leonard, playwright-producer-director, whose sound knowledge of the method and understanding of its applications to various branches of the stage, screen, radio and television persuaded me to impose upon him the editorial work for this final version of the manuscript. His invaluable craftsmanship has placed me deeply in his debt.

Michael Chekhov
Beverly Hills, California
1952

A MEMO TO THE READER

I need your help.

The abstruse nature of the subject requires not only concentrated reading, not alone clear understanding, but *co-operation* with the author. For that which could easily be made comprehensible by personal contact and demonstration, must of necessity depend on mere words and intellectual concepts.

Many of the questions that may arise in your mind during or after the reading of each chapter can best be answered through the practical application of the exercises prescribed herein. Unfortunately, there is no other way to co-operate: the technique of acting can never be properly understood without *practicing it*.

M.C.

The technique of any art is sometimes apt to dampen, as it were, the spark of inspiration in a mediocre artist; but the same technique in the hands of a master can fan that spark into an unquenchable flame.

– Josef Jasser

1

THE ACTOR'S BODY AND PSYCHOLOGY

Our bodies can be either our best friends or worst enemies.

It is a known fact that the human body and psychology influence each other and are in constant interplay. Either an undeveloped or muscularly overdeveloped body may easily dim the activity of the mind, dull the feelings or weaken the will. Because each field and profession is prey to characteristic occupational habits, diseases and hazards which inevitably affect its workers and practitioners, it is seldom that we find a complete balance or harmony between the body and psychology.

But the actor, who must consider his body as an instrument for expressing creative ideas on the stage, *must* strive for the attainment of complete harmony between the two, body and psychology.

There are certain actors who can feel their roles deeply, can comprehend them pellucidly, but who can neither express nor convey to an audience these riches within themselves. Those wonderful thoughts and emotions are somehow chained inside their undeveloped bodies. The process of rehearsing and acting is for them a painful struggle against their own "too too solid flesh," as

Hamlet said. But no need to be dismayed. Every actor, to a greater or lesser degree, suffers from some of his body's resistance.

Physical exercises are needed to overcome this, but they must be built on principles different from those used in most dramatic schools. Gymnastics, fencing, dancing, acrobatics, calisthenics and wrestling are undoubtedly good and useful for what they are, but the body of an actor must undergo a special kind of development in accordance with the particular requirements of his profession.

What are these requirements?

First and foremost is extreme *sensitivity of body to the psychological creative impulses*. This cannot be achieved by strictly physical exercises. The psychology itself must take part in such a development. The body of an actor must absorb psychological qualities, must be filled and permeated with them so that they will convert it gradually into a sensitive membrane, a kind of receiver and conveyor of the subtlest images, feelings, emotions and will impulses.

Since the last third of the nineteenth century a materialistic world outlook has been reigning, with ever-increasing power, in the sphere of art as well as in science and everyday life. Consequently, only those things which are tangible, only that which is palpable and only that which has the outer appearance of life phenomena seem valid enough to attract the artist's attention.

Under the influence of materialistic concepts, the contemporary actor is constantly and out of sheer necessity suborned into the dangerous practice of eliminating the psychological elements from his art and overestimating the significance of the physical. Thus, as he sinks deeper and deeper into this inartistic milieu, his body becomes less and less animated, more and more shallow, dense, puppet-like, and in extreme cases even resembles some kind of automaton of his mechanistic age. Venality becomes a convenient substitute for originality. The actor begins to resort to all sorts of theatrical tricks and clichés and soon accumulates a number of peculiar acting habits and bodily mannerisms; but no matter how good or bad they are or seem to be, they are only a replacement for his real artistic feelings and emotions, for real creative excitement on the stage.

Moreover, under the hypnotic power of modern materialism, actors are even inclined to neglect the boundary which must separate everyday life from that of the stage. They strive instead to bring life-as-it-is onto the stage, and by doing so become ordinary photographers rather than artists. They are perilously prone to forget that the real task of the creative artist is not merely to copy the outer appearance of life but to *interpret* life in all its facets and profoundness, to show what is behind the phenomena of life, to let the spectator look beyond life's surfaces and meanings.

For is not the artist, the actor in the truest sense, a being who is endowed with the ability to see and experience things which are obscure to the average person? And is not his real mission, his joyous instinct, to convey to the spectator, as a kind of revelation, *his* very own impressions of things as *he* sees and feels them? Yet how can he do that if his body is chained and limited in its expressiveness by the force of unartistic, uncreative influences? Since his body and voice are the only physical instruments upon which he can play, should he not protect them against constraints that are hostile and deleterious to his craft?

Cold, analytical, materialistic thinking tends to throttle the urge to imagination. To counteract this deadly intrusion, the actor must systematically undertake the task of feeding his body with other impulses than those which impel him to a merely materialistic way of living and thinking. The actor's body can be of optimum value to him only when motivated by an unceasing flow of artistic impulses; only then can it be more refined, flexible, expressive and, most vital of all, sensitive and responsive to the subtleties which constitute the creative artist's inner life. For the actor's body must be molded and re-created from *inside*.

As soon as you start practicing you will be astonished to see how much and how avidly the human body, especially an actor's

body, can consume – and respond to – all kinds of purely psychological values. Therefore, for an actor's development, special
psychophysical exercises must be found and applied. The first
nine exercises are designed to fill this requirement.

This brings us to the delineation of the second requirement,
which is the *richness of the psychology itself*. A sensitive body and a
rich, colorful psychology are mutually complementary to each
other and create that harmony so necessary to the attainment of
the actor's professional aim.

You will achieve it by constantly enlarging the circle of your
interests. Try to experience or assume the psychology of persons of
other eras by reading period plays, historical novels or even
history itself. While doing so, try to penetrate their thinking
without imposing upon them your modern points of view,
moral concepts, social principles or anything else that is of a
personal nature or opinion. Try to understand them through
their way of living and the circumstance of their lives. Reject
the dogmatic and misleading notion that the human personality
never changes but remains the same at all times and in all ages.
(I once heard a prominent actor say, "Hamlet was just a guy
like myself"! In an instant he had betrayed that inner laziness
which failed to enter more thoroughly into Hamlet's personality, and his lack of interest in anything beyond the limits of his
own psychology.)

Similarly, try to penetrate the psychology of different nations;
try to define their specific characteristics, their psychological features, interests, their arts. Make clear the main differences that
distinguish these nations from one another.

Further, endeavor to penetrate the psychology of persons
around you toward whom you feel unsympathetic. Try to find
in them some good, positive qualities which you perhaps failed
to notice before. Make an attempt to experience what they
experience; ask yourself *why* they feel or act the way they do.

Remain objective and you will enlarge your own psychology

immensely. All such vicarious experiences will, by their own weight, sink gradually into your body and make it more sensitive, noble and flexible And your ability to penetrate the inner life of the characters you are studying professionally will become sharper. You will first begin to discover that inexhaustible fund of originality, inventiveness and ingenuity you are capable of displaying as an actor. You will be able to detect in your characters those fine but fugitive features which nobody but you, the actor, can see and, as a consequence, reveal to your audiences.

And if, in addition to the foregoing suggestions, you acquire the habit of suppressing all unnecessary criticism, whether in life or in your professional work, you will hasten your development considerably.

The third requirement is *complete obedience of both body and psychology to the actor*. The actor who would become master of himself and his craft will banish the element of "accident" from his profession and create a firm ground for his talent. Only an indisputable command of his body and psychology will give him the necessary self-confidence, freedom and harmony for his creative activity. For in modern everyday life we do not make sufficient or proper use of our bodies, and as a result the majority of our muscles become weak, inflexible and insensitive. They must be reactivated and made resilient. The entire method suggested in this book leads us to the accomplishment of this third requirement.

Now let us get down to practical work and start doing our exercises. Avoid doing them mechanically, and always try to keep in mind the final aim of each.

EXERCISE 1

Do a series of wide, broad but simple movements using a maximum of space around you. Involve and utilize your whole body. Make the movements with sufficient strength, but without straining your muscles unnecessarily. Movements can be made that will "enact" the following:

Open yourself completely, spreading wide your arms and hands, your legs far apart. Remain in this expanded position for a few seconds. Imagine that you are becoming larger and larger. Come back to the original position. Repeat the same movement several times. Keep in mind the aim of the exercise, saying to yourself, "I am going to awaken the sleeping muscles of my body; I am going to revivify and use them."

Now close yourself by crossing your arms upon your chest, putting your hands on your shoulders. Kneel on one or both knees, bending your head low. Imagine that you are becoming smaller and smaller, curling up, contracting as though you wanted to disappear bodily within yourself, and that the space around you is shrinking. Another set of your muscles will be awakened by this contracting movement.

Resume a standing position, then *thrust* your body forward on one leg, stretching out one or both arms. Do the same *stretching* movement sideways to the right, to the left, using as much space around you as you can.

Do a movement that resembles a blacksmith *beating* his hammer upon the anvil.

Do different, wide, well-shaped, full movements – as though you were in turn *throwing* something in different directions, *lifting* some object from the ground, *holding* it high above your head, or *dragging*, *pushing* and *tossing* it. Make your movements complete, with sufficient strength and in moderate tempo. Avoid dancing movements. Do not hold your breath while moving. Do not hurry. Pause after each movement.

This exercise will gradually give you a glimmer of the sensations of *freedom and increased life*. Let these sensations sink into your body as the first psychological qualities to be absorbed.

EXERCISE 2

After you have taught yourself by means of this preparatory exercise to produce these simple, wide and free movements, continue doing them another way. Imagine that within your chest there is a *center* from which flows the actual impulses for all your movements. Think of this imaginary center as a source of inner activity and *power* within your body. Send this power into your head, arms, hands, torso, legs and feet. Let the sensation of strength, harmony and well-being penetrate the whole body. See to it that neither your shoulders, elbows, wrists, hips nor knees stanch the flow of this energy from the imaginary center, but let it course freely. Realize that the joints are not given you to make your body stiff but, on the contrary, to enable you to use your limbs with utmost freedom and flexibility.

Imagining that your arms and legs originate from this center within your chest (not from the shoulders and hips), try a series of natural movements: lift your arms and lower them, stretch them in different directions, walk, sit down, get up, lie down; move different objects; put on your overcoat, gloves, hat; take them off, and so on. See that all the movements you make are actually instigated by that power which flows from the imaginary center within your chest.

While doing this exercise keep in mind another important principle: let the power which flows from the imaginary center within your chest and leads you through space *precede* the movement itself; that is, first send out the impulse for the movement, and then, an instant later, do the movement itself. While walking forward, sideways or backward, let even the center itself go out, as it were, from your chest, a few inches ahead of you in the direction of your movement. Let your body *follow* the center. It will make your walk as well as every movement smooth, graceful and artistic, as pleasant to fulfill as to look at.

After the movement is accomplished, do not cut short the stream of power generated from the center, but let it flow and radiate for a while beyond the boundaries of your body and into the space around you. This power must not only precede each of your movements but also *follow* it, so that the sensation of freedom will be bolstered by that of power, thus placing another psychophysical achievement at your command. Gradually, you will experience more and more of that strong feeling which may be called an actor's presence on the stage. While facing the audience you will never be self-conscious, never suffer from any kind of fear or lack of confidence in yourself as an artist.

The imaginary center in your chest will also give you the sensation that your whole body is approaching, as it were, an "ideal" type of human body. Like a musician who can play only on a well-tuned instrument, so you will have the feeling that your "ideal" body enables you to make the greatest possible use of it, to give it all kinds of characteristic features demanded by the part you are working upon. So continue these exercises until you feel that the powerful center within your chest is a natural part of you and no longer requires any special attention or concentration.

The imaginary center also serves other purposes, which will be discussed later on.

EXERCISE 3

As before, make strong and broad movements with your whole body. But now say to yourself: "Like a sculptor, I *mold* the space surrounding me. In the air around me I leave forms which appear to be chiseled by the movements of my body."

Create strong and definite forms. To be able to do this, think of the beginning and the end of each movement you make. Again say to yourself: "Now I begin my movement which creates a form," and, after completing it: "Now I *finished* it; the form is there." Along with this, think and feel your body itself as a *movable* form. Repeat each movement several times until it becomes free and most enjoyable to fulfill. Your efforts will resemble the work of a designer who, again and again, draws the same line, striving for a better, clearer and more expressive form. But in order not to lose the molding quality of your movement imagine the air around you as a medium which resists you. Also try the same movements in different tempos.

Then try to reproduce these movements by using only different parts of your body: mold the air around you with only your shoulders and shoulder blades, then with your back, your elbows, knees, forehead, hands, fingers, etc. In all these movements preserve the sensation of strength and inner power flowing through and out of your body. Avoid unnecessary muscular tension. For the sake of simplicity do your molding movements at first without imagining a center within your chest, and after a while with the imagined center.

Now, as in the previous exercise, return to simple natural movements and everyday business, using the center and preserving, as well as combining, the sensations of strength, molding power and form.

When coming in contact with different objects, try to pour your strength into them, to fill them with your power. This will develop your ability to handle the objects (hand props on the stage) with utmost skill and ease. Likewise, learn to extend this power to your partners (even at a distance); it will become one of the simplest means of establishing true and firm contacts with those on the stage, which is an important part of the technique and will be dealt with later. Spend your power lavishly; it is inexhaustible, and the more you give, the more it will accumulate in you.

Conclude this exercise (as well as Exercises 4, 5, and 6) with an attempt to train your *hands* and *fingers* separately. Make any natural series of movements; take, move, lift up, put down, touch and transpose different objects, large and small. See to it that your hands and fingers are filled with the same molding power and that they, too, create forms with each movement. No need to exaggerate your movements, and no need to be discouraged because at first they may look slightly awkward and overdone. An actor's hands and fingers can be most expressive on the stage if well developed, sensitive and economically used.

Having acquired sufficient technique in doing these molding movements, and experienced pleasure in making them, next say to yourself: "Every movement I make is a little piece of art, I am doing it like an artist. My body is a fine instrument for producing molding movements and for creating forms. Through my body I am able to convey to the spectator my inner power and strength." Let these thoughts sink deeply into your body.

This exercise will constantly enable you to create forms for whatever you do on the stage. You will develop a taste for form and will be artistically dissatisfied with any movements that are vague and shapeless, or with amorphous gestures, speech, thoughts, feelings and will impulses when you encounter them in yourself and others during your professional work. You will understand and be convinced that vagueness and shapelessness have no place in art.

EXERCISE 4

Repeat the wide and broad movements of the previous exercises, utilizing the whole body; then switch to the simple natural movements, and finally exercise with your hands and fingers only.

But now awaken in yourself still another thought: "My movements are *floating* in space, merging gently and beautifully one into another." As in the previous exercise, all the movements must be simple and well shaped. Let them ebb and flow like big waves. As before, avoid unnecessary muscular tension, but, on the other hand, do not let the movements become weak, vague, unfinished or shapeless.

In this exercise imagine the air around you as a surface of water which supports you and over which your movements lightly skim.

Change tempos. Pause from time to time. Consider your movements as little pieces of art, as with all exercises suggested in this chapter. A sensation of calm, *poise* and psychological *warmth* will be your reward. Preserve these sensations and let them fill your whole body.

EXERCISE 5

If you have ever watched flying birds, you will easily grasp the idea behind these next movements. Imagine your whole body *flying* through space. As in the previous exercises, your movements must merge into each other without becoming shapeless. In this exercise the physical strength of your movements may increase or diminish according to your desire, but it must never disappear altogether. Psychologically you must constantly maintain your strength. You may come to a static position outwardly, but inwardly you must continue your feeling of still soaring aloft. Imagine the air around you as a medium which instigates your flying movements. Your desire must be to overcome the weight of your body, to fight the law of gravity. While moving, change tempos. A sensation of joyful *lightness* and *easiness* will permeate your entire body.

Start this exercise, too, with the wide, broad movements. Then proceed to the natural gestures. While carrying out the everyday movements, be sure to preserve their truthfulness and simplicity.

EXERCISE 6

Begin this exercise, as always, with the broad, wide movements of the previous exercises, then go into the simple, natural movements next suggested. Lift your arm, lower it, stretch it forward, sideways; walk around the room, lie down, sit down, get up, etc.; but continuously and in advance send the *rays* from your body into the space around you, in the direction of the movement you make, and after the movement is made.

You may wonder perhaps how you can continue, for instance, sitting down after you have actually sat down. The answer is simple if you remember yourself as having sat down, tired and worn out.

True, your *physical* body has taken this final position, but *psychologically* you still continue to "sit down" by *radiating* that you are sitting. You experience this radiation in the sensation of enjoying your relaxation. The same with getting up while imagining yourself tired and worn-out: your body resists it, and long before you really get up you are already doing it inwardly: you are radiating "getting up" and you continue to get up when you are already standing. Of course, this is not to suggest that you must "act" or pretend to be tired during this example. It is merely an illustration of what might happen in a given real-life circumstance. In this exercise this should be done with every movement that comes to a *physically* static position. Radiation must precede and follow all your actual movements.

While radiating strive, in a sense, to go out and beyond the boundary of your body. Send your rays in different directions from the whole body at once and afterward through its various parts – arms, hands, fingers, palms, forehead, chest and back. You may or may not use the center in your chest as the mainspring of your radiation. Fill the entire space around you with these radiations. (Actually it is the same process as sending out your power, but has a much lighter quality. Also, be alert to the subtle differences between the flying and radiating movements, until practice makes them easily apparent to you.) Imagine that the air around you is filled with light.

You must not be disturbed by doubts as to whether you are actually radiating or whether you are only imagining that you are. If you sincerely and convincingly imagine that you are sending out rays, the imagination will gradually and faithfully lead you to the real and actual process of radiating.

A sensation of the actual existence and significance of your *inner being* will be the result of this exercise. Not infrequently actors are unaware of or overlook this treasure within themselves, and while acting rely far more than necessary upon merely their outer means of expression. The use of outer expressions alone is glaring evidence of how some actors forget or ignore that the characters they portray have living souls, and that these souls can be made manifest and convincing through powerful *radiation*. In fact, there is nothing within the sphere of our psychology which cannot thus be radiated.

Other sensations you will experience will be those of freedom, happiness and inner warmth. All these feelings will fill your entire body, permeating it and making it more and more alive, sensitive and responsive. (Additional comments on Radiation may be found at the end of this chapter.)

EXERCISE 7

When you are thoroughly familiar with these four kinds of movements (molding, floating, flying and radiating) and are able to fulfill them easily, try to reproduce them in your imagination only. Repeat this until you can easily duplicate the same psychological and physical sensations you experienced while actually moving.

In every true, great piece of art you will always find four qualities which the artist has put into his creation: *Ease*, *Form*, *Beauty*, and *Entirety*. These four qualities must also be developed by the actor; his body and speech must be endowed with them because they are the only instruments available to him on the stage. His body must become a piece of art within itself, must acquire these four qualities, must experience them inwardly.

Let us first deal with the quality of *Ease*. While acting, heavy movements and inflexible speech are capable of depressing and even repulsing an audience. Heaviness in an artist is an uncreative power. On the stage it may exist only as a *theme*, but never as a *manner* of acting. "It is the lightness of touch which more than anything else makes the artist," said Edward Eggleston. In other words, your *character* on the stage can be heavy, awkward in movements and inarticulate in speech; but you yourself, as an *artist*, must always use lightness and ease as a means of expression. Even heaviness itself must be performed with lightness and ease. You will never confuse the qualities of the character and those of yourself as an artist if you will learn to distinguish between *what* you act (the theme, the character) and *how* you do it (the way, the manner of acting).

Ease relaxes your body and spirit; therefore, it is also much akin to humor. Some comedians resort to a heavy means of humorous expression, such as getting red in the face, "mugging," contorting their bodies and punishing their vocal chords – and yet the laughs fail to come off. Other comedians use the same heavy devices, but with ease and finesse, and are highly successful with them. An even better illustration is a fine clown who falls "heavily" to the ground, but with such artistic grace and ease that you cannot restrain your laughter. The ultimate and incomparable examples are, of course, the easy manner behind the heavy grotesqueries of a Charlie Chaplin or a clown like Grock.

The quality of Ease is best acquired through the exercises on the flying and radiating movements which are now familiar to you.

Of similar importance is the sense of *Form*. You may be called upon to play a stage character which the author has written as a vague, slack type of person, or you may have to perform a bewildered, chaotic type of man with no sense of form, with unclear and even stuttering speech. But such a character must be considered only thematically, as *what* you are playing. *How* you, the artist, play it will depend on how complete and perfect is your feeling of *form*. The tendency toward clarity of form is apparent even in the unfinished works and sketches of the great masters. To create with clear-cut forms is an ability which artists in all crafts can and perforce must develop to a high degree.

The exercises on the molding movements can best serve you in acquiring the quality of Form.

But what about *Beauty*? It has frequently been stated that beauty is the result of a conglomeration of many psychophysical elements. This is undoubtedly true. But the actor who attempts exercises on beauty should not try to experience beauty analytically or vicariously but, rather, instantly and intuitively. For the actor to understand beauty as solely a confluence of many elements would lead to much confusion and result in many errors of training.

Before the actor starts exercising on beauty he must think of it as having its good and bad sides, its right and wrong, its apposite and opposite. For beauty, as does each positive thing, has its shadowy side. If daring is a virtue, then thoughtless, senseless bravado is its negative side; if caution is a positive quality, then blinding fear is its negative, and so on. The same must be said of beauty. True beauty has its roots *inside* the human being, whereas false beauty is only on the *outside*. "Showing off" is the negative side of beauty, and so are sentimentality, sweetness, self-love and other such vanities. An actor who develops a sense of beauty simply to enjoy *himself* fosters only a surface gloss, a thin veneer. His aim must be to acquire this sense only for his art. If he is able to extract the sting of egotism from his sense of beauty, he is out of danger.

But you may ask: "How can I perform ugly situations and repulsive characters if my creation has to be beautiful? Won't this beauty rob me of expressiveness?" The answer, in principle, remains the same as that of distinguishing between *what* and *how*, between the theme and the way of performing it, between the character or situation and the artist with a well-developed sense of beauty and fine taste. Ugliness expressed on the stage by unaesthetic means irritates the nerves of the audience. The effect of such a performance is *physiological* rather than psychological. The uplifting influence of art remains paralyzed in such cases. But aesthetically performed, an unpleasant theme, character or situation preserves the power of uplifting and inspiring the audience.

The beauty with which such a theme is performed transforms the particular ugliness into its *idea*; behind the particular there then looms the archetype, and at once it appeals chiefly to the mind and spirit of the spectator instead of jangling his nerves.

An apt illustration of this might be King Lear's speeches wherein he curses his daughters, heaping one malediction upon the other. Taken separately they certainly do not belong to the realm of beauty, but in context all of them create the impression of a most beautifully executed segment of the play. Here we see Shakespeare's genius applying beautiful means (*how*) to treat a highly unpleasant theme (*what*). This classic example alone tells us, more than any number of words can, the meaning and uses of histrionic beauty.

With these explanations in mind one can start doing these simple exercises on Beauty.

EXERCISE 8

Begin with observations of all kinds of beauty in human beings (putting aside sensuousness as negative), in art and in nature, however obscure and insignificant the beautiful features in them may be. Then ask yourself: "*Why* does it strike me as beautiful? Because of its form? Harmony? Sincerity? Simplicity? Color? Moral value? Strength? Gentleness? Significance? Originality? Ingenuity? Selflessness? Idealism? Mastery?" Etc.

As a result of long and patient processes of observation, you will notice that a sense of true beauty and fine artistic taste gradually becomes responsive within you. You will feel that your mind and body have accumulated beauty and that you have sharpened your ability to detect it everywhere. It becomes a kind of habit in you. Now you are ready to proceed with the following exercise:

Begin, as before, with broad, simple movements. trying to do them with the beauty which rises from *within* you, until your entire body is permeated with it and begins to feel an aesthetic satisfaction. Do not do your exercises before a mirror; this will tend to stress beauty as only a surface quality when the purpose is to *fathom it deep within yourself*. Avoid dancing movements. Afterward, move with the imaginary center within your chest. Go over the four kinds of movements: molding, floating, flying, radiating. Speak a few words. Then do everyday movements and simple business. And even in your everyday life carefully avoid ugly movements and speech. Resist the temptation to *appear* beautiful.

Now to the last of the four qualities inherent in the actor's art, *Entirety*.

The actor who plays his part as so many separate and unrelated moments between each entrance and exit, without regard for what he did in his previous scenes or what he will be doing in scenes to follow, will never understand or interpret his part as a whole or in its *entirety*. Failure or inability to relate a part to its entirety might make it inharmonious and incomprehensible to the spectator.

On the other hand, if in the beginning or from the very first entrance you already have a vision of yourself playing (or rehearsing) your last scenes – and, conversely, remembering the first scenes as you play (or rehearse) the very last scenes – you will better be able to see your whole part in every detail, as though you were viewing it in perspective from some elevation. The ability to evaluate the details within the part as a well-integrated whole will further enable you to play each of these details as little entities which blend harmoniously into the all-embracing *entirety*.

What new qualities will your acting gain because of this *entirety* feeling? You will intuitively stress *essentials* in your character and follow the *main line* of events, thus holding firmly the attention of the audience. Your acting will become more powerful. It will also help you from the very outset to grasp your character without much floundering.

EXERCISE 9

Review in your mind the events of the day just past, trying to pick out those periods which are complete in themselves. Pretend that they are separate scenes in a play. Define their beginnings and ends. Again and again go over them in your memory until each one stands out as an entity and yet coheres with the others as an *entirety*.

Do the same with longer periods of your entire past life and, finally, try to foresee the future in connection with your plans, ideals and aims.

Do the same in connection with the lives of historical personages and their destinies. And do the same with plays.

Now turn to things and objects displayed before your eyes (plants, animals, architectural forms, landscapes, etc.), looking at them as entire forms by themselves. Then find within them separate parts which can stand out as complete little pictures. Imagine them as being put into frames, so that they resemble snapshots or sections of a film.

You may also do that with your sense of hearing. Listen to a musical composition and try to perceive its separate phrases as more or less independent units. The relationship of the variation within each to the whole theme, as with the kinship of the separate scenes to a play, will at once become apparent to you.

Conclude your exercise as follows: Divide the room in which you do your exercises into two parts. Step from one part, which represents off stage, into the other, which represents the stage itself, and try to establish the moment of your appearance before the imaginary audience as a significant *beginning*. Stand still before your "audience" and speak one or two sentences, pretending that you are playing a part, then leave your "stage" as though your disappearance were a definite *end*. Grasp the entire process of appearance and disappearance as an entirety in itself.

An acute sense of the beginning and end is only one means

of developing your feeling of entireness. Another means is to conceive your character as *unchangeable in its core*, in spite of all the transformations it might undergo in the play. This aspect of the exercise will be touched upon in later chapters dealing with the Psychological Gesture and the Composition of the Performance.

A few supplementary remarks on *radiation* are in order here.

To radiate on the stage means *to give*, to send out. Its counterpart is *to receive*. True acting is a constant exchange of the two. There are no moments on the stage when an actor can allow himself – or rather his character – to remain passive in this sense without running the risk of weakening the audience's attention and creating the sensation of a psychological vacuum.

We know how the actor radiates and why, but what should he (the character) *receive*, and *when* and *how*? He can receive the presence of his partners, their actions and words, or he can receive his surroundings specifically or in general as required by the play. He can also receive the atmosphere in which he finds himself, or he can receive things or events. In short, he receives everything that should make an impression upon him as a character according to the meaning of the moment.

When the actor must receive or radiate depends on the content of the scene, the director's suggestions, the actor's own free choice or perhaps a combination of these factors.

As to *how* the receiving should be executed and felt, the actor must bear in mind that it is more than merely a matter of looking. and listening on the stage. To actually receive means to *draw toward* one's self with the utmost inner power the things, persons or events of the situation. Even though your partners may not know this technique, you must never, for the sake of your own performance, stop receiving whenever you choose to do so. You will find that your own efforts will intuitively awaken other players and inspire their collaboration.

Thus, in our first nine exercises, we have laid the foundation for the attainment of the four requirements which are basic to the actor's technique. By means of the suggested psychophysical exercises the actor can increase his *inner strength*, develop his abilities to *radiate* and *receive*, acquire a fine sense of *form*, enhance his feelings of *freedom*, *ease*, *calm* and *beauty*, experience the significance of his *inner being*, and learn to see things and processes in their *entirety*. If the suggested exercises are patiently complied with, all these and all the other qualities and abilities we have covered will permeate his body, making it finer and more sensitive, enrich his psychology and at the same time give him, even at this stage of his development, a degree of mastery over them.

2

IMAGINATION AND
INCORPORATION OF IMAGES

Not that which *is* inspires the creation, but that which *may* be;
not the *actual*, but the *possible*.

– Rudolf Steiner

It is evening. After a long day, after much work and many impressions, experiences, actions and words – you let your tired nerves rest. You sit quietly with your eyes closed. What is it that appears out of the darkness before your mind's eye? You review the faces of people you've met during the day, their voices, movements, their characteristic or humorous features. You run again through the streets, pass familiar houses, read the signs. Passively, you follow the motley images of your memory.

Unnoticed by yourself you step back over the boundaries of today, and in your imagination slowly arise visions of your past life. Your forgotten and half-remembered wishes, daydreams, life's aims, successes and failures appear as pictures before your mind. True, they are not so faithful to the facts as the recollections of the day just passed. Now they are, in retrospect, slightly changed. But you still recognize them. With your mind's eye you now follow them with greater interest, with more awakened attention, because they *are* changed, because they now bear some traces of imagination.

But much more happens. Out of the visions of the past there flash here and there images totally unknown to you! They are pure products of your *Creative Imagination*. They appear, disappear, they come back again, bringing with them new strangers. Presently they enter into relationships with one another. They begin to "act," to "perform" before your fascinated gaze. You follow their heretofore unknown lives. You are absorbed, drawn into strange moods, atmospheres, into the love, hatred, happiness and unhappiness of these imaginary guests. Your mind is now fully awake and active. Your own reminiscences grow paler and paler; the new images are stronger than they. You are amused by the fact that these new images possess their own independent lives; you are astonished that they appear without your invitation. Finally these newcomers force you to watch them with greater poignancy than the simple pictures of everyday memory; these fascinating guests, who made their appearance from nowhere, who live their own lives full of emotions, awaken your responsive feelings. They force you to laugh and to cry with them. Like magicians, they call up in you an unconquerable desire to become one of them. You enter into conversations with them, you now see yourself among them; you want to act, and you do so. From a passive state of mind the images have uplifted you to a *creative* one. Such is the power of imagination.

Actors and directors, like all creative artists, are well acquainted with this power. "I am always surrounded by images," said Max Reinhardt. The whole morning, wrote Dickens, he sat in his study expecting Oliver Twist to appear. Goethe observed that inspiring images appear before us of their own accord, exclaiming, "Here we are!" Rafael saw an image pass before him in his room and this was the Sistine Madonna. Michelangelo exclaimed in despair that images pursued him and forced him to carve their likenesses out of rocks.

But although Creative Images are independent and changeable within themselves, although they are full of emotions and desires, you, while working upon your parts, must not think that they will come to you fully developed and accomplished. They don't. To complete themselves, to reach the degree of expressiveness that would satisfy you, they will require your active collaboration. What must you do to perfect them? You must ask questions of these images, as you would ask questions of a friend. Sometimes you must even give them strict orders. Changing and completing themselves under the influence of your questions and orders, they give you answers visible to your inner sight. Let us take an example:

Suppose you are going to play Malvolio in *Twelfth Night*. Suppose you want to study the moment when Malvolio approaches Olivia in the garden, after having received a mysterious letter which he supposes to be "from her." Here is where you begin to ask questions such as "Show me, Malvolio: how would you enter the gates of the garden and with a smile move toward your 'sweet lady?'" The question immediately incites the image of Malvolio to action. You see him in the distance. Hastily he hides the letter under his cloak, to produce it later with triumphant effect! His neck stretched, his face deadly serious, he looks for Olivia. Here she is! How the smile distorts his face! Didn't she write to him, "Thy smiles become thee well . . ."? But his eyes, do they smile? Oh, no! They are alarmed, anxious and watchful! They peer from behind the mask of a madman! His concern is his pace, his beautiful walk! His yellow, cross-gartered stockings seem fascinating and seductive to him. But what is that? Maria! This intrusive creature, this plague is here, too, watching him out of the comer of her mischievous eye! The smile fades from his face, he forgets his legs for a moment and his knees bend slightly, involuntarily, and the whole figure betrays his not-so-youthful body. Hatred now flashes in his gaze! But time is short. His "sweet lady" awaits! Signs of love, of passionate desire, must be given to her without delay! Tighter his cloak, faster his walk, nearer to her he goes! Slowly, secretly, seductively a little tiny corner of "her" letter appears from under his cloak. . . . Doesn't she see it? No! She looks at his face. . . . Oh, the smile! It has been forgotten, and now it turns on when she greets him with:

"How now, Malvolio!"

"Sweet lady, ho, ho!"

"Smilest thou? . . ."

What was this little "performance" Malvolio offered you? I was his first answer to your question. But you may feel dissatisfied. It does not seem right to you; the "performance" left you cold. You ask further questions: Should not Malvolio at this moment be more dignified? Was not his "performance" too much of a carica-ture? Was he not too old? Would it not be better to "see" him as rather pathetic? Or maybe at this moment, when he believes he has achieved the aim of his whole life, he reaches the point where his mind is shaken and he verges on madness. Maybe he should bear more resemblance to a clown. Shouldn't he be even more old and undignified? Shouldn't his lecherous desires be stressed more? Or perhaps his appearance would be enhanced if he made a rather humorous impression. What if he looked like a naïve and rather innocent child? Is he entirely bewildered or still able to keep his senses under control?

Many questions like these may arise in your mind while you are working upon a part. Here your collaboration with the image begins. You guide and build your character by asking it new questions, by ordering it to show you different variations of pos-sible ways of acting, according to your taste (or the director's interpretation of the character). The image changes under your questioning gaze, transforms itself again and again until gradually (or suddenly) you feel satisfied with it. Thereupon you will find your emotions aroused, and the desire to act flares up in you!

By working this way you will be able to study and create your character more profoundly (and more quickly, too); you will not be relying only on ordinary thinking instead of "seeing" these little "performances." Dry reasoning kills your imagination. The more you probe with your analytical mind, the more silent become your feelings, the weaker your will and the poorer your chances for inspiration.

There is no question that cannot be answered in this way. Of course, not all questions will be answered immediately; some are more intricate than others. Were you to ask, for instance, what the *relationship* is between your character and the others in the play, the right answer would not always come at once. Sometimes hours, even days, are required before you "see" your character in these different relationships.

The more you work upon your imagination, strengthening it by means of exercises, the sooner a sensation will arise within you which you can describe as something like this: "The images which I see with the mind's eye have their own psychology, like the people surrounding me in my everyday life. However, there is one difference: In everyday life, seeing people by their outer manifestations alone and not seeing behind their facial expressions, movements, gestures, voices and intonations, I might misjudge their inner lives. But it is not so with my creative images. *Their* inner lives are completely open for me to behold. All their emotions, feelings, passions, thoughts, their aims and innermost desires are revealed to me. Through the outer manifestation of my image – that is to say, of the character I am working upon by means of my imagination – I see its inner life."

The oftener and more intently you look *into* your image, the sooner it awakens in you those feelings, emotions and will impulses so necessary to your performance of the character. This "looking" and "seeing" is nothing but rehearsing by means of your well-developed and flexible imagination. Michelangelo creating his Moses not only "saw" the muscles, the ripples of the beard, the folds of the garment, but, undoubtedly, also "saw" that *inner might* of Moses which had created those muscles, veins, beard, garment folds and the whole rhythmical composition. Leonardo da Vinci was tormented by the fiery inner life of the images he "saw." This is one of the most valuable and important functions of imagination, provided you take the pains to develop it to a high degree. You will begin to appreciate it as soon as you realize that you need not "squeeze" your feelings out of yourself, that they will rise from within you by themselves, and with ease, as soon as you learn to "see" the psychology, the inner life, of your images. And just as Michelangelo "saw" the inner might which created Moses' outer appearance, so your "seeing" and experiencing your character's inner life will always prompt you to new, more original, more correct and more suitable means of outer expressiveness on the stage.

The more developed your imagination through systematic exercises, the more flexible and fleeting it becomes. Images will follow images with increasing rapidity; they will form and vanish too hastily. This may result in your losing them before they can kindle your feelings. You must possess enough will power, more than you normally exert in everyday activities, to keep them before your mind's eye long enough for them to affect and awaken your own feelings.

And what is this additional will power? It is the power of concentration.

I anticipate your asking: "Why should I take such pains to develop my imagination and apply it to work upon modern, naturalistic plays when all the characters are so obvious and easy to comprehend; when the lines, situations and business provided by the author take care of everything?" If that is your question, permit me to take issue with it. What the author has given you in the form of a written play is *his* creation, not yours; he has applied *his* talent. But what is your contribution to the writer's work? To my understanding, it is, or should be, the discovery of the psychological depths of the characters given you in the play. There is no human being who is obvious and easy to comprehend. The true actor will not glide over the surfaces of the characters he plays nor impose upon them his personal and unvarying mannerisms. I know perfectly well that that is the widely recognized and practiced custom in our profession today. But, for whatever impression it may make upon you, let me take the liberty of expressing myself unrestrainedly on this point.

It is a crime to chain and imprison an actor within the limits of his so-called "personality," thus making of him an enslaved laborer rather than an artist. Where is his freedom? How can he use his own creativeness and originality? Why should he always appear before his audiences as a puppet compelled to make the same kind of movements when the strings are pulled? The fact that modern writers, audiences, critics and even actors themselves have become habituated to this degradation of the actor-artist does not make the charge less true or the evil less execrable.

One of the most disappointing results stemming from this accustomed treatment of the actor has been that it makes him a less interesting human being on the stage than he invariably is in private life. (It would be infinitely better for the theater if the opposite prevailed.) His "creations" are not worthy of himself. Using only his mannerisms, the actor becomes *unimaginative*; all characters become the same to him.

To create, in the real sense, means to discover and show new things. But what novelty is there in the stilted mannerisms and clichés of the fettered actor? The deeply hidden, and nowadays almost completely forgotten, desire of every true actor is to express himself, to assert his ego, through the medium of his parts. But how can he do it if he is encouraged, more often required, to resort to his mannerisms instead of his creative imagination? He can't because the creative imagination is one of the main channels through which the artist in him finds the way to express his *own*, individual (and therefore always unique) interpretation of the characters to be portrayed. And how is he going to express his creative individuality if he does not or cannot penetrate deeply into the inner life of the characters themselves by means of his creative imagination?

I am quite prepared for some disagreement with these views; it is a sign that the actor is at least giving some thought to the problem. Nevertheless, for the sake of argument, let us find the best arbitrator. In this case I recommend the power of imagination itself. Start doing the suggested exercises that follow and you may change your mind upon seeing and experiencing how much penetration you develop while working upon your parts; how interesting and intricate your characters will appear to you, whereas they seemed so ordinary, flat and obvious before; how many new, human and unexpected psychological features they will reveal to you, and how, as a consequence, your acting will become less and less monotonous!

EXERCISE 10

Start your exercise with recollections of simple, impersonal events (not of your own emotions or inner, real-life experiences). Try to recall as many details as possible. Concentrate on these recollections, trying not to break the flow of your concentration.

Simultaneously with this exercise, begin to train yourself in *catching the very first image* the moment it appears before your mind's eye. Do it this way: Take a book, open a page at random, read a word from it and see which image it conjures up before you. This will teach you to *imagine* things rather than confine yourself to abstract, lifeless conceptions of them. Abstractions are of very little use to a creative artist. After a little practice you will notice that every word, even words like "but," "and," "if," "because" and so on, will evoke certain images, some of them perhaps strange and fantastic. Fix your attention upon these images for a moment, then continue your exercise in the same way with new words.

After a while proceed to the next step of the exercise: Having caught an image, look at it and wait until it begins to move, to change, to speak and to "act" *on its own*. Realize that each image has its own *independent life*. Don't interfere with this life, but follow it for at least several minutes.

Next step: Again create an image and let it develop its independent life. Then, after a while, begin to interfere with it by asking questions or giving orders. "Will you show me how you sit down? Get up? Walk? Ascend or descend a staircase? Meet other people?" And so forth. If the independent life of the image becomes too strong and the image turns obstinate (as it often does), turn the requests into orders.

Proceed with questions and orders of a more psychological nature: "How do you appear in despair? In a happy mood? . . . Give a hearty welcome to your friend. Meet your enemy. Become suspicious, thoughtful. Laugh. Cry." And many other similar questions and orders. Ask the same question as many times as you have to, until your image shows you what you want to "see." Repeat the same procedure for as long as you wish to continue your exercises. While interfering with the independent life of your image you might also put it in different situations, order it to change its outer appearance, or set other tasks for it. Alternate by giving it its freedom several times and then making your demands upon it again.

From a play choose a short scene having few characters. Act out the scene with all its characters several times in your imagination. Then put before the characters a series of questions and give them a number of suggestions – "How would you act if the atmosphere of the scene were different?" – and suggest to them several different atmospheres. Watch their reactions, then order: "Now change the tempo of the scene." Give them suggestions to play the scene with more reserve, or with more abandon. Ask them to make certain feelings stronger and certain others weaker, and vice versa. Interpolate some new pauses or discard the previous ones. Change their *mise-en-scènes*, business, or whatever will make for a different interpretation.

Thus you will learn to *collaborate* with your creative image while working upon your part. On the one hand, you will get used to accepting the suggestions which your character (as an image) gives you, while on the other, by means of your questions and orders, you will elaborate and lead it to perfection according to your own (and your director's) taste and desire.

Now, as the next step of your exercise, try to learn to penetrate through the outer manifestation of an image into its *inner* life.

In our everyday existence it is not unusual to observe people around us closely and most attentively, and yet not be able to penetrate their inner lives deeply enough. Some areas of their psychology will always be obscured to you; there will always be some secrets which you will not be able to discover. But not so with your images; they can have no secrets from you. Why? Because however new and unexpected your images may be, they are, after all, your own creations; their inner experiences are your own. True, they often reveal to you feelings, emotions and desires of which you were not aware before you started using your creative imagination, but from whatever deep levels of your subconscious life they may have emerged they are nonetheless *yours*. Therefore, train yourself to watch the images as long as it is necessary to become *affected* by their emotions, desires, feelings and all else they have to offer; that is, until you *yourself* begin to feel and wish what your image feels and wishes. This is one of the ways of awakening and kindling your feelings without laboriously and painfully "squeezing" them out of yourself. Choose simple psychological moments at first.

Next proceed to the exercise for developing the *flexibility* of your imagination. Take some image, study it in detail. Then make it *transform* slowly into another image. For instance: A young man gradually becomes old, and vice versa; a young shoot of a plant slowly develops into a big, many-branched tree; a winter landscape fluently transforms itself into one of spring, summer and autumn.

Do this same exercise with images of fantasy. Make a bewitched castle transform itself into a poor hut, and vice versa; an old witch become a beautiful young princess; a wolf turn into a handsome prince. Then start working with moving images, such as a tournament of knights, a growing forest fire, an excited crowd of people, a ballroom with dancing couples or a factory busily at work. Try to hear the speeches and sounds of your images. Don't allow your attention to be distracted or jump from one stage to another and so miss the transitory stages. The transformation of images must be a smooth, continuous flow, as in a film.

Next create a character *entirely by yourself*. Start developing it, elaborating it in detail; work upon it through many days or perhaps weeks by asking questions and getting visible answers. Put it in different situations, different environments, and watch its reactions; develop its characteristic features and peculiarities. Then ask it to speak, and follow its emotions, desires, feelings, thoughts; open yourself to it so that its inner life will influence your own inner life. Co-operate with it by accepting its "suggestions" if you like them. Create dramatic as well as humorous characters.

Working that way, the time may come at any moment when your image will become so powerful that you will be unable to resist the desire to *incorporate* it, to act it even if it is only a bit of a short scene. When such a desire flares up in you, do not resist it, but act *freely* for as long as you wish.

This sound desire to incorporate your image can be systematically cultivated by means of a special exercise, one which will give you the *technique of incorporation*:

EXERCISE 11

Imagine yourself doing, at first, some simple movement: raising your arm, getting up, sitting down or taking an object. Study this movement of yours in your imagination, and then *actually* fulfill it. Imitate it, as it were, as faithfully as you can. If, when fulfilling it, you notice that your actual movement is not quite that which you saw in your imagination – study it again in your imagination and try it again, until you are satisfied that you have copied it faithfully. Repeat this exercise until you are sure that your body obeys even the slightest detail you developed when imagining, your movement. Continue the exercise with more and more complicated movements and business.

Apply the same exercise to imagining a character from a play or a novel, starting with simple movements, business and psychological content. Let your image speak a few words. In your imagination. study the character with utmost attention to as many details as possible, until the feelings of the character arouse your own feelings. Then try to incorporate your new vision as faithfully as you can.

When incorporating, you may notice that you sometimes deviate from what you have visualized and studied in detail. If this deviation is the result of sudden inspiration *while* incorporating, accept it as a positive and desirable fact.

This exercise will gradually establish those fine connections so necessary to the linking of your vivid imagination with your body, voice and psychology. Your means of expression will thus become flexible and obedient to your commands.

When working this way with the character you are going to play on the stage, you might, to begin with, choose only one feature from all that stand before your inner vision. By doing so you will never experience the shock (which actors know only too well!) that comes of trying to incorporate the whole image *at once*, in one greedy gulp. It is this strangling shock that often forces you to abandon imaginative efforts and relapse into clichés and old, worn-out theatrical habits. You know that your body, voice and whole psychological make-up are not always able to adjust themselves to your vision on short notice. Going over your image bit by bit, you avoid this difficulty. You enable your means of expression to go quietly through the necessary transformation and be ready to comply with the respective tasks they have to fulfill. You will be better able to incorporate the entire character you are working upon if you do it gradually. It sometimes happens that after only a few attempts to incorporate its separate features, the character will suddenly leap ahead and incorporate itself as a whole.

While thus incorporating your character, whether exercising or while working professionally, add to your imagination all the things you did not foresee and now encounter only in reality – new business, your partners' ways of acting, tempos suggested by your director, and other such contingencies. With these new additions, "rehearse" the scene you are studying in your imagination, then incorporate it again on the stage or while doing your exercise.

These exercises of attempting to incorporate your images will soon prove themselves the most effective means of developing your body as well. For in the process of incorporating strong, well-elaborated images you mold your body from within, as it were, and permeate it throughout with artistic feelings, emotions and will impulses. Thus the body becomes more and more the "sensitive membrane" previously described.

The more time and effort you spend on *conscious* work for developing the strength of your imagination and on the technique of incorporating your images, the sooner your imagination will serve you subconsciously, without your even noticing it at work. Your characters will grow and develop by themselves while you are seemingly not thinking about them, or while you are dreamlessly asleep at night, or even in your dreams. You will also notice that sparks of inspiration will strike oftener and oftener and with greater accuracy.

To sum up the exercises on Imagination:

1   Catch the first image.
2   Learn to follow its independent life.

3   Collaborate with it, asking questions and giving orders.

4   Penetrate the inner life of the image.

5   Develop the flexibility of your imagination.

6   Try to create characters entirely by yourself.

7   Study the technique of incorporating characters.

3

IMPROVISATION AND ENSEMBLE

Only artists united by true sympathy into an Improvising Ensemble can know the joy of unselfish, common creation.

As pointed out in the preceding chapter, the highest and final aim of every true artist, whatever his particular branch of art, may be defined as the desire to express himself freely and completely.

Each of us has his own convictions, his own world outlook, own ideals and ethical attitude toward life. These deeply rooted and often unconscious creeds constitute part of man's individuality and its great longing for free expression.

Profound thinkers impelled to express themselves create their own philosophical systems. Similarly, an artist who strives to express his inner convictions does so by improvising with his own tools, his particular form of art. The same, without exception, must be said for the actor's art: *his* compelling desire and highest aim also can be achieved only by means of free *improvisation*.

If an actor confines himself merely to speaking the lines provided by the author and executing the "business" ordered by the director, and seeks no opportunity to improvise independently, he makes himself a slave to the creations of others and his profession a borrowed one. He erroneously believes that both author and director have already improvised for him and that there is little room left for the free expression of his own creative individuality. This attitude, unfortunately, prevails among too many of our actors today.

Yet every role offers an actor the opportunity to improvise, to collaborate and truly co-create with the author and director. This suggestion, of course, does not imply improvising new lines or substituting business for that outlined by the director. On the contrary. The given lines and the business are the firm bases upon which the actor must and can develop his improvisations. *How* he speaks the lines and *how* he fulfills the business are the open gates to a vast field of improvisation. The "hows" of his lines and business are the *ways* in which he can express himself freely.

More than that, there are innumerable other moments between the lines and business when he can create wonderful psychological transitions and embroider his performance on his own, where he can display his true artistic ingenuity. His interpretation of the whole character down to its minutest features offers a wide range for his improvisations. He need only begin by refusing to play just himself or resorting to worn-out clichés. If he but stop considering all his parts as "straight" ones and will try to find some *fine characterization* for each – that, too, will be a rewarding step toward improvisation. The actor who has not felt the pure joy of transforming himself on the stage with each new part can scarcely know the real, creative meaning of improvisation.

Furthermore, as soon as an actor develops the *ability* to improvise, and discovers within himself this inexhaustible well from which every improvisation is drawn, he will enjoy a sense of *freedom* hitherto unknown to him, and will feel himself much richer inwardly.

The following exercises are designed to develop the ability to improvise. Try to keep them as simple as they are given here.

EXERCISE 12 (*for individual work*):

First decide which are the starting and concluding moments of your improvisation. They must be definite pieces of action. In the beginning, for instance, you may get up quickly from a chair and with firmness of tone or gesture say, "Yes," while in the concluding moment you may lie down, open a book and start reading quietly and leisurely. Or you may start with gaily and hastily putting on your overcoat, hat and gloves, as if intending to go out, and end by sitting down depressed and perhaps even in tears. Or you may begin by looking out the window with fear or great concern, trying to hide yourself behind the curtain and then, exclaiming, "Here he is again!" recoil from the window; and for the concluding moment you might play the piano (real or imaginary) in a very happy and even hilarious mood. And so on. The more contrasted the starting and concluding moments, the better.

Do not try to anticipate what you are going to do *between* the two chosen moments. Do not try to find any logical justification or motivation for either the starting and concluding moments themselves. Choose them at random. Choose any two things that first pop into your head, and not because they will suggest or bracket a good improvisation. Just a contrasting beginning and end.

Do not try to define the theme or plot. Define only the mood or feelings of that beginning and end. Then give yourself over to whatever momentary suggestions occur to you by pure intuition. Thus, when you get up and say, "Yes" – if that is your beginning – you will freely and with full confidence in yourself begin to "act," mainly following your feelings, emotions and moods.

And the middle part, the whole transition from starting to concluding points, is *what* you will improvise.

Let each successive moment of your improvisation be a *psychological* (not logical!) result of the moment preceding it. Thus, without any previously thought-out theme, you will move from the starting to the concluding moment, improvising all the way. By doing so you will go through the whole gamut of different sensations, emotions, moods, desires, inner impulses and business, all of which will be found by you spontaneously, on the spot, as it were. Perhaps you will become indignant, then pensive, then irritated; perhaps you will go through the stages of indifference, humor, gaiety; or perhaps you will write a letter in great agitation, or go to the telephone and call someone, or anything else.

Any and every possibility is open to you according to your mood at the particular moment, or according to the accidental things you may encounter during the improvisation. All you have to do is listen to that "inner voice" which prompts all the changes of your psychology and all the business you resort to. Your subconscious will suggest things which cannot be foreseen by anyone, not even by yourself, if you will but yield freely and completely to the inspiration of your own improvising spirit. With the concluding moment present in your imagination, you will not flounder aimlessly and endlessly, but will constantly and inexplicably be drawn to it. It will loom before you as a magnetic guiding light.

Go on exercising this way, each time establishing a new beginning and a new end, until you have confidence in yourself, until you no longer have to stop and guess about things to do between the start and finish.

You may wonder why the beginning and end of this exercise, whatever they may prove to be, must be clearly defined at the outset. Why should what you are doing or the position of your body and mood be established at the start and finish, but the improvisation in between be permitted to flow spontaneously? Because real and true freedom in improvising must always be based upon *necessity*; otherwise it will soon degenerate into either arbitrariness or indecision. With no definite beginning to impel your actions and no definite end to complete them, you would only wander pointlessly. Your sense of freedom would be meaningless without a place to start or without direction or destination.

When rehearsing a play you naturally encounter a great number of "necessities" which demand your facile improvisational activity and ability. The plot, lines, tempo, the author's and director's suggestions, the acting of the others in the cast – all determine the necessities and the varying lengths between them to which you must accommodate yourself. Therefore, to prepare yourself for such professional conditions and to be able to adapt yourself to them, you develop your exercise by establishing similar necessities or limitations.

At first, in addition to the exact beginning and end, you will also define as one of the necessities the approximate duration of each exercise. For working alone, about five minutes is sufficient for each improvisation.

Next add to the same starting and concluding points one more point (necessity) somewhere in the middle of the improvisation. This must be just as definite a piece of action, with definite feeling, mood or emotion, as the start and finish.

Now go from the beginning to the middle point, and from there to the end, in the same way that you traversed the two points alone, but try not to spend more time on them than before.

After a while add one more point wherever you choose, and fulfill your improvisation by going through the four points in approximately the same amount of time that it took you to go through the two.

Continue to add more and more such points between start and finish. Choose them all at random and without attempt at coherence or logical selection; leave this task to your improvising psychology. But in this variation of the exercise *do not* take a new beginning and end each time.

Having thus accumulated a sufficient number of points and satisfactorily bridged them as so many steps, you may start to impose new necessities upon yourself in still another way: try to act the first part in a slow tempo and the last part in a fast tempo; or try to create a certain atmosphere around you and maintain it in either a chosen section or throughout the entire improvisation.

You can then heap further necessities into the improvisation by using different qualities, such as molding, floating, flying or radiating movements, separately or in any combinations you wish to set for yourself; or you may even try the improvisation with various characterizations.

Later on you can imagine a definite setting in which you have to improvise; then the location of the audience; then decide whether your improvisation is tragedy, drama, comedy or farce. Also try to improvise as though you were performing a period play, and in this case dress yourself in an imaginary costume of the chosen period. All these things will serve as additional necessities upon which to develop your free improvisation.

It is to be expected that, in spite of all the new and varying necessities you introduce, a certain pattern of plot will inevitably creep into your improvisation. In order to avoid this during your exercises you can, after a while, try transposing the beginning and the end; later you can change the order of the points in the middle section as well.

When you have exhausted this series of combinations, start the whole exercise afresh with a new beginning and end and all kinds of necessities; and, as before, without any premeditated plot.

The result of this exercise is that you develop the *psychology of an improvising actor*. You will retain this psychology while going over all the necessities you have chosen for your improvisation, regardless of their number. Later on, when rehearsing and performing on the stage, you will feel that the lines you have to speak, the business you have to do and all the circumstances imposed upon you by the writer and director, and even the plot of the play, will lead and direct you as did the necessities you found for your exercise. You will not notice any substantial difference between the exercise and your professional work. Thus you will eventually be confirmed in the belief that dramatic art is nothing more than a *constant improvisation*, and that there are no moments on the stage when an actor can be deprived of his right to improvise. You will be able to fulfill faithfully all the necessities imposed upon you and at the same time preserve your *spirit of an improvising actor*. A new and gratifying sensation of complete confidence in yourself, along with the sensation of freedom and inner richness, will be the reward of all your efforts.

The exercises on developing the ability to improvise also can, and should be, employed in ensembles of two, three and more partners. And although they are in principle the same as for the individual, there is nevertheless an essential difference which must be considered.

The dramatic art is a collective art and therefore, however talented the actor may be, he will not be able to make full use of his ability to improvise if he isolates himself from the ensemble, his partners.

Of course, there are many unifying impulses on the stage, such as the atmosphere of the play, its style, a well-executed performance, or exceptionally fine staging. And yet a true stage ensemble needs more than these ordinary consolidations. The actor must develop within himself a sensitivity to the creative impulses of others.

An improvising ensemble lives in a constant process of giving and taking. A small hint from a partner – a glance, a pause, a new or unexpected intonation, a movement, a sigh, or even a barely perceptible change of tempo – can become a creative impulse, an invitation to the other to improvise.

Therefore, before starting exercises on group improvisation it is recommended that the members concentrate for a while on a preparatory exercise designed to develop what we shall call the *ensemble feeling*.

EXERCISE 13 (*for a group*)

Each member of the group begins by making an effort to open himself inwardly, with the greatest possible sincerity, to every other member. He tries to be aware of the *individual presence* of each. He makes an effort, figuratively speaking, "to open his heart" and admit everyone present, as though he were among his dearest friends. This process is much the same as that of *receiving*, which was described in Chapter One. At the beginning of the exercise each member of the group should say to himself:

"The creative ensemble consists of individuals and must never be considered by me as an impersonal mass. I appreciate the individual existence of each and every one present in this room and in my mind they do not lose their identity. Therefore, being here among my colleagues, I deny the general concept of 'They' or 'We' and instead I say: 'He and She, and She and I.' I am ready to receive any impressions, even the subtlest, from each one taking part with me in this exercise and I am ready to react to these impressions harmoniously."

You will help yourself immeasurably by ignoring all shortcomings or unsympathetic features of the members of the group, but trying instead to find their attractive sides and the better qualities of their characters. To avoid unnecessary embarrassment and artificiality, do not overdo it with prolonged and overly sentimental stares into their eyes, too friendly smiles or other unnecessary devices.

It is quite natural that you may develop a warm attitude toward your partners, but this should not be misconstrued as an invitation to float around in the group or lose yourself in vague feelings. The exercise is intended, rather, to give you the psychological means for establishing a firm professional contact with your partners.

With the inner contact between themselves solidly established, the members of the group then go to the next step of the exercise. They outline a succession of simple actions to choose from. These might be walking quietly around the room, running, standing motionless, changing places, assuming positions against the walls or coming together in the center of the room. Three or four such definite actions will be sufficient.

No one must be told *which* of these movements will be the

specific group action when the exercise begins. Each participant must divine, with his newly developed "openness," which of the agreed-upon actions the group as a whole desires to fulfill, then proceed to carry it out. Several false starts may be made by one or all, but eventually the common action will be arrived at in concert.

Still inherent in this guessing is the constant observation of the others by each member of the group. The closer and sharper the observation, the better the receptivity. The object is for all the members to select and perform the same action at the same time without prearrangement or hint of any kind. Whether they succeed or not is of no consequence, because the real value of the exercise lies in the *effort* to open one's self to the others and to intensify the actor's ability to observe his partners at all times, thus strengthening sensitivity toward the entire ensemble.

After a while, when the members of the group genuinely feel the sensation of being intimately united by the exercise, they should go to the exercise for group improvisation. This is different from the individual exercise. This time the *theme* must also be defined, but only in general or outline form. Will the group, to offer only a few suggestions, perform work in a factory of some kind, attend an elegant ballroom affair or house party, arrive or depart at a railway station or airport, be caught in a gambling raid, dine at a restaurant or make merry at a carnival? Whatever theme is chosen, the group next agrees on the setting. Here are the doors, tables, work-benches, orchestra, gates – whatever is called for by the particular locale which the chosen theme suggests.

The group then "distributes the parts." Neither premeditated plot nor any succession of events should be permitted. No more than the starting and concluding moments, with their initial business and corresponding moods, should be stated, as they were in the individual exercise. Also, the group should agree on the approximate duration of the improvisation.

Do not use too many words. Do not monopolize the dialogue, but speak only when it is natural and necessary to do so. Furthermore, the ability to improve or expand upon dialogue is not the actor's function, therefore you should not distract your attention from the improvisation with efforts to create the perfect lines for your part or the situation. The meaning of the exercise will not suffer if your words have no literary value and even sound awkward.

In all probability the first attempt at group improvisation will be chaotic despite everyone's sharpened sensitivity, openness and sense of unity. But everyone will receive a number of impressions from his partners. Each will recognize the others' intentions to create and develop the given situation, feel their moods and guess their conceptions of the scene imagined. He will also know his own unfulfilled intentions, his failure to conform to the plot, his partners, and so on. All these things, however, should *not* be discussed, but the members of the group should at once make another attempt to do the same improvisation, still relying upon their sense of unity and the contact they have established among themselves.

The second time the improvisation will undoubtedly assume a more definite shape, and many neglected intentions will find fulfillment. The group must repeat its efforts again and again until the improvisation reaches the point where it begins to look like a well-rehearsed little sketch. Meantime, in spite of inevitable repetitions of words, business and situations here and there, each member must maintain the psychology of an improvising artist.

Do not repeat yourself if you can help it, but instead try to find a new way of performing the same situation. Although you will have a natural inclination to retain and repeat the best achievements of the previous improvisations, do not hesitate to alter or discard them if your "inner voice" prompts you to hazard more expressive business or a more artistic interpretation of the moment, or even a new attitude toward the other participants. Your taste, your tact will tell you what can be altered and when, and what should be preserved for the sake of the ensemble and the plot in development. You will soon learn to be unselfish on one hand and still pursue your artistic freedom and desires on the other.

No matter how many times the group will want to repeat the same improvisation, its beginning and end should always remain clearly and *exactly* defined.

In group improvisation, it is well to remember, there is no need to establish any additional points between the start and the finish. They will gradually be found and crystallized as the improvisation progresses, the theme establishes itself and the plot grows and develops.

As soon as the improvisation assumes the appearance of a well-rehearsed sketch, the members of the group might decide to make it more interesting by adding a few necessities – atmospheres, characterizations, different tempos – all of which can be introduced one at a time.

When one theme is exhausted, the group can choose another and begin exercising it, again starting by establishing contact and unity as described in the beginning of this exercise.

Now the group is ready for the following experiment: Choose a scene from a play which none of the members has seen on the stage or screen, or perhaps acted in. Distribute the parts. Let one of you be made the "director" and asked to stage *exactly* the beginning and the end of the chosen scene. Then, knowing the content of the scene, start to improvise upon the whole middle part. Do not deviate too much from the psychology of the characters you are playing. Do not memorize the lines, except perhaps those of the beginning and the end. Let all the business and the *mise-en-scène* arise from your improvising initiative, as in previous exercises. You may speak a few lines here and there to approximate the author's, but if by chance you have retained some of them in your memory there is no need to mispronounce them deliberately in order to make them sound "improvised."

Do not as yet try to develop your characterization; otherwise your attention will be distracted from that "inner voice" which guides your improvisational activity. However, if the characteristic features of the role you are playing "insist" on coming to the fore and being incorporated, do not suppress them.

Having thus arrived at the end of the scene, ask your "director" to stage for you, again *exactly*, a little section of the scene somewhere in the middle. Then start your improvisation anew from the beginning to the "directed" middle point, and proceed from there to the end. In this way, filling in the gaps step by step, you will soon be able to play the entire scene as it is written by the author, maintaining throughout the *psychology of the improvising ensemble*. You will become more and more convinced that even while working upon an actual play, with all the director's and author's suggestions (necessities), you are still free to improvise creatively, and soon this conviction will become your new ability, your *second nature*, as it were.

Next the group can begin to develop the characterizations.

This exercise, as you undoubtedly see for yourself, is intended to familiarize you with the richness of your own actor's soul.

In concluding this chapter it is necessary to add a word of caution. If, while improvising, you begin to feel that you are becoming untrue or unnatural, you can be sure that it results either from the interference of your "logic" or from using too many unnecessary words. You must have the courage to rely completely on your improvising spirit. Follow the *psychological succession of inner events* (feelings, emotions, wishes and other impulses) that speak to you from the depths of your creative individuality and you will soon be convinced that this "inner voice" you possess never lies.

Simultaneously with the group exercises, it is highly advisable to continue the individual exercises, because both complement but do not substitute for each other.

4

THE ATMOSPHERE AND INDIVIDUAL FEELINGS

The idea of a play produced on the stage is its *spirit*; its atmosphere is its *soul*; and all that is visible and audible is its *body*.

I don't think it is erroneous to say that two different conceptions exist among actors concerning the stage in which they invest all their hopes and on which they would spend the greater part of their lives. To some of them it is nothing but an empty space which from time to time is filled with actors, stagehands, settings and properties; to them, all that appears on the stage is only the visible and the audible. To the others, the small space of the stage is an entire world permeated with an *atmosphere* so strong, so magnetic that they can hardly bear to part with it after the performance is over.

· In bygone days, when an aura of romance still pervaded our profession, actors frequently spent enchanted nights in their empty dressing rooms, or among pieces of scenery, or wandering on the half-lit stage like the old tragedian in Anton Chekhov's *Swan Song*. Their experiences of many years welded them to this stage filled with a magic spell. They needed this *atmosphere*. It gave them inspiration and power for their future performances.

But atmospheres are limitless and to be found everywhere. Every landscape, every street, house, room; a library, a hospital, a cathedral, a noisy restaurant, a museum; morning, noon, twilight, night; spring, summer, fall, winter – every phenomenon and event has its own particular atmospheres.

The actors who possess or who have newly acquired a love and understanding for atmosphere in a performance know only too well what a strong bond it creates between them and the spectator. Being enveloped by it too, the spectator himself begins to "act" along with the actors. A compelling performance arises out of *reciprocal action* between the actor and the spectator. If the actors, director, author, set designer and, often, the musicians have truly created the atmosphere for the performance, the spectator will not be able to remain aloof from it but will respond with inspiring waves of love and confidence.

Significant also is the fact that the atmosphere *deepens* the perception of the spectator. Ask yourself how you as a spectator would perceive the same scene if it were played before you in two ways, one without atmosphere and the other with it. In the first case, you would undoubtedly grasp the content of the scene with your intellect, but you would not be able to penetrate its psychological aspects as profoundly as you might if you let the atmosphere of the scene help you in this. In the second case, with the atmosphere reigning on the stage, your *feelings* (and not only your intellect) will be stirred and awakened. You will feel the content and very essence of the scene. Your understanding will be broadened by these feelings. The content of the scene will become richer and more significant to your perception. What would become of the content of that vitally important opening scene of Gogol's *Inspector General* were it perceived without its atmosphere? Blandly stated, the scene consists of the bribing officials absorbed in discussions of escape from punishment which they expect with the arrival of the Inspector from Petersburg. Endow it with its proper atmosphere, and you will see it and react to it quite differently; through the atmosphere you will perceive the content of this same scene as one of impending catastrophe, conspiracy, depression and almost "mystical" horror. Not only the psychological finesse of a sinner's soul will be revealed to you through the atmosphere of the opening scene, not only the humor of the flogging to which Gogol sentenced his heroes ("Don't blame the mirror when it's your own kisser that's crooked"), but all the officials will take on a new and greater significance, becoming *symbols*, portraying sinners of all kinds, of all times and of all places, and yet at the same time remaining individual characters with all their peculiar features. Or imagine Romeo speaking his beautiful words of love to Juliet without the atmosphere that must surround these two enamored beings You might still enjoy Shakespeare's incomparable poetry, but you definitely will feel a distinct lack of that something which is real, vital and inspirational. What? Is it not *love* itself, *the atmosphere* of love?

Have you as a spectator ever experienced that peculiar sensation of "I am looking into a *psychologically void space*" while watching a scene played on the stage? It was a scene deprived of atmosphere. Have not many of us also received similarly unsatisfactory sensations when a *wrong* stage atmosphere had misrepresented the true content of the scene? I well remember a performance of *Hamlet* where, in the scene of Ophelia's madness, the actors accidentally created an atmosphere of slight fear rather than one of profound tragedy and pain. It was startling to see how much unintentional humor this wrong atmosphere provoked in all of poor Ophelia's movements, words and looks!

Atmosphere exerts an extremely strong influence upon your acting. Have you ever noticed how, unwittingly, you change your movements, speech, behavior, thoughts and feelings as soon as you create a strong, contagious atmosphere, and how it increases its influence upon you if you accept it and succumb to it willingly?

Each evening while performing, yielding yourself to the atmosphere of the play or the scene, you can take delight in observing the self-sprung new details and nuances of your portrayal. You will not need to cling cowardly to the clichés of yesterday's acting. The space, the air around you filled with atmosphere will always support and arouse in you new feelings and fresh creative impulses. The atmosphere *urges* you to act in harmony with it.

What is this urge, where does it come from? Figuratively speaking, from the *will*, from the dynamic or driving power (call it what you like) which lives within the atmosphere. Experiencing, for instance, an atmosphere of happiness, you will find that its *will* awakens in you the desire to expand, extend, open, spread yourself, burst forth, gain space. Now take the atmosphere of depression or grief. Would not the *will* of this atmosphere be completely the reverse? Would you not, now, feel the urge to contract, close, even to diminish yourself?

But suppose we challenge that for a moment with: "In strong, dynamic atmospheres such as catastrophe, panic, hatred, exultation or heroism, their *will*, their urging power is obvious enough. But what happens to that forceful power amid calm and peaceful atmospheres, such as a forgotten cemetery, the tranquility of a summer morning, or the silent mystery of an aged forest?" The explanation is a simple one: in these cases the *will* of the atmosphere is seemingly less strong only because it is not so obviously violent. Nevertheless, it is there and it influences you with as much power as any other atmosphere. A nonactor or a person who is deprived of artistic sensitivity will probably remain passive in the atmosphere of a calm, moonlit night; hut an actor giving himself to it wholly will soon feel a kind of creative activity engendered within him. Images, one after the other, will appear before him and will gradually draw him into their own sphere. The *will* of such a tranquil night will soon transform itself into beings, events, words and movements. Was it not the atmosphere of coziness, charm and love which surrounded the fireplace in the little house of John Piribingle (*The Cricket on the Hearth*) which brought to life in Dickens' imagination the obstinate teapot, the fairy, John's Little Dot with her eternal companion, Tilly Slowboy, and even John Piribingle himself? There is no atmosphere deprived of the inner dynamic, life and will. All you need to get inspiration from it is to open yourself toward it. A little practice will teach you how to do it.

Now, for practical purposes we must state two facts: First, we must make a clear distinction between the *individual feelings* of the characters and the atmospheres of the scenes. Although both of them belong equally to the realm of feelings, they are entirely independent of each other and can exist simultaneously even if they are complete contrasts. Let us take some examples from life. Imagine a street catastrophe. A large group of people surrounds the place. Everyone feels the strong, depressing, torturous, frightful atmosphere of the scene. The whole group is enveloped by it, and yet it is not likely that you will find identical feelings in any two individuals within the entire crowd. One remains cold and untouched by the event, another feels a strong egotistical satisfaction that he is not the victim; the third (perhaps the policeman) is in an active, business-like mood, and the fourth is full of compassion.

An atheist can maintain his skeptical feelings in an atmosphere of religious awe, or a man in grief can still carry his sorrow in his soul when entering an atmosphere of gaiety and happiness. Therefore, making a distinction between the two, we must call atmospheres *objective feelings* as opposed to individual *subjective feelings*. Next, we must be aware of the principle that two different atmospheres (objective feelings) *cannot exist simultaneously*. The stronger atmosphere inevitably defeats the weaker. Again let us take an example:

Imagine an old deserted castle, where time itself seems to have ceased many centuries ago and preserved in invisible but haunting glory the thoughts and deeds, sorrows and joys of its long-forgotten inhabitants. A mysterious, tranquil atmosphere pervades these empty halls, corridors, cellars and towers. A group of people enters the castle, bringing with them a noisy, gay and hilarious atmosphere. What happens now? The two atmospheres clash at once in deadly combat, and before long one of them proves victorious. Either the group of merry people with its atmosphere submits to the stately atmosphere of the old castle, or the castle becomes "dead" and "empty," bereft of its ancient spirit, and stops telling its wordless tale!

These two facts, if taken into consideration, give actors and directors the practical means for creating certain effects on the stage: the conflict between two contrasting atmospheres and the slow or sudden but inevitable defeat of one of them, or the individual feelings of a character engaging in a fight with a hostile atmosphere, resulting either in a victory or defeat of the atmosphere over individual feelings.

Such psychological events on the stage will always create suspense for the audience because all the contrasts, collisions, combats, defeats and victories that take place on the stage must be accounted to the strong, if not the strongest, dramatic effects of the performance. Contrasts on the stage create that sought-after tenseness in an audience, while the victory or defeat that concludes the fight gives the audience a strong aesthetic satisfaction which can be compared to that arising from a resolved musical chord.

Much can be done for a play in this way, even if the atmospheres are only slightly hinted at by the author. There are many purely theatrical means by which to create atmospheres on the stage even if they are not indicated by the author: lights with their shadows and colors; settings with their shapes and forms of compositions; musical and sound effects; grouping of actors, their voices with a variety of timbres, their movements, pauses, changes of tempo, all kinds of rhythmical effects and manner of acting.

Practically all that the audience perceives on the stage can serve the purpose of enhancing atmospheres or even creating them anew.

It is well known that the realm of art is primarily the realm of feelings. A good and true definition would be that the atmosphere of every piece of art is its *heart*, its *feeling soul*. Consequently it is also the soul, the heart, of each and every performance on the stage. So that this is clearly understood let us make a comparison. Each of us knows that every normal human being exercises three main psychological functions: thoughts, feelings and will impulses.

Now imagine for a moment a human being completely deprived of the ability to *feel*, a human being who can be called entirely "heartless." Imagine further that his thoughts, ideas, and abstract intellectual conceptions on one hand, and his will impulses and actions on the other hand, contact each other and meet without any intervening link, without feelings between them. What kind of impression would such a "heartless" person make upon you? Would he still be a man, a human being? Would he not appear before you as a clever, refined and extremely complicated "machine"? Would not such a machine seem to be on a lower level than the human being whose three functions (thoughts, feelings and will) must work together in full harmony with one another?

Our feelings harmonize our ideas and will impulses. Not only that; they modify, control and perfect them, making them "human." A tendency to destruction arises in such human beings who are deprived of or who neglect their feelings. If you want examples, turn the pages of history. How many of the political or diplomatic ideas that were put straight into action without being controlled, modified and purified by the influence of feelings would you call human, benevolent or constructive? There are identical effects in the realm of art. A performance deprived of its atmospheres bears the impression of a *mechanism*. Even if the audience is able to appreciate the fine technique and skill of the performers and the value of the play; it might, nevertheless, remain cold and untouched by the whole performance. The emotional life of the characters on the stage is, with rare exceptions, only a substitute for atmosphere. This is especially true of our dry and intellectual era, when we are afraid of our own and others' feelings. Let us not forget that in the realm of art, in the theater, there is no excuse for banishing atmospheres. An individual, if he wishes, can dispense with his feelings for a while in his private life; but the arts, and the theater in particular, will slowly approach death if the atmospheres cease to radiate through their creations. The great mission of the actor as well as the director and the playwright is to save the *soul* of the theater and with it the future of our profession.

Should you desire to increase your sense of atmosphere and also acquire a certain technique for creating it at will, here are some suggested exercises:

EXERCISE 14

Start with the observation of life surrounding you. Look systematically for different atmospheres which you may encounter. Try not to overlook or disregard atmospheres because they happen to be weak, subtle or hardly noticeable. Pay special attention to the fact that each atmosphere you observe is actually *spread in the air*, enveloping people and events, filling the rooms, floating through landscapes, pervading the life of which it is a part.

Watch people while they are surrounded by a certain atmosphere. See whether they move and speak in harmony with it, surrender to it, fight against it or to what extent they are sensitive or indifferent to it.

After a period of observation, when your ability to perceive the atmospheres is sufficiently trained and sharpened, begin to experiment with yourself. Consciously and deliberately try to submit to certain atmospheres, "listening" to them as you listen to music, and let them influence you. Let them call up in you your own individual feelings. Begin to move and speak in harmony with the different atmospheres you encounter. Then choose cases where you can fight with a specific atmosphere, trying to develop and preserve feelings which are contrary to it.

After having worked for a while with atmospheres you encounter in real life, start to *imagine* events and circumstances with their corresponding atmospheres. Take them from literature, history, plays, or invent them yourself. Visualize, for instance, the storming of the Bastille. Imagine the moment when the people of Paris burst into one of the cells of the prison. Observe closely the figures of the men and women. Let this scene, created by your imagination, appear before your mind's eye with utmost clarity, and then say to yourself, "The crowd is inspired by an atmosphere of *extreme agitation, intoxicated with force and boundless might*. Everyone is enveloped in this atmosphere." And now observe the faces, movements, the separate figures and the groups in the crowd. Watch the tempo of the event. Listen to the shrieks, to the timbres of the voices. Peer into all the details of the scene and see how the atmosphere stamps its impression upon everything and everyone in this agitated event.

Now change the atmosphere a little and once again watch your "Performance." This time let the atmosphere assume the character of *evil and revengeful ruthlessness*. See with what power and authority this altered atmosphere will change all that is happening in the cell of the prison! Faces, movements, voices, groups – all will be different now, all will express the vengeful will of the crowd. It will be a different "performance" although the theme is the same.

Change the atmosphere once more. Here let it be *proud, dignified and majestic*. Again a transformation will take place.

Now learn to create the atmospheres *without imagining any*

occurrence or circumstance at all. You can do it by imagining *the space, the air,* around you as filled with a certain atmosphere, just as it can be filled with light, fragrance, warmth, cold, dust or smoke. Imagine at first, any simple, quiet atmosphere like coziness, awe, solitude, foreboding, etc. Don't ask yourself how it is possible to imagine a feeling of awe, or any other feeling floating in the air around you, before you actually try it, *practice it.* Two or three efforts will convince you that it is not only possible but extremely easy. In this exercise I appeal to your imagination, not to your cold, analytical reason. What is our entire art but a beautiful "fiction" based on our creative imagination? Take this exercise as simply as I am trying to convey it to you. Don't do anything but *imagine feelings spreading around you, filling the air.* Do this exercise with a series of different atmospheres.

Take the next step. Choose a definite atmosphere, imagine it spread around you in the air, and then make a slight movement with your arm and hand. See that the movement is in *harmony* with the atmosphere surrounding you. If you have chosen a *calm and peaceful* atmosphere, your movement will also be calm and peaceful. An atmosphere of *caution* will lead your arm and hand with caution. Repeat this simple exercise until you feel the sensation of your arm and hand being *permeated* with the chosen atmosphere. The atmosphere should fill your arm and fully express itself through your movement.

Avoid two possible mistakes. Don't be impatient to "perform" or "act" the atmosphere with your movement. Don't deceive yourself; have confidence in the power of the atmosphere and imagine and woo it long enough (it will not be long at all!), and then move your arm and hand *within it.* Another possible mistake you may make is trying to *force yourself to feel* the atmosphere. Try to avoid such an effort. You *will* feel it around and within you as soon as you concentrate your attention on it properly. It will stir your feelings by itself, without any unnecessary and disturbing violence on your part. It will happen to you exactly the way it happens in life: when you encounter the atmosphere of a street disaster, you can't help *feeling* it.

Proceed to more complicated movements. Get up, sit down, take an object and carry it to some other place, open and close the door, rearrange things on the table. Strive to get the same results as before.

Now speak a few words, first without an accompanying gesture and then with it. The words and gestures must be utterly simple at first. Try it with everyday dialogue like: "Please sit down!" (an inviting gesture); "I don't need it anymore" (a gesture of tearing a paper); "Give me this book, please" (a gesture of indication). As before, see that they are in full harmony with it. Do this exercise in different atmospheres.

Carry the exercise a step further. Create an atmosphere around you. Let it grow strong enough, until you feel fully familiar and intimate with it. Fulfill a simple action born out of the chosen atmosphere, and then little by little develop this simple piece of business further, continuing to be guided by the atmosphere flowing to you from your surroundings, until it gradually becomes a short scene. Do this exercise in different atmospheres, with those having more violent characters such as ecstasy, despair, panic, hatred or heroism.

Again create around you a certain atmosphere and, having lived in it for a while, try to imagine circumstances which would harmonize with it.

Read plays and try to define the atmospheres within them by *imagining* the scenes over and over again (rather than by using your reasoning). For each play you might chart a kind of "score" of succeeding atmospheres. By creating such a "score" you don't need to take into account the division of acts or scenes given by the author, because the same atmosphere can encompass many scenes or change several times in one scene.

Also, do not overlook the general, over-all atmosphere of the play as a whole. Each play has such a general atmosphere in accordance with its category of tragedy, drama, comedy or farce; and each play has in addition a particular individual atmosphere.

Exercises on atmosphere can be done most successfully by a group. In group work the atmosphere will show its unifying power for all participants. Besides, the common effort to create an atmosphere by imagining the air or space as filled with a certain feeling always produces a much stronger effect than when done by the individual alone.

Here we return to the matter of individual feelings and how to handle them professionally.

The individual feelings of an actor are, or might at any time become, very mercurial and capricious. You can't *order* yourself to *feel* truly sorry or gay, to love or to hate. Too often are actors compelled to *pretend* that they are feeling on the stage, too numerous their unsuccessful attempts to *squeeze* these feelings out of themselves. Is it not, in the majority of cases, merely a "happy accident" rather than a triumph of technical skill when an actor is able to awaken his feelings whenever he wants or needs them? True artistic feelings, if they refuse to appear by themselves, must be coaxed by some technical means which will make an actor the master over them.

There seem to be several ways to awaken creative feelings. A well-trained imagination and living within an atmosphere have already been mentioned. Now let us consider still another means and, step by step, *fulfill it in practice*.

Lift your arm. Lower it. What have you done? You have fulfilled a simple physical *action*. You have made a gesture. And you have made it without any difficulty. Why? Because, like every *action*, it is completely within your will. Now make the same gesture, but this time color it with a certain *quality*. Let this quality be *caution*. You will make your gesture, your movement *cautiously*. Have you not done it with the same ease? Do it again and again and then see what happens. Your movement, made cautiously, is no longer a mere physical action; now it has acquired a certain *psychological* nuance. What is this nuance?

It is a *Sensation* of caution which now fills and permeates your arm. It is a psychophysical sensation. Similarly, if you moved your entire body with the quality of caution, then your entire body would naturally be filled with this sensation.

Sensation is the vessel into which your genuine artistic feelings pour easily and by themselves; it is a kind of magnet which draws to it feelings and emotions akin to whatever quality you have chosen for your movement.

Now ask yourself if you *forced* your feelings. Did you order yourself to "feel caution"? No. You only made a *movement with a certain quality*, thus creating *a sensation of caution* through which you aroused your feelings. Repeat this movement with various other qualities and the feeling, your desire, will grow stronger and stronger.

Therein you have the simplest *technical* means for kindling your feelings if they should become obstinate, capricious and refuse to function exactly when you need them in your professional work.

After some practice you will find that having chosen a certain quality, and having turned it into a sensation, you will get much more than you expected for your efforts. The quality of caution, for just one example, might awaken in you not only a feeling of caution alone, but also the whole gamut of feelings akin to that of caution, according to the circumstances given in the play. As a byproduct of this cautious quality you might feel irritated or alert, as if facing danger; you might feel warm and tender, as if protecting a child; cold and reserved, as if protecting yourself; or kind of astonished and curious as to why you should be cautious. All these nuances of feelings, however varied, are connected with the sensation of caution.

But how, you may wonder, does this apply when the body is in static positions?

Any bodily position can be permeated with qualities in exactly the same way as any movement. All you need to do is say to yourself: "I am going to stand, to sit or to lie with this or that quality in my body," and the reaction will come immediately, calling up from within your soul a kaleidoscope of feelings.

It might easily happen that while working upon a scene you will be in doubt as to which quality, sensation, you have to choose. In such a dilemma don't hesitate to take two or even three qualities for your action. You can try them one after the other in search of the one that's best, or you can combine them all at once. Let us suppose that you take the quality of heaviness and at the same time the qualities of despair, thoughtfulness or anger. No matter how many suitable qualities you may select and combine, they will always merge into one sensation for you, like a dominant chord in music.

As soon as your feelings are kindled, they will carry you away with them, and your exercise, rehearsal or performance will have found true inspiration.

EXERCISE 15

Do a simple, natural action. Take an object from the table, open or close a window or a door, sit down, get up, walk or run around the room. Do this action several times so that you can fulfill it easily. Now invest it with certain qualities, doing the action calmly, surely, irritably, sorrowfully, grievously, slyly or tenderly. Next try the action with molding, floating, flying and radiating qualities. Then give your action the qualities of staccato, legato, ease, form, etc. Repeat this exercise until the sensation fills your entire body and your feelings respond to it easily. Be careful that you do not *force* your feelings out of yourself instead of following and relying upon the suggested technique. Don't hurry the result.

Do the same with broad, wide movements as in Exercise 1.

Again take a quality of movement or action and add to it two or three words. Speak these words also with the sensation which arises in you.

If you exercise with partners, do simple improvisations and use words. You might improvise a salesman and prospective purchaser; a host and guest; a tailor or hairdresser and the client. Before starting agree upon the qualities you and your partners are going to use in each instance.

Do not use too many unnecessary words while exercising with partners.

Superfluous speeches very often lead you astray; they give the impression that you are actively doing your exercise, while in reality they paralyze the action and substitute for it the intellectual content of the words. Thus a word-heavy exercise degenerates into an ordinary, uninspired conversation.

These simple exercises will also develop a strong sensation of harmony between your inner life and its outer manifestations.

It may be well to summarize this chapter on Atmosphere and Individual Feelings with these highlights:

1   The atmosphere inspires the actor.
2   It unites the audience with the actor as well as the actors with one another.
3   It deepens the perception of the spectator.
4   Two contrasting atmospheres cannot coexist. But individual feelings of the characters, even though they may contrast with the atmosphere, can exist simultaneously with it.
5   The atmosphere is the soul of the performance.
6   Observe atmospheres in life.
7   Imagine the same scene within different atmospheres.
8   Create atmospheres around you without any given circumstances.

9   Move and speak in harmony with whatever atmosphere you create.

10   Imagine suitable circumstances for the atmosphere you have created.

11   Chart and keep a "score" of the atmospheres you create.

12   Carry out movements (business) with qualities – sensations – feelings.

5

THE PSYCHOLOGICAL GESTURE

The soul desires to dwell with the body because without the
members of the body it can neither act nor feel.
— Leonardo da Vinci

In the previous chapter I said that we cannot directly command
our feelings, but that we can entice, provoke and coax them by
certain indirect means. The same should be said about our wants,
wishes, desires, longings, lusts, yearnings or cravings, all of
which, although always mixed with feelings, generate in the
sphere of our will power.

In the qualities and sensations we found the key to the treasury
of our feelings. But is there such a key to our will power? Yes, and
we find it in the *movement* (action, gesture). You can easily prove it
to yourself by trying to make a *strong*, well-shaped but simple
gesture. Repeat it several times and you will see that after a while
your will power grows stronger and stronger under the influence
of such a gesture.

Further, you will discover that the *kind* of movement you make
will give your will power a certain direction or inclination; that is,
it will awaken and animate in you a *definite* desire, want or wish.

So we may say that the *strength* of the movement stirs our will power in general; the *kind* of movement awakens in us a definite corresponding *desire*, and the quality of the same movement conjures up our *feelings*.

Before we see how these simple principles can be applied to our profession, let us take a few examples of the gesture itself in order to get a broad idea of its connotations.

Imagine that you are going to play a character which, according to your first general impression, has a strong and unbending *will*, is possessed by dominating, despotic *desires*, and is filled with *hatred* and *disgust*.

You look for a suitable over-all gesture which can express all this in the character, and perhaps after a few attempts you find it (see Drawing 1).

It is *strong* and well shaped. When repeated several times it will tend to strengthen your *will*. The direction of each limb, the final position of the whole body as well as the inclination of the head are such that they are bound to call up a *definite desire* for *dominating* and *despotic* conduct. The *qualities* which fill and permeate each muscle of the entire body, will provoke within you feelings of *hatred* and *disgust*. Thus, through the gesture, you penetrate and stimulate the depths of your own psychology.

Another example:

This time you define the character as aggressive, perhaps even fanatical, with a rather fiery will. The character is completely opened to influences coming from "above," and is obsessed by the desire to receive and even to force "inspirations" from these influences. It is filled with mystical qualities but at the same time stands firmly on the ground and receives equally strong influences from the earthly world. Consequently, it is a character which is able to reconcile within itself influences both from above and below (see Drawing 2).

For the next example we will choose a character that in a way contrasts with the second. It is entirely introspective, with no desire to come in contact either with the world above or below, but not necessarily weak. Its desire to be isolated might be a very strong one. A brooding quality permeates its whole being. It might enjoy its loneliness (see Drawing 3).

For the following example, imagine a character entirely attached to an earthly kind of life. Its powerful and egotistical will is constantly drawn downward. All its passionate wishes and lusts are stamped with low and base qualities. It has no sympathy for anyone or anything. Mistrust, suspicion and blame fill its whole limited and introverted inner life. The character denies a straight and honest way of living, always choosing roundabout and crooked paths. It is a self-centered and at times an aggressive type of person (see Drawing 4).

Still another example. You might see the strength of this particular character in its protesting, negative will. Its main quality may seem to you to be suffering, perhaps with the nuance of anger or indignation. On the other hand, a certain weakness permeates its entire form (see Drawing 5).

The last example. This time your character is again a weak type, unable to protest and fight his way through life; highly sensitive, inclined to suffering and self-pity, with a strong desire to complaints (see Drawing 6).

Here also, as in the previous cases, by studying and exercising the gesture and its final position, you will experience its threefold influence upon your psychology.

You are strongly urged to bear in mind that all the gestures and their interpretations, as demonstrated, are only examples of possible cases and are in no way obligatory to your individual approach when searching for over-all gestures.

Let us call them *Psychological Gestures* (hereinafter referred to as

PG's), because their aim is to influence, stir, mold and attune your whole inner life to its artistic aims and purposes.

Now to the problem of applying the PG to professional work.

There is a written play before you with your part in it. It is only an inanimate literary work as yet. It is your task and your partners' to transform it into a living and scenic piece of theatrical art. What are you to do to fulfill this task?

To begin with, you have to make a first attempt to investigate your character, to penetrate it in order to know whom you are going to perform on the stage. You can do this either by using your analytical mind or by applying the PG. In the former case you choose a long and laborious way because the reasoning mind, generally speaking, is not imaginative enough, is too cold and abstract to be able to fulfill an artistic work. It might easily weaken and for a long time retard your ability to act. You may have noticed that the more your mind "knows" about the character, the less you are able to perform it. This is a psychological law. You might know only too well what the feelings and desires of your character are, but that knowledge alone would not enable you to fulfill the desires truthfully or experience its feelings sincerely on the stage. It is like knowing everything about a science or an art and ignoring the fact that this intelligence per se is far removed from being proficient in it. Of course, your mind can and will be very helpful to you in evaluating, correcting, verifying, making additions and offering suggestions, *but it should not do all these before your creative intuition has asserted itself and spoken fully*. This is by no means an implication that reason or intellect should be done away with in preparing the part, but it is an admonition that you should not appeal to it, should not rest your hopes on it, and that it must at the outset remain in the background so that it will not obtrude and hamper your creative efforts.

But if you choose another and more productive way, if you apply the PG in order to study your character, you appeal to your creative forces directly and do not become a "bookish" or rote actor.

Many an actor has asked, "How can I find the PG without first knowing the character for which the PG should be found, if use of the intellect is not recommended?"

From the results of previous exercises you certainly will have to admit that your sound intuition, your creative imagination and your artistic vision always give you at least some idea of what the character is, even upon the very first acquaintance with it. It might be just a guess, but you can rely upon it and use it as a springboard for your first attempt to build the PG. Ask yourself what the *main* desire of the character might be, and when you get an answer, even if it is only a hint, start to build your PG step by step, using at first your *hand* and *arm* only. You might thrust them forward aggressively, clenching your fist, if the desire reminds you of grasping or catching (greed, avarice, cupidity, miserliness); or you might stretch them out slowly and carefully, with reserve and caution, if the character wishes to grope or search in a thoughtful and diffident manner; or you might direct both your hands and arms upward, lightly and easily, with palms open, in case your intuition prompts that the character wants to receive, to implore, to beseech with awe; or maybe you will want to direct them downward, roughly with palms turned earthward, with clawing and crooked fingers, if the character lusts to overpower, to possess. Having once started this way, you will no longer find it difficult (in fact, it will happen by itself) to extend and adjust your particular gesture to your shoulders, your neck, the position of your head and torso, legs and feet, until your *entire* body is thus occupied. Working this way, you will soon discover whether your first guess as to the main desire of the character was correct. The PG itself will lead you to this discovery, without too much interference on the part of the reasoning mind. In some instances you might feel the need to do your PG by starting not from a neutral position but from one that the character suggests to you. Consider our second

PG (see Drawing 2), which expresses a complete openness and expansion. Your character might be introspective or introverted and his main desire might be defined as an urge to be open and receptive to the influences coming from above. In that case you might start from a more or less closed instead of neutral position. In choosing a starting position you are, of course, just as free as in creating any PG.

Now you continue developing the PG, correcting and improving it, adding to it all the qualities you find in the character, slowly leading it to the stage of perfection. After a short experience you will be able to find the correct PG practically at once, and will have only to improve it according to your or your director's taste while aiming at its final version.

By using the PG as a means of exploiting the character, you actually do more than that. You prepare yourself for acting it. By elaborating, improving, perfecting and exercising the PG you are, more and more, becoming the very character yourself at the same time. Your will, your feelings are stirred and awakened in you. The more you progress in this work, the more the PG reveals to you the entire character in *condensed* form, making you the possessor and master of its *unchangeable core* (as alluded to at the end of Chapter 1).

To assume a PG means, then, to prepare the entire part in its *essence*, after which it will become an easy task to work out all the details in actual rehearsals on the stage. You will not have to flounder and grope aimlessly, as often happens when you start dressing a part with flesh, blood and sinews without first having found its spine. The PG gives you this very spine. It is the shortest, easiest and the most artistic way of transforming a literary creation into a theatrical piece of art.

Until now I have spoken of the PG as applicable to the *entire* character. But you can use it just as well for any segment of the role, for separate scenes or speeches if you wish, or even separate sentences. The way to find and apply it in these shorter instances is exactly the same as for the entire character.

If you have any doubts about how to reconcile the general, overall PG for the whole part with particular, smaller PG's for separate scenes, the following illustration should serve to clarify the point:

Imagine three different characters – Hamlet, Falstaff and Malvolio. Each of these characters can become angry, grow pensive or start laughing. But they will not do any of these things in the same way because they are *different characters* Their difference will influence their anger, pensiveness and laughter. The same with different PG's. Being an *essence* of the whole character, the over-all PG will of its own accord influence all smaller, particular PG's. Your well-developed sensitivity to the PG (see the following Exercise) will show you intuitively which nuances in all the minor PG's must be elaborated to make them match up with the major PG. The more you work upon PG's, the more you will realize how flexible they are, what unlimited possibilities they offer you in coloring them the way you like. What may seem an insoluble problem for the dry and calculating mind, is resolved most simply by creative intuition and imagination, from which the PG springs.

On the other hand, you might use these minor PG's only so long as you need them to study your scene, your speech, etc., and then drop them entirely. But the over-all PG for the character will remain with you *always*.

Another question that may arise in your mind is, "Who tells me whether the PG I find for my character is the right one?" The answer: *Nobody but yourself.* It is your own free creation, through which your individuality expresses itself. *It is right if it satisfies you as an artist.* However, the director is entitled to suggest alterations to the PG you have found.

The only question you can permit yourself in this connection is whether you fulfill the PG correctly; that is, whether you observe all the necessary conditions for such a gesture. Let us investigate these conditions.

There are two kinds of gestures. One we use both while acting on the stage and in everyday life – the natural and usual gesture. The other kind is what might be called the *archetypal gesture*, one which serves as an original model for all possible gestures of the same kind. The PG belongs to the second type. Everyday gestures are unable to stir our will because they are too limited, too weak and particularized. They do not occupy our whole body, psychology and soul, whereas the PG, as an archetype, takes possession of them *entirely*. (You prepared yourself for making archetypal gestures through Exercise 1 (see Chapter 1), when you learned to do wide, broad movements, using the maximum space around you.)

The PG must be *strong* in order to be able to stir and increase our will power, but it should never be produced by means of *unnecessary* muscular tension (which weakens the movement rather than increases its power). Of course, if your PG is a violent one, like that chosen as our first example (see Drawing 1), then you can't avoid using your muscular strength; but even in that case the real power of the gesture is more psychological than physical. Think of a loving mother hugging her baby to her bosom with the great strength of maternal ardor, and yet with muscles almost completely relaxed. If you have properly and sufficiently exercised the molding, floating, flying and radiating movements (see Chapter 1), you will know that real power has actually nothing to do with overstraining one's muscles.

In our two last examples (5 and 6) we assumed that the characters were more or less weak. Hence the question may arise as to whether, in producing a weak character, the gesture itself should also lose its power. The answer is, absolutely no. The PG must always remain strong and the weakness must be regarded only as its quality. Thus the psychological strength of your PG will suffer little whether you produce it gently, tenderly, warmly, lovingly, or even with such qualities as laziness or tiredness combined with weakness. Besides, it is the actor and not the character who produces a strong PG and it is the character, not the actor, who is lazy, tired or weak.

Further, the PG should be as *simple* as possible, because its task is to summarize the intricate psychology of a character in an easily surveyable form, to compress it into its essence. A complicated PG cannot possibly do so. A true PG will resemble the broad charcoal stroke on an artist's canvas before he starts on the details. It is, to restate it, a scaffolding upon which the whole complicated architectural construction of the character will be erected.

The PG must also have a very clear and definite *form*. Any vagueness existing in it should prove to you that it is not yet the essence, the core, of the psychology of the character you are working upon. (The sense of form, you will remember, was implicit in the Exercise on molding, floating and other movements, Chapter 1.)

Much, too, depends on the *tempo* in which you exercise the PG once you have found it. Everybody goes through life in different tempos. It depends mainly on the temperament and the destiny of a person. The same must be said for the characters in plays. The general tempo in which the character lives depends largely on your *interpretation* of it. Compare Drawings 2 and 3. Do you recognize and feel how much faster is the life tempo of the former?

The same PG made in different tempos might change all its qualities, its strength of will and its susceptibility to different coloration. Take any of our PG examples and try to produce them first in slow and then in quick tempos.

Study the gesture of the first drawing, for example: slowed in tempo, it conjures up in our imagination a dictatorial character, rather thoughtful, clever, capable of planning and plotting and, in a way, patient and self-controlled; made quickly, in lightning-like tempo, it becomes a ruthless, criminal character of unbridled will, incapable of any rational conduct.

Many transformations through which the characters might go in the course of the play can often be expressed by a mere change of tempo in the same PG you have found for the part. (The problem of tempo on the stage will be discussed in greater detail later on.)

Having achieved the physical limit of the PG, when your body is unable to extend it further, you must still continue to try for a while (ten to fifteen seconds), going beyond the boundaries of your body by means of *radiating* its power and qualities in the direction indicated by the PG. This radiation will greatly strengthen the true psychological power of the gesture, enabling it to produce a greater influence upon your inner life.

The foregoing are the few conditions which should be observed in order to create a correct PG.

Now your task will be to develop a fine *sensitiveness* to the gesture you make.

EXERCISE 16

Take as one illustration the PG of *calmly closing yourself* (see Drawing 7). Find a sentence corresponding to it, perhaps: "I wish to be left alone." Rehearse both the gesture and the sentence simultaneously, so that qualities of restrained will and calmness penetrate your psychology and voice. Then start making *slight* alterations in the PG. If, let us say, the position of your head had been erect, incline it slightly downward and cast your glance in the same direction. What change did it effect in your psychology? Did you feel that to the quality of calmness was added a slight coloring of *insistence, stubbornness*?

Drawing 1

Drawing 2

Drawing 3

Drawing 4

Drawing 5

Drawing 6

Drawing 7

Do this altered PG several times, until you are able to speak your sentence in full harmony with the change that has occurred.

Do a new alteration. This time bend your right knee slightly, transferring the weight of your body to the left leg. The PG might now acquire a nuance of *surrender*. Lift your hands up to your chin and the quality of surrender can become stronger and new slight nuances of *unavoidability* and *loneliness* will introduce themselves. Throw your head back and close your eyes: *pain* and *pleading* qualities may appear. Turn your palms outward: *self-defense*. Incline your head to one side: *self-pity*. Bend the three middle fingers of each hand: a slight hint of *humor* might occur. With each alteration speak the same sentence to conform with it.

Remember that these examples are also only a few of the possible experiences which the PG might call up in you; the range can be limitless. Always be free in interpreting all the gestures with their alterations. *The slighter the change in your gesture, the finer the sensitivity that will develop in you.*

Continue this exercise until your *whole body* – the position of your head, shoulders, neck, the movements of your arms, hands, fingers, elbows, torso, legs, feet, the direction of your sight – will awaken in you psychologically corresponding reactions.

Take any PG, exercise it for a while in slow tempo and then increase it by *degrees* until you reach the quickest possible tempo. Try to experience whatever psychological reaction each degree calls up in you (you may use the suggested examples as a start). For each degree of tempo find a *new*, suitable sentence and speak it while making your gesture.

This exercise on sensitivity will, also, greatly increase the sense of *harmony* between your body, psychology and speech. Developed to a high degree, you should be able to say, "I feel my body and my speech as a direct continuation of my psychology. I feel them as visible and audible parts of my soul."

Soon you will notice that, while acting, fulfilling your business, speaking the lines, making simple and natural gestures, the PG is somehow *ever-present* in the back of your mind. It helps and leads you like an invisible director, friend and guide who never fails to inspire you when you need inspiration most. It preserves your creation for you in a condensed and crystallized form.

You will also notice that the strong and colorful inner life which you invoked within you through the PG gives you greater expressiveness, however economical and reserved your acting may be. (I don't think it is even necessary to mention that the PG itself must never be shown to the audience, no more than an architect would be expected to show the public the scaffolding of his building instead of the completed masterwork. A PG is the scaffolding of your part and it must remain your technical "secret.")

If you exercise in a group, make short improvisations, using different PG's for each of the participants.

In addition to the exercises begun with Drawing 7, the following is recommended:

Choose a short sentence and speak it, taking different natural positions or making different everyday movements (not PG's). These may consist of sitting, lying, standing, walking around the room, leaning against the wall, looking through the window, opening or closing a door, entering or leaving a room, taking and putting down or throwing away some object, and so forth. Each bodily movement or position, calling up a certain psychological state, will prompt *how* you are to speak your sentence, with what intensity, quality and in which tempo. Change your positions or movements, but speak the same sentence each time. It will increase in you the sense of harmony between your body, psychology and speech.

Now, having developed sufficient sensitivity, try to create a series of PG's for different characters, observing all the conditions previously described – archetype, strength, simplicity, etc. At first take characters from plays, literature and history; then find

PG's for living people well known to you; then for people you have accidentally and briefly met on the streets. Finally, create some characters in your imagination and find PG's for them.

As the next step of this exercise, choose a character from a play which you have never seen or acted in. Find and elaborate a PG for it. Absorb it completely and then, at first, try to rehearse a very short scene from the play on the basis of the PG. (If possible, do it with partners.)

A few final words concerning tempo are in order here.

Our usual conception of tempo on the stage fails to distinguish between the *inner* and *outer* varieties. The inner tempo can be defined as a quick or slow change of thoughts, images, feelings, will impulses, etc. The outer tempo expresses itself in quick or slow actions and speech. Contrasting outer and inner tempos can run simultaneously on the stage. For instance, a person can expect something or somebody impatiently; the images in his mind follow each other in quick succession, thoughts and desires flare up in his mind, chasing one another, appearing and disappearing; his will is stirred to a high pitch; and yet, at the same time, the person can control himself so that his outer behavior, his movements and speech, will remain calm and slow in tempo. An outer slow tempo can run concurrently with a quick inner tempo, or vice versa. The effect of two contrasting tempos running simultaneously on the stage unfailingly makes a strong impression on an audience.

You should not confuse slow tempo with *passiveness* or a lack of energy in the actor himself. Whatever slow tempo you use on the stage, your self as an artist must always be *active*. On the other hand, the quick tempo of your performance must not become an obvious *haste* or an unnecessary psychological and physical tension. A flexible, well-trained and obedient body and a good technique of speech will help you to avoid this mistake and make possible the correction and simultaneous usage of two contrasting tempos.

EXERCISE 17

Do a series of improvisations with contrasting *inner* and *outer* tempos.

For example: A big hotel at night. Porters with quick, skillful, habitual movements carry the luggage from the elevator, sort it out and put it into waiting automobiles that must hurry to catch the night train. The *outer tempo* of the servants is quick, but they are indifferent to the excitement of the guests who are checking out. The *inner tempo* of the porters is slow. The departing guests, on the contrary, trying to preserve an outer calm, are inwardly excited, fearing they will miss the train; their *outer tempo* is slow, their *inner tempo* is quick.

For further exercises on inner and outer tempos, you might use the examples contained in Chapter 12.

Read plays with the purpose of trying to trace different tempos in different combinations.

Summary on the Psychological Gesture:

1 The PG stirs our will power, gives it a definite direction, awakens feelings, and gives us a condensed version of the character.
2 The PG must be archetypal, strong, simple and well formed; it must radiate and be performed in the correct tempo.
3 Develop sensitiveness to the PG.
4 Distinguish between inner and outer tempos.

6

CHARACTER AND CHARACTERIZATION

Transformation – that is what the actor's nature, consciously or sub-consciously, longs for.

Now let us discuss the problem of creating the *Character*.

There are no parts which can be considered so-called "straight" parts or parts in which the actor always shows his audience the same "type" – himself as he is in private life. There are many reasons for the unfortunate misconceptions about "true dramatic art," but we need not dwell upon them here. It is sufficient to point out the tragic fact that the theater as such will never grow and develop if this destructive "himself" attitude, already deeply rooted, is permitted to thrive. Every art serves the purpose of discovering and revealing new horizons of life and new facets in human beings. An actor cannot give his audience new revelations by unvaryingly displaying only himself on the stage. How would you evaluate a playwright who in all his plays unfailingly dramatizes himself as the leading character, or a painter who is unable to create anything but self-portraits?

As you will never meet two persons precisely alike in life, so you will never find two identical parts in plays. That which constitutes their *difference* makes them *characters*. And it will be a good starting point for an actor, in order to grasp the initial idea about the character he is going to perform on the stage, to ask himself: "What is the *difference* – however subtle or slight this difference may be – between myself and the character as it is described by the playwright?"

By doing so you will not only lose the desire to paint your "self-portrait" repeatedly but discover the main psychological characteristics or features in your character.

Then you face the need to incorporate these characteristic features that make the difference between yourself and the character. How will you approach this task?

The shortest, most artistic (and amusing) approach is *to find an imaginary body for your character*. Imagine, as a case in point, that you must play the role of a person whose character you define as lazy, sluggish and awkward (psychologically as well as physically). These qualities should not necessarily be pronounced or emphatically expressed, as perhaps in comedy. They might show themselves as mere, almost imperceptible indications. And yet they are typical features of the character which should not be overlooked.

As soon as you have outlined those features and qualities of your role – that is, compared with your own – try to imagine *what kind of body* such a lazy, awkward and slow person would have. Perhaps you will find that he might possess a full, plump, short body with drooping shoulders, thick neck, long arms hanging listlessly, and a big, heavy head. This body is, of course, a far cry from your own. Yet you must look like that and do as it does. How do you go about effecting a true resemblance? Thus:

You are going to imagine that in the same space you occupy with your own, real body there exists another body – the imaginary body of your character, which you have just created in your mind.

You clothe yourself, as it were, with this body; you put it on like a garment. What will be the result of this "masquerade"? After a while (or perhaps in a flash!) you will begin to feel and think of yourself as *another person*. This experience is very similar to that of a real masquerade. And did you ever notice in everyday life how different you feel in different clothes? Are you not "another person" when wearing a dressing gown or an evening dress; when in an old, worn-out suit or one that's brand-new? But "wearing another body" is more than any raiment or costume. This assumption of the character's imaginary physical form influences your psychology ten times more strongly than any garment!

The imaginary body stands, as it were, *between* your real body and your psychology, influencing both of them with equal force. Step by step, you begin to move, speak and feel in accord with it; that is to say, your character now dwells within you (or; if you prefer, you dwell within it).

How strongly you express the qualities of your imaginary body while acting will depend on the type of play and on your own taste and desire. But in any case, your *whole being, psychologically and physically*, will be changed – I would not hesitate to say even *possessed* – by the character. When really taken on and exercised, the imaginary body stirs the actor's will and feelings; it harmonizes them with the characteristic speech and movements, it transforms the actor into another person! Merely discussing the character, analyzing it mentally, cannot produce this desired effect, because your reasoning mind, however skillful it may be, is apt to leave you cold and passive, whereas the imaginary body has the power to appeal directly to your will and feelings.

Consider creating and assuming a character as a kind of quick and simple game. "Play" with the imaginary body, changing and perfecting it until you are completely satisfied with your achievement. You will never fail to win with this game unless your impatience hurries the result; your artistic nature is bound to be carried away by it if you do not force it by "performing" your imaginary body prematurely. Learn to rely upon it in full confidence and it will not betray you.

Do not exaggerate outwardly by stressing, pushing and overdoing those subtle inspirations which come to you from your "new body." And only when you begin to feel absolutely free, true and natural in using it should you start rehearsing your character with its lines and business, whether at home or on the stage.

In some cases you will find it sufficient to use only a part of your imaginary body: long, depending arms, for example, might suddenly change your whole psychology and give your own body the necessary stature. But always see to it that your *entire* being has transformed itself into the character you must portray.

The effect of the imaginary body will be strengthened and acquire many unexpected nuances if you add to it the *imaginary center* (see Chapter 1).

So long as the center remains in the middle of your chest (pretend it is a few inches deep), you will feel that you are still yourself and in full command, only more energetically and harmoniously so, with your body approaching an "ideal" type. But as soon as you try to shift the center to some other place within or outside your body, you will feel that your whole psychological and physical attitude will change, just as it changes when you step into an imaginary body. You will notice that the center is able to draw and concentrate your whole being into one spot from which your activity emanates and radiates. If, to illustrate the point, you were to move the center from your chest to your head, you would become aware that the thought element has begun to play a characteristic part in your performance. From its place in your head the imaginary center will suddenly or gradually co-ordinate all your movements, influence the entire bodily attitude, motivate your behavior, action and speech, and tune your psychology in such a way that you will quite naturally experience the sensation that the thought element is germane and important to your performance.

But no matter where you choose to put the center, it will produce an entirely different effect as soon as you change its *quality*. It is not enough to place it in the head, for example, and leave it there to do its own work. You must further stimulate it by investing it with various desired qualities. For a wise man, let us say, you would imagine the center in your head as big, shining and radiating, whereas for a stupid, fanatic or narrow-minded type of person you would imagine a small, tense and hard center. You must be free from any restraint in imagining the center in many and different ways, so long as the variations are compatible with the part you are playing.

Try a few experiments for a while. Put a soft, warm, not too small center in the region of your abdomen and you may experience a psychology that is self-satisfied, earthy, a bit heavy and even humorous. Place a tiny, hard center on the tip of your nose and you will become curious, inquisitive, prying and even meddlesome. Move the center into one of your eyes and notice how quickly it seems that you have become sly, cunning and perhaps hypocritical. Imagine a big, heavy, dull and sloppy center placed outside the seat of your pants and you have a cowardly, not too honest, droll character. A center located a few feet outside your eyes or forehead may invoke the sensation of a sharp, penetrating and even sagacious mind. A warm, hot and even fiery center situated within your heart may awaken in you heroic, loving and courageous feelings.

You can also imagine a movable center. Let it sway slowly before your forehead and circle your head from time to time, and you will sense the psychology of a bewildered person; or let it circle irregularly around your whole body, in varying tempos, now going up and now sinking down, and the effect will no doubt be one of intoxication.

Innumerable possibilities will be opened to you if you experiment in this way, freely and playfully. You will soon get used to the "game" and appreciate it as much for its enjoyment as for its great practical value.

The imaginary center serves you mainly for the character as a whole. But you can use it for different scenes and separate movements. Suppose you are working upon the part of Don Quixote. You see his old, lean, gentle body; you see his noble, enthusiastic but eccentric and flighty mind, and you decide to place a small but powerful, radiating and constantly twirling center high above your head. This might serve you for the entire Don Quixote character. But now you come to the scene where he is fighting his imaginary enemies and sorcerers. The Knight hunches, jumps into emptiness with lightning speed. His center, now dark and hard, shoots from the heights into his chest, choking his breath. Like a ball on a long rubber band, the center flies forward and snaps back, darting to the right and to the left in search of enemies. Again and again the Knight darts after the "ball" in all directions, until the fight is over. The Knight exhausted, the center sinks slowly to the ground and then, just as slowly, rises up again to its original place, radiating and whirling restlessly as before.

For the sake of clarity you were given some obvious and, perhaps, grotesque examples. But the use of the imaginary center in the majority of cases (especially in modern plays) requires a much finer application. However strong the sensation which the center produces in you may be, the extent to which you wish to display that sensation while acting will always depend on your judgment.

Both the imaginary body and the center, whether you use them in combination or only one at a time, will help you to create the character.

Now let us try to distinguish between the character as a whole and the *characterization*, which can be defined as a small, *peculiar feature* of the character. A characterization or peculiar feature can be anything indigenous to the character: a typical movement, a characteristic manner of speech, a recurrent habit, a certain way of laughing, walking or wearing a suit, an odd way of holding the hands, or a singular inclination of the head, and so forth. These small peculiarities are a kind of "finishing touches" which an artist bestows upon his creation. The whole character seems to become more alive, more human and true, as soon as it is endowed with such a peculiar little feature. The spectator begins to love and expect it as soon as his attention is drawn to it. But such a characterization should be born out of the character as a whole, derived from the important part of its psychological make-up.

Let us take a few examples. An idle and garrulous person, unable to do any work, could have a characterization that expresses itself in arms pressed closely to his sides, elbows at right angles, hands hanging limply. An absent-minded character, while holding a conversation with another person, could show a characteristic manner of quickly blinking his eyes, at the same time directing a finger-pointing gesture at his interlocutor and pausing with mouth slightly ajar before he collects his thoughts and puts them into words. An obstinate character, a squabbler, while listening to other people, may have an unconscious habit of slightly shaking his head as though preparing a negative reply. A self-conscious person will fumble with his suit, touching the buttons and straightening the folds. A cowardly man might keep his fingers together, trying to hide his thumbs. A pedantic character might unconsciously touch things around him, straightening and arranging them more or less symmetrically; a misanthrope, just as unconsciously, will perhaps push away from himself things within his reach. A not quite sincere or sly person might acquire the habit of throwing quick glances at the ceiling while speaking or listening. Etc.

Sometimes the characterization alone can suddenly call forth the entire character.

While creating a character and a characterization for it, you might find great help and perhaps many inspiring suggestions by observing people around you. But in order to avoid a mere copying of life, I would not recommend such observations before you have first made good use of your own creative imagination. Besides, the ability to observe becomes more acute when you know exactly *what* you are looking for.

There is no need to outline any special exercises here. Rather, you can devise them for yourself by "playing" with imaginary bodies and movable, changeable centers, and inventing suitable characterizations for them. It will help if, in addition to such "playing," you try to observe and discover *where* and *what kind* of center this or that person possesses in real life.

7

CREATIVE INDIVIDUALITY

To create by inspiration one must become aware of one's own individuality.

Here some explanation is necessary for the term "the creative individuality of an artist" as used in this book. Even a brief acquaintance with some of its qualities can be useful to the actor who seeks ways for the free expansion of his inner forces.

If, for example, you were to ask two equally talented artists to paint the same landscape with the utmost exactitude, the result would be two markedly different pictures. The reason is obvious: each will inevitably paint his individual impression of that landscape. One of them might prefer to convey the landscape's atmosphere, its beauty of line, or its form; the other would probably stress the contrasts, the play of light and shadows, or some other aspect peculiar to his own taste and mode of expression. The point is that the same landscape invariably will serve as the medium for both to display their *creative individualities*, and how they differ in that respect will be apparent in their pictures.

Rudolf Steiner defines the creative individuality of Schiller as characterized by the poet's moral tendency: Good fights Evil. Maeterlinck seeks subtle mystical nuances behind outer events. Goethe sees archetypes unifying the multitudinous phenomena.

Stanislavsky states that in *The Brothers Karamazov* Dostoievsky expresses his search for God; which, incidentally, is true of all his major novels. The individuality of Tolstoy is manifest in the tendency toward self-perfection, and Chekhov quarrels with the triviality of bourgeois life. In short, the creative individuality of every artist always expresses itself in a dominant idea which, like a leitmotif, pervades all his creations. The same must be said for the creative individuality of the actor-artist.

It has been reiterated that Shakespeare created only one Hamlet. But who will say with equal certainty what kind of Hamlet existed in Shakespeare's imagination? In reality there are, there must be, as many Hamlets as there are talented and inspired actors to undertake their conceptions of the character. The creative individuality of each will invariably determine his own unique Hamlet. For the actor who wishes to be an artist on the stage must, with modesty as well as daring, strive for an individualistic interpretation of his roles. But how does he experience this creative individuality in moments of inspiration?

In everyday life we identify ourselves as "I"; we are the protagonists of "I wish, I feel, I think." This "I" we associate with our body, habits, mode of life, family, social standing and everything else that comprises normal existence But in moments of inspiration the *I* of an artist undergoes a kind of metamorphosis. Try to remember yourself in such moments. What happened to your everyday "*I*"? Did it not retreat, give place to another I, and did you not experience it as the true artist in you?

If you have ever known such moments, you will recall that, with the appearance of this new *I*, you felt first of all an influx of power never experienced in your routine life. This power permeated your whole being, radiated from you into your surroundings, filling the stage and flowing over the footlights into the audience. It united you with the spectator and conveyed to him all your creative intentions, thoughts, images and feelings. Thanks to this power, you are able to feel to a high degree that which we previously called your real presence on the stage.

Considerable changes which you cannot help experiencing take place in your consciousness under the influence of this powerful other *I*. It is a higher-level *I*; it enriches and expands the consciousness. You begin to distinguish *three different beings*, as it were, within yourself. Each has a definite character, fulfills a special task and is comparatively independent. Let us pause and examine these beings and their particular functions.

While incorporating your character on the stage you use your emotions, voice and your mobile body. These constitute the "building material" from which the higher self, the real artist in you, creates a character for the stage. The higher self simply takes possession of that building material. As soon as this happens, you begin to feel that you are standing apart from, or rather above, the material and, consequently, above your everyday self. That is because you now identify yourself with that creative, higher *I* which has become active. You are now aware of both your expanded self and your usual, everyday "I" existing within you simultaneously, side by side. While creating you are two selves, and you are able to distinguish clearly between the different functions they fulfill.

Once the higher self has that building material well in hand, it begins to mold it from within; it moves your body, making it flexible, sensitive and receptive to all creative impulses; it speaks with your voice, stirs your imagination and increases your inner activity. Moreover, it grants you genuine feelings, makes you original and inventive, awakens and maintains your ability to improvise. In short, it puts you in a *creative* state. You begin to act under its inspiration. Everything you do on the stage now surprises you as well as your audience; all seems entirely new and unexpected. Your impression is that it is happening spontaneously and that you do nothing but serve as its medium of expression.

And yet, although your higher self is strong enough to take command over the entire creative process, it has its tendon of Achilles: it is inclined to break the boundaries, overstep the necessary limits set during rehearsals. It is too eager to express itself and its dominant idea; it is too free, too powerful, too ingenious, and therefore too near the precipice of chaos. The power of inspiration is always more intense than the means of expression, said Dostoievsky. It needs restricting.

That is the task of your everyday consciousness. What does it do during those inspired moments? It controls the canvas upon which the creative individuality draws its designs. It fulfills the mission of a common-sense regulator for your higher self in order that the business should be carried through correctly, the established *mise-en-scène* kept unchanged and communication with stage partners unbroken. Even the psychological pattern for the whole character, as discovered during rehearsals, must be followed faithfully. Upon the common sense of your everyday self devolves the protection of the forms that have been found and fixed for the performance. Thus, by the co-operation of both the lower and higher consciousnesses, the performance is made possible.

But where is that third consciousness previously referred to, and to whom does it belong? The bearer of the third consciousness is the Character as created by yourself. Although it is an illusory being, it also, nonetheless, has its own independent life and its own "I." Your creative individuality lovingly sculptures it during the performance.

On previous pages the terms "genuine," "artistic" and "true" were frequently used to describe an actor's feelings on the stage. A closer inspection, however, will reveal that human feelings fall into two categories: those known to everybody and those known only to artists in moments of creative inspiration. The actor must learn to recognize the important distinctions between them.

The usual, everyday feelings are adulterated, permeated with egotism, narrowed to personal needs, inhibited, insignificant and often even unaesthetic and spoiled by untruths. They should not be used in art. Creative individuality rejects them. It has at its disposal another kind of feelings – those completely impersonal, purified, freed from egotism and therefore aesthetic, significant and artistically true. These your higher self grants you while inspiring your acting.

All you experience in the course of your life, all you observe and think, all that makes you happy or unhappy, all your regrets or satisfactions, all your love or hate, all you long for or avoid, all your achievements and failures, all you brought with you into this life at birth – your temperament, abilities, inclinations, whether they remain unfulfilled, underdeveloped or overdeveloped – all are part of the region of your so-called subconscious depth. There, being forgotten by you, or never known to you, they undergo the process of being purified of all egotism. They become feelings per se. Thus purged and transformed, they become part of the material from which your individuality creates the psychology, the illusory "soul" of the character.

But who purifies and transforms these vast riches of our psychology? The same higher self, the individuality that makes artists of some of us. Therefore, it is quite evident that this individuality does not cease to exist between creative moments, though it is only when being creative that we become aware of it. On the contrary, it has a continuous life of its own, unknown to our everyday consciousness; it goes on evolving its own, higher kind of experiences, those it lavishly offers up as inspiration for our creative activity. It is hardly conceivable that Shakespeare, whose everyday life, as far as it is known to us, was so insignificant, and Goethe, whose lot was so placid and contented, drew all their creative ideas from personal experiences only. Indeed, the exterior lives of many lesser literary figures have yielded up far richer biographies than those of the masters, and yet their works will scarcely bear comparison with those of Shakespeare and Goethe. It is the degree of inner activity of the higher self, producing those purified feelings, that is the final determinant of quality in the creations of all artists.

Further, all the feelings derived by the character from your individuality are not only purified and impersonal, but have two other attributes. No matter how profound and persuasive, these feelings are still as "unreal" as the "soul" of the character itself. They come and go with the inspiration. Otherwise they would become forever yours, indelibly impressed upon you after the performance is over. They would enter your everyday life, would be poisoned by egotism and would become an inseparable part of your inartistic, uncreative existence. You would no longer be able to draw the line of demarcation between the illusory life of your character and that of your own. In no time you would be driven mad. If creative feelings were not "unreal" you would not be able to enjoy playing villains or other undesirable characters.

Here you can also see what a dangerous as well as inartistic mistake some conscientious actors make by trying to apply their real, everyday feelings on the stage, squeezing them out of themselves. Sooner or later such attempts lead to unhealthy, hysterical phenomena; in particular, emotional conflicts and nervous breakdowns for the actor. Real feelings exclude inspiration and vice versa.

The other attribute of creative feelings is that they are compassionate. Your higher self endows the character with creative feelings; and because it is able at the same time to observe its creation, it has compassion for its characters and their destinies. Thus the true artist in you is able to suffer for Hamlet, cry with Juliet, laugh about the mischief-making of Falstaff.

Compassion may be called the fundamental of all good art because it alone can tell you what other beings feel and experience. Only compassion severs the bonds of your personal limitations and gives you deep access into the inner life of the character you study, without which you cannot properly prepare it for the stage.

To summarize the foregoing quickly, the true creative state of an actor-artist is governed by a threefold functioning of his consciousness: the higher self inspires his acting and grants him genuinely creative feelings; the lower self serves as the commonsense restraining force; the illusory "soul" of the character becomes the focal point of the higher self's creative impulses.

There is yet another function of the actor's awakened individuality which should be dealt with here, and that is its ubiquity.

Being comparatively free from the lower self and the illusory existence of the character, and possessing an immensely extended consciousness, individuality appears to be capable of straddling both sides of the footlights. It is not only a creator of the character but also its spectator. From the other side of the footlights it follows the spectators' experiences, shares their enthusiasm, excitement and disappointments. More than that, it has the ability to foretell audience reaction an instant before it takes place. It knows what will satisfy the spectator, what will inflame him and what will leave him cold. Thus, for the actor with an awakened awareness of his higher *I*, the audience is a living link which connects him as an artist with the desires of his contemporaries.

Through this ability of the creative individuality the actor learns to distinguish between the real needs of contemporary society and the bad tastes of the rabble. Listening to the "voice" speaking to him from the audience during the performance, he slowly begins to relate himself to the world and his brothers. He acquires a new "organ" which connects him with life outside the theater and awakens his contemporary responsibilities. He begins to extend his professional interest beyond the footlights, he begins to ask questions: "What is my audience experiencing tonight, what is its mood? Why is this play needed in our time, how will this mixture of people benefit from it? What thoughts will this play and this kind of portrayal arouse in my contemporaries? Will this kind of play and this kind of performance make the spectators more sensitive and receptive to the events of our life? Will it awaken in them any moral feelings, or will it give them only pleasure? Will play or performance perhaps arouse the audience's baser instincts? If the performance has humor, what kind of humor does it evoke?" The questions are always there, but only Creative Individuality enables the actor to answer them.

To test this, the actor need only make the following experiment: He can imagine the house as filled with a specific type of audience, such as only scientists, teachers, students, children, farmers, doctors, politicians, diplomats, simple or sophisticated people, people of different nationalities, or even actors. Then, by asking himself the foregoing or similar questions, he should try to sense intuitively what the reaction of each audience might be.

Such an experiment will gradually develop in the actor a new kind of audience sense, through which he will become receptive to the meaning of the theater in present-day society and be able to respond to it consciously and correctly.

In fact, the actor would do well to experiment with all the thoughts expressed in this chapter, going over them until he is certain that he has them in his grasp. By so doing he will understand why this or that particular exercise was suggested as sequential to the professional approach. Eventually the principles of this book will clarify themselves and become a well-integrated whole, wherein every step is designed to attract the actor's individuality and draw it into his work in order to make him always an inspired artist and his profession an important instrument of human utility. Properly understood and applied, the method becomes so much a part of the actor that, in time, he is able to make free use of it, at will, and even modify it here and there according to his own needs and desires.

8

COMPOSITION OF THE PERFORMANCE

The thing isolated becomes incomprehensible.
— Rudolf Steiner

Each art constantly strives to resemble music.
— W. Paret

The same fundamentals which govern the universe and the life of earth and man, and the principles which bring harmony and rhythm to music, poetry and architecture, also comprise the *Laws of Composition* which, to a greater or lesser degree, can be applied to every dramatic performance. A few of the tenets most germane to the actor's craft have been selected for introduction at this point.

Shakespeare's tragic *King Lear* has been chosen to demonstrate all the laws to be dealt with, mainly because it is replete with opportunities to illustrate their practical application. And while on the subject it may not be amiss to voice a purely personal admonishment, that for the modern theater all Shakespearean plays should be shortened and scenes even transposed in order to give them their proper tempo and increase their driving force. But for our purposes here no detailed description of such alterations is necessary.

This chapter will also endeavor to draw closer together the different psychologies of the actor and director. For a good actor must acquire the director's broad, all-embracing view of the performance as a whole if he is to compose his own part in full harmony with it.

The first law of composition might be called the *law of triplicity*. In every well-written play the battle rages between the primary powers of Good and Evil, and it is this battle which constitutes the life impulse of the play, its driving force, and is basic to all plot structures. But the battle itself inevitably falls into three sections: the plot generates, unfolds and concludes. Every play, no matter how complicated and involved its construction, follows this process and is therefore divisible into these three sections.

So long as Lear's kingdom is still intact and the evil powers are passive, we are clearly within the first section. The transition to the second section is apparent with the beginning of the destructive activity, and we are well within it as the destruction takes effect and swells the tragedy to its peak. We are led into the third section when the conclusion develops and we see the evil powers disappear after having destroyed everyone and ruined everything around them.

The law of triplicity is connected with another law, that of *polarity*. In any true piece of art (in our case an inspired performance), the beginning and the end are, or should be, polar in principle. All the main qualities of the first section should transform themselves into their opposites in the last section. It is obvious, of course, that the beginning and the end of a play cannot be defined merely as the first and last scenes; beginning and end in themselves usually embrace a series of scenes each.

The process that transforms the beginning into its polarity at the end takes place in the middle section, and it is this *transformation* which represents our third law of composition.

The director and actors can gain much from knowing these closely connected laws of *triplicity*, *polarity* and *transformation*. By obeying them their performances will acquire more than aesthetic beauty and harmony.

Polarity alone, for instance, will save the performance from monotony and give it greater expressiveness, as contrasts always do; it will also deepen the meaning of both extremes. In art, as in life, we begin to evaluate, to understand and experience things differently if we see them in the light of true contrasts. Think of such opposites, for instance, as life and death, good and evil, spirit and matter, true and false, happiness and unhappiness, health and illness, beauty and ugliness, light and darkness; or more specific phenomena such as short and long, high and low, quick and slow, legato and staccato, big and small, and so on. The very essence of one without the other might easily escape us. Contrast between the beginning and the end is truly the quintessential of a well-composed performance.

Let us pursue this example a little further. Imagine the *King Lear* tragedy again and again with the idea of seeing its beginning and end as polar to each other. Leave out for the time being the middle or transformative section.

Vast, gorgeous and opulent, and yet somewhat dark and gloomy, enveloped in the oppressive atmosphere of despotism, appears the legendary kingdom of Lear. Its boundaries seem to be limitless, and still it is isolated and closed, like a huge fortress. It is drawn toward its center, and the center is Lear himself. Tired, and feeling as ancient as his kingdom, Lear longs for peace and quiet. He speaks of death. Tranquility and immobility shackle his whole environment. The evil, hiding under the guises of submission and obedience, escapes his sleepy mind. He does not yet know compassion and does not distinguish between good and evil. In his earthly grandeur he has no enemies and does not long for friends. He is blind and deaf to human and spiritual values. The earth gave him all its treasures, forged his iron will and taught him to dominate. He is unique, he brooks no equal, he is the kingdom itself.

So the beginning of the tragedy might appear to you. But what is its opposite pole?

We all know what happens to Lear's despotic world. It crumbles, collapses, its boundaries are wiped out. Instead of "shadowy forests and with champains rich'd, with plenteous rivers and wide-skirted meads," it becomes the heath, woeful and desolated. Naked rocks and tents replace the sumptuous halls and chambers of the castle. The deathlike tranquility of the beginning is now transformed into battle cries and clash of steel. Evil which hid under the guise of loyal love now unveils itself: Goneril, Regan, Edmund and Cornwall, spineless at first, now show their stubborn, relentless will. Earthly life has lost its significance for Lear. Pain, shame and despair have broken the boundaries of his consciousness; now he sees and hears and is able to distinguish between good and evil. His crude and heartless will now emerges as a pulsating fatherly love. Again Lear stands there as a center, but as a new Lear and in a new world. He is as unique as before, but now he is desperately lonely as well. The absolute ruler has become a powerless captive and a ragged beggar.

Such is the composition between the beginning and the end. Each throws light upon the other, explaining and complementing through the power of their contrasts. The beginning of the performance rises again like a vision in the mind of the spectator as he watches the end of the performance, and it is the law of polarity which conjures up this vision.

The means by which this polarity is invoked will depend, of course, entirely upon the director and his collaborators. For the stately but gloomy and dark beginning they might choose, for instance, a depressing atmosphere. The music accompanying the performance here and there will increase the power of such an atmosphere. Perhaps they will design the scenery in massive and heavy architectural forms, in dark purple, deep blue and gray colors. Probably they will use stiff and simple costumes in harmony with the scenic architecture and colors. A somewhat dimly lit stage will further help to achieve this aim. The director might stage the acting in moderate tempo; with spare, well-formed and rather definite movements; with compact, stately and unvarying groupings, resembling sculpture, and with voices rather muted. The tragedy (according to Rudolf Steiner's suggestion) might in the beginning be played in a comparatively slow tempo with pauses. These and similar means of expression might be good preparation for creating contrast with the end of the performance.

Tragic still, atmosphere and music of an uplifting nature can now prevail at the end. Brighter lights, flat scenery which creates the feeling of much space and emptiness, yellow and orange colors, lighter costumes, faster tempo without pauses, freer movements and rather mobile groups – these the director can choose for the end of the performance in order to make it polar to the beginning.

To make the composition even more complete the director and actors should look for other, smaller contrasts within the framework of the large one.

For such an example take the three speeches of Lear in the heath:

"Blow, winds, and crack your cheeks!"
(Act III, Scene 2.)
"Poor naked wretches, wheresoe'er you are."
(Act III, Scene 4.)
"Why, thou wert better in thy grave."
(Act III, Scene 4.)

Play all three of these speeches over several times in your imagination and you will see that psychologically they originate from three different sources. The first, like a storm, bursts out of the *will* of Lear as he revolts against the elements of nature; the second is born within the sphere of *feelings* which heretofore were so little known to him; the third ensues from *thoughts* as he tries to penetrate into the essence of a human being, as he now understands it.

The first and third speeches are in contrast to each other, as *will* and *thought* are. Between them, as the transitional connecting link, stands the second speech born of feelings. By different means of expression the director and actor will convey the contrasts to the spectator. Different will be the *mise-en-scènes* presented by the director. Different movements and speech[1] will be displayed by the actor. Different psychologically will be the attitudes the actor will awaken in himself for each of these speeches.

Contrast of a different kind will be found in the juxtaposition of the tragedy's two leading characters, Lear and Edmund. From the very beginning Lear appears before us as one who possesses all the privileges of an earthly, despotic ruler. In contrast to him we see Edmund, known to no one, deprived of all privileges, the bastard son of Gloucester; he starts life with nothing, he is "a nothingness." Lear loses, Edmund gains. At the end of the tragedy, Edmund is covered with glory, powerful, and possesses the love of Goneril and Regan. He becomes "everything" and Lear "nothing." Their situations are reversed, the compositional gesture of the contrast is completed.

But the true meaning of this polarization exists on a higher level. The *whole* tragedy at the end becomes a contrast to its beginning; from its earthly level it aspires to a spiritual one, the values are revalued. "Everything" and "nothing" acquire different meanings: in his earthly "nothingness" Lear at the end becomes "everything" in the spiritual sense, while Edmund as the earthly "everything" becomes a spiritual zero.

Again the director and the actors will easily find the means of expressing this contrast. In the beginning Lear might use a strong molding quality in his movements and speech (heavy, but noble

[1] In *Lauteurhythmy*, by Rudolf Steiner, you will find indications of how to use artistic speech for expressing either will, feelings or thoughts.

and dignified), while Edmund's acting and speech can take on the quality of ease and lightness (by no means a spiritual and uplifting quality, but rather one with cunning, thievish nuances which will create the impression of false modesty and self-effacement). While in motion Edmund can hug the walls and shadows, never occupying prominent places on the stage. At the end, when the whole tragedy moves to a higher sphere, both leading characters can exchange qualities, with Lear using lightness and easiness as spiritual, noble, uplifting qualities, whereas Edmund remolds his quality to become heavy, rude, ill-mannered and gruff-voiced.

The more the director stresses this polarity by such means, the more it will reveal a part of the main idea of the tragedy and one of the most profound: *The value of things changes in the light of the spiritual or in the dark of the material.*

Now let us return to the three main units of the tragedy and discuss the second, which serves as the transition between the two contrasting poles.

Imagining it as a *continuous process* of transformation, you can perceive every moment of it simultaneously in the light of beginning and end. Simply ask yourself: To what extent and in which sense does this or that particular moment of the middle part depart from the beginning and approach the end? In other words, in which sense has the beginning *already* transformed itself into the end?

In our example of *King Lear*, in the stately atmosphere of the beginning, the action taking place includes the division of the kingdom, the false profession of love by the two daughters, the courageous truth of Cordelia, the banishment of Kent, the destruction of the kingdom by tossing away the crown, etc. The transformation has begun! The world of the play, so stable, so seemingly durable in the beginning, now shatters and empties itself. Lear calls but his voice remains unheard: "I think the world's asleep." "Thou hadst little wit in thy bald crown," says the

Fool, "when thou gavest thy golden one away." Grave suspicions creep into Lear's mind, and only the Fool dares to put them into words. "Does any here know me?" exclaims Lear. "Who is it that can tell me who I am!" Fool: "Lear's shadow." The beginning of the tragedy gradually transforms into its middle part. Lear has already lost his kingdom but has not yet realized it; Goneril, Regan and Edmund have already lifted a bit of their masks but have not yet torn them off; Lear has already received his first wound but has not yet neared the moment when his heart starts bleeding; his despotic mind is already shaken but there is as yet no sign of the new thoughts which replace the old.

Step by step, to the very end, the director and actor follow the transformation of the King into a beggar, of a tyrant into a loving father. These "alreadies" and "not yets" spin living threads, weaving each and every given point of the past (beginning) into the present and simultaneously prophesying the pattern of the future (end). Each scene and character reveals its true meaning and significance in each moment of the transformation, which takes place in the ever-present middle part. The Lear who gives up his stately throne and the Lear who first appears at Goneril's castle are two different Lears. The second rises out of the first, as the third will rise out of the second, etc., until the very end, where the "not yets" are no more and all the "alreadies" merge into the final, majestic design of the tragedy.

Bearing in mind how all the scenes transform one into the other under the influence of the three laws of composition, the director and actors can easily distinguish between the important and the unimportant, between the major and the minor. They will be able to follow the basic line of the play and the battle raging in it without getting lost in the details. Seen in the light of composition, the scenes themselves will prompt the director as to how they should best be staged, because their significance to the whole play is unmistakably revealed to him.

The laws of triplicity, polarity and transformation lead us to the next law of composition, which consists of finding *climaxes* for the three big sections or units.

Each of the units has its own meaning, characteristic qualities and prevailing powers, all of which are not evenly distributed within them; they wax and wane in strength, they rise and fall like waves. Their moments of maximum tension we shall call *climaxes*.

In a well-written and well-performed play there are three main climaxes, one for each unit. They are as related to each other as the three units themselves: the climax of the first unit is a kind of summary of the plot thus far; the second climax also shows in condensed form how the plot of the second or middle unit develops, and the third climax crystallizes the finale of the plot within the framework of the last unit. Therefore, all three climaxes are also as regulated by the laws of triplicity, transformation and polarity as the units are. Another example from *King Lear* will illustrate this.

Negative, earthly powers, depressing atmosphere, dark deeds and thoughts threaten in the first unit of the tragedy. If you were to ask yourself just where in this unit its qualities, powers and meaning are expressed with the utmost clarity and intensity, in their most concentrated form, in all probability your attention would be drawn to the scene in which Lear condemns Cordelia, throws the crown into the hands of his enemies and banishes his faithful and devoted servant, Kent (Act I, Scene 1). This comparatively short scene may be likened to one in which a seed suddenly breaks through its cover and the growth of the plant begins. In this scene you see the first manifestation of the evil powers that were hidden around and within Lear. Breaking violently from within Lear's being, these forces now release the negative powers around him. The world of King Lear, heretofore so complete and harmonious, begins to disintegrate. In his egocentric blindness Lear is not able to see Cordelia. Goneril and Regan snatch the power that goes with the crown, the ominous atmosphere grows and spreads. All the mainsprings of the tragedy are loosed during this short scene. This is the *climax* of the first unit (Act I, Scene 1, beginning with Lear's speech, "Let it be so," and ending with Kent's exit).[2]

Before trying to find the climax of the second unit it is prerequisite that we probe the climax of the third unit.

The positive, spiritual powers and qualities, in contrast to the beginning, are dominant in the third unit. An enlightened atmosphere, illuminated by the suffering of Lear and the disappearance of evil, prevails at the end. Here you also find the scene where all the powers and qualities merge into the majestic finale which comprises the meaning of the third unit. It is the fruit of the seed which grew and developed during the tragedy. The climax begins with the moment of Lear's appearance, bearing the dead Cordelia in his arms (Act V, Scene 3). The earthly, material world has disappeared for him. A new world permeated with spiritual values emerges instead. The suffering he has endured from the evil, with which he wrestled from within and without,

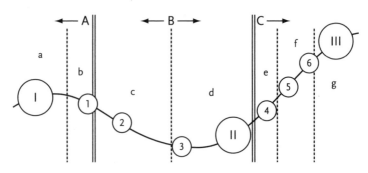

A,B,C – Three Big (Main) Units
I,II,III – Main Climaxes

1,2,3,4,5,6 – Auxiliary Climaxes
a,b,c,d,e,f,g – Subdivisions

CHART

[2] See CHART, I.

has transformed him into a new and purified Lear. His eyes are now opened and he sees the true Cordelia, sees her as he could not when she stood before him at his throne. The death of Lear himself concludes the third climax.[3] The polarity of both main climaxes is the same as the polarity of the beginning and the end of the play.

Now we can return to the climax of the second unit, that crucible wherein the transformation takes place.

Chaotic, tempestuous, destructive powers, relentlessly pursuing and persecuting Lear, mark this second unit. Then the storm ceases and the atmosphere of emptiness and solitude spreads itself. Lear's former consciousness is distraught and he wanders the heath as a madman. Where, then, do we find the climax of this unit? Is there any scene which expresses the transformation of the tragedy's beginning into the end, a scene wherein we are aware of the dying past and the dawning future at one and the same time? Yes, there is, there must be, such a scene. It is the one in which Shakespeare shows us *two* Lears at the same time: one is expiring (the past), another is beginning to grow (the future). It is interesting to note that the transformation in this case finds its expression not so much in the content of the lines or the meaning of specific words, but rather in the situation itself, in the fact of Lear's madness. This climax starts with the entrance of the mad Lear in the field near Dover and ends with his departure (Act IV, Scene 6).[4]

Now look into the meaning of this scene and ask yourself, "Is it the same Lear I saw and knew in the beginning, and in subsequent scenes?" The answer must be: No, it is only his outer shell, a tragic caricature of the former, royal Lear. True, the destruction of his mind and the humbling of his outer appearance have reached their apex, but you feel that these are not the finials of Lear's destiny. All his suffering, tears, despair, remorse – were they intended to fall upon Lear's white head only to produce a madman? Hardly. It would be unjust and purposeless. Were his

[3] See CHART, III.
[4] See CHART, II.

torn heart, his pride and dignity all in vain, or his courage, fierce fight and proud, unbending kingly will? If so, what a waste of magnificent character! But you know and feel that Lear's tragedy is not yet resolved, and you wait for that which hides behind the madman's disguise. You wait for a *new* Lear, whose future you can only guess at now but for whom there must be a more ennobling resolution. You wait for him, and in your mind's eye you already envisage the Lear of the future. You know that behind his feckless façade he is in the process of being regenerated into the new Lear, and that he will soon emerge. You will see him in his new appearance when, on his knees in Cordelia's tent, he will beg her forgiveness. But right now there are two Lears before you: one as an empty, spiritless body, the other as a bodiless spirit. What takes place before you is the *process of transformation of the past into the future*. The polarity is in the process of being shaped. You experience the climax of the middle, transitory unit.

The three main climaxes (if they are found correctly, by artistic intuition rather than by reasoning) give you the key to the main idea and to the basic dynamic of the play. Each climax expresses the essence of that unit which it represents. Three comparatively short scenes trace Lear's whole inner and outer path, his whole destiny: Lear commits a number of sins and frees dark powers; chaos, suffering and madness tear apart Lear's former consciousness as well as his old body and his world; a new consciousness, a new Lear and a new world begin to dawn as a result of it. The tragedy is lifted from the earthly plane into the spiritual, and positive powers are victorious in it. If you try to see only these three climaxes in your imagination, you can express the content and the meaning of the whole tragedy in three words: *sin*, *judgment* and *enlightenment*. Thus the three climaxes crystallize one more facet of the main idea of the play.

At this juncture it might be suggested to the director that he start his rehearsals with the three main climaxes. It is an erroneous impression that rehearsals of a play should start with the very first scene and continue in undeviating succession; it is prompted by habit and not inspired by creative necessity. There is no need or reason to start from the beginning if the whole play is vivid in the imagination. It would be better to start with scenes which express the gist of the play, then proceed to scenes of secondary importance.

Each of the three main units of the play can be subdivided into any number of smaller ones. These smaller units also have their own climaxes, which we will call *auxiliary climaxes* to distinguish them from the main climaxes. *King Lear* lends itself to the following subdivisions:

The main first unit (A) falls into two smaller ones. In the first (*a*) Lear appears before the audience in all his grandeur, exuding unlimited despotic power. He commits three sins: condemns Cordelia, gives away the crown and banishes Kent. In the second subdivision (*b*) the negative, evil powers begin their subversive, destructive activity.

The first main climax (I) is also the climax of the first subdivision (*a*), but the second subdivision (*b*) has its own auxiliary climax (1). After the enraged Lear leaves the throne and the King of France leads Cordelia away, we first hear the whispering voices of Goneril and Regan in an atmosphere of conspiracy and secrecy (Act I, Scene 1). Goneril: "Sister, it is not little I have to say . . ." They are scheming their plot, and this is the beginning of the auxiliary climax (1). The theme of Evil which had begun mutedly (it was rather felt in the atmosphere from the very rise of the curtain) and then suddenly burst violently with Lear's wrath, now enters its third and most important stage of development. It acquires a definite form of conscious, deliberate plotting. This climax also embraces Edmund's soliloquy (Act I, Scene 2), because from the point of view of composition, the author's divisions into acts and scenes should be disregarded. Thus the climax ends with the entrance of Gloucester.

The middle unit (B) can also be subdivided into two smaller parts (*c* and *d*). The first part is passionate, stormy and chaotic; the elemental powers are raging in it, slowly penetrating into the depths of Lear's consciousness, tormenting and tearing it. The auxiliary climax (2) of this subdivision (*c*) begins with Lear's soliloquy, "Blow winds and crack your cheeks! . . ." (Act III, Scene 2), and ends with his line, " . . . So old and white as this. O! O! 'tis foul!"

The second subdivision (*d*) begins when the storm subsides, when the world seems to be empty and the exhausted and forlorn Lear falls into a deep, deathlike sleep. Here, by the way, I would like to call your attention to the fact that the middle unit (B) in its two subdivisions (*c* and *d*) shows a strong contrast or polarity. In the second subdivision (*d*) you find two climaxes: the main climax (II) and the auxiliary climax (3) which precedes it. The auxiliary climax (3) shows the extreme tension of the dark powers, their forte-fortissimo in the cruelest scene of the entire tragedy, the blinding of Gloucester (Act III, Scene 7). The climax begins with Gloucester's entrance and ends with the wounded Cornwall's exit. This wild scene breaking into the general atmosphere of desolation, solitude and emptiness only emphasizes it by its contrasting qualities. At the same time it is a turning point in the theme of Evil. If you follow the developments of positive and negative powers, you can see the essential difference between them. The positive, good powers have no turning point. They develop and grow almost in a straight line, to the very end, whereas the negative, evil powers turn their destructive activity upon themselves after they have ruined everything around them. That is their turning point. Therefore it is most important to observe their birth in the first auxiliary climax (1), their bloom in the third auxiliary climax (3), and their complete annihilation. The latter also will have its climactic scene in the duel between the two brothers (the sixth auxiliary climax).

Even before the third big unit (C) begins, the dawn of rising light is felt in the long sequence of scenes. Behind the cloak of the madman we already anticipate a new, enlightened Lear; Evil begins to destroy itself; Gloucester meets his faithful son; the brief appearance of Cordelia. From the point of view of composition they are all a preparation for the third, uplifting, spiritual part of the tragedy. And with the appearance of Lear in Cordelia's tent, the theme of light (Good) flares up with great strength. Thus the third unit (C) begins.

The theme of light goes through three successive stages, which make for three subdivisions. The first (e), in the tent of Cordelia (Act IV, Scene 7), is soft and romantic. The new Lear awakens into a new world, surrounded by loving people. This is the "second Lear" for whose appearance we have been waiting. From the moment of Lear's awakening and up to his exit constitutes the auxiliary climax (4) of this romantic part.

The second subdivision (f) is passionate and heroic. Lear and Cordelia are led off to prison (Act V, Scene 3). Here the new consciousness of Lear grows and gains strength. Into Lear's voice again creep the overtones of the former mighty King, but now his voice does not sound despotic. It has become more spiritual than earthly. The auxiliary climax (5) of this part starts with the entrance of Lear and Cordelia and ends with their exit.

It is in this same heroic part (f), as its concluding moment, that the duel between Edmund and Edgar takes place. This is another auxiliary climax (6), the one referred to earlier.

The third and last subdivision (g) has a tragic, uplifting quality. This is the concluding, final chord for the whole composition. The climax of this subdivision is the third main climax (III) of the entire tragedy.

All the climaxes are correlated, complementing or contrasting each other. As already stated, the three main climaxes absorb in themselves the whole idea of the play and express it in three successive stages. The auxiliary climaxes build transitions and connecting links between them. They are the elaborations of the main idea, which can be expressed as follows:

Having committed his three decisive sins (I), Lear unleashes evil powers (1) which pursue and torment him, growing in Shakespeare's burning imagination into the majestic symbol of a raging storm (2). Meeting no resistance, the evil powers increase their destructive activity until they reach their climax (3), then begins their decline and self-destruction. Lear's punishment also attains its climactic height (the juncture of the two Lears), when he becomes mad from his suffering and torment (II), after which the process of tragic enlightenment advances through three successive stages: romantic (4), heroic (5) and finally, after the evil powers destroy themselves (6), the most spiritual and uplifting stage, when the purified Lear passes into the other world to join his beloved Cordelia (III).

Therefore, the director might do well, having started his rehearsals with the main climaxes, to take up the auxiliary climaxes, until gradually the details group themselves around the spine.

The main and auxiliary climaxes do not embrace all the moments of conflict or tension spread throughout the entire play. Their number does not depend on any laws and may be freely defined in accordance with the taste and interpretation of the director and actors. To distinguish the moments of lesser tension we will call them *accents*. As an example of how accents are defined we will take the first main climax of the tragedy.

This climax begins with a tense, meaningful pause immediately following Cordelia's crucial answer, "Nothing, my lord" (Act I, Scene 1). This pause is the first accent within the first

main climax. In this pause the whole ensuing scene is germin-
ated, and from this germ issues the impulse which forces Lear to
commit the three sins that show us the dark features of his
nature. That is what turns this first pause into an accent and
makes this accent so significant and strong from the point of view
of composition.

Another such pause is found at the end of the first main climax.
It is the concluding accent of the climax and follows immediately
after Kent's exit. In it, as in a focus, is concentrated the moral
result of all that has taken place. The first pause-accent predicts
the coming events, the last summarizes them.

Between the first and concluding accents just delineated Lear
condemns Cordelia and thrusts her away, gives the crown to his
other daughters and, finally, banishes Kent from the boundaries of
the kingdom. The first of these sins committed by Lear has a
purely spiritual significance: casting off Cordelia, he condemns
himself to a future of solitude; he empties his own being. The
soliloquy, "Let it be so," is the second accent of the climax.

Lear's second sin has a more external character: he destroys his
surroundings, his kingdom. Instead of the implication that he is
nobly transferring his crown to his rightful heirs, as befits his
stately manner, he virtually discards it with hatred as a protest
against the truth from Cordelia and Kent. This misguided
bestowal of his regal powers is the third accent of the scene,
starting with the speech, "Cornwall and Albany, with my two
daughters' dowers," and ending with, "that troops with majesty."

The banishment of Kent, Lear's third sin, has an entirely outer
character: he banishes Kent from his earthly possessions, whereas
Cordelia was banished from his spiritual realm. The last speech of
Lear, "Hear me, recreant!" is the fourth accent of the scene. The
fifth accent-pause concludes the climax.

Here the director, after having rehearsed the climaxes, can proceed
with the rehearsal of the accents. Thus he and the actors will hew

to the main line of the play and will not be diverted or distracted by its less essential moments during the staging.

The next principle of composition we shall call the *law of rhythmical repetitions*. This law also manifests itself in various ways in the life of the universe, earth and man. Only two of these ways need be mentioned in connection with dramatic art. First, when phenomena repeat themselves regularly in space or time, or both, and remain unchanged; second, when phenomena change with each successive repetition. These two kinds of repetition evoke different reactions in the spectator.

In the first case the spectator gets the impression of "eternity" if the repetition takes place in time, or of "endlessness" if it occurs in space. This kind of repetition, applied to the stage, often helps to create a certain atmosphere. Consider the rhythmical sounding of a bell, the ticktock of a clock, the sound of waves beating against the shore, recurring gusts of wind, etc.; or contemplate the repetitions in a setting, such as equally distributed rows of windows, pillars, tiers, or human figures passing evenly across the stage.

In *King Lear* it is most advantageous to use this kind of rhythmical repetition in the beginning of the play in order to create the impression of the "eternal" (ancient) and "endless" (immensely large) legendary kingdom. The settings, the distribution of light such as torches, lanterns and illuminated windows, the sounds and movements, can easily be used to achieve this aim. Rhythmical appearances of the characters and courtiers upon the stage, their spacing as to distance, rhythmically established short pauses before and after Lear's entrance, even the sound of Lear's approaching steps – all these and kindred means will create the desired impression. The same technique of rhythmical repetition can be used in the scenes when the storm rages in the heath: flashes of lightning, claps of thunder, gusts of wind, as well as the actors' movements alternately becoming sharp (staccato) or soft (legato). The director will undoubtedly be able to find innumerable other means and devices with which to create the impression of the "endless," torturous storm which holds Lear and his companions in its grip.

The effect produced by the second type of repetition, when phenomena do change, is a different one. It either increases or diminishes certain impressions, making them more spiritual or material; it increases or diminishes the humor or tragedy or any other facet of a situation. *King Lear* gives us good opportunity to demonstrate this second kind of repetition, too:

1. Three times in the course of the tragedy does the *kingly theme* come forth with great strength. Upon Lear's first appearance in the Room of State the spectator greets him as a king in all his earthly glory. The image of the pompous tyrant is firmly impressed upon the mind. The *repetition* of the theme strikes the audience when the mad King appears in the heath (Act IV, Scene 6). This repetition emphasizes to the spectator the decline or decrease of the earthly, kingly grandeur and the rise or increase of the spiritual. Nowhere does Shakespeare dim the *kingly* qualities of his main character. On the contrary, he does everything to stress that it is a *King* and not an average person who undergoes the transformation from earthly to *spiritual* majesty. Not alone words, but the contrast with the situation at the beginning – the outer appearance of the King, his torn and distracted mind – force the spectator to see him in retrospect in order to follow the King's cruel destiny with greater compassion. The dramatic effect would not be so striking were the spectator allowed to forget even for a moment that it is a *King*: "I am the King himself! . . . Ay, every inch a King. . . . I am a King, my masters, know you that!"

At the end of the tragedy "The King" appears for the third time, when Lear dies with the dead Cordelia in his arms. It is then that Lear stands in still greater contrast before the spectator. The mighty despot on the throne and the helpless pauper on the battlefield, true, but he is still a King withal. He dies at the end of the tragedy. But now try asking yourself as a spectator if the *King* really died for you, even though you saw it so performed. Not very likely. If the role has been well performed and the repetitions properly handled, the spectator's conclusion undoubtedly will be that what died in the King was only his earthly, despotic "I" but that the other, *spiritual King* with the purified "I" had won a worthy immortality. After the performance is over he continues to live in the spectator's mind and heart. If this is idle theory, then compare Lear's death to Edmund's. What remains with the spectator after Edmund's death? Emptiness, the "nothingness" that characterized his life. He vanishes from memory. The death of Lear, on the other hand, is a transcendent transformation: he still exists, though as another being; in the course of the tragedy his kingly "I" has accumulated such spiritual energy that he remains intensely alive to the spectator long after his physical death. Hence the repetition of the "King" theme serves to increase the spiritual meaning of the "King" concept. This rhythmical repetition again reveals to us one of the aspects of the main idea of the tragedy: *"The King," the higher self in man, has the power to live and grow and transform itself under the blows of ruthless destiny, and is able to transcend the boundaries of physical death.*

2. Five times Lear meets Cordelia. Each meeting is a step toward their eternal union. Lear meets her in the Room of State and thrusts her away. In a compositional sense this is a preparatory gesture, a kind of springboard for their meetings to come. The harder he thrusts her away, the more impressive will their final meeting become. The second meeting takes place in Cordelia's tent after a long, long separation. It has an entirely different character. The roles are reversed. Lear's weakness and helplessness are juxtaposed to his former might. On his knees he implores her forgiveness. But in the higher sense which the tragedy seeks to convey they have not found each other as yet. In this second

meeting Lear is too humiliated, too much on a lower plane. Cordelia is not yet able to raise him to her level. An elevational step is needed, another meeting is necessary. This happens in the third repetition of the rhythmical figure: Lear and Cordelia are led off to prison. But here too, total equality is not yet attained. In Lear's unbending "I" egotism flares up again, although now it is already tinted with spiritual qualities. He despises the courtiers, these "gilded butterflies," these "poor rogues," and it is this disdain which reawakens the pride which had alienated Cordelia. By this very proof we see that Lear is not yet worthy of her. The spectator still feels that another meeting is needed, hence he sees them together again when Lear carries Cordelia's body in his arms. This is their fourth meeting. Now Lear is rid of his pride and all desires except one – to merge the inexpressible love of his whole being with Cordelia's, to give of himself even more than she had given of herself. But there is between them the boundary of two worlds. In the world in which he still stands, he had once thrust her away. Now, in his despair, he tries to call her back, for how else can he now attain the only worthy goal of his existence? "Cordelia, Cordelia, stay a little. Ha! What is't thou say'st?" (Act V, Scene 3.) So still another step forward, another meeting is needed, and that is the passing of Lear himself into Cordelia's world. And Lear dies. His death concludes the rhythmical repetition. The two who sought each other for so long are now united beyond the boundaries of the physical world. This last, fifth meeting the spectator acknowledges as the highest form of human love, the ultimate union of true devotion. Now Lear and Cordelia have not only given of themselves equally, but are each other's equal, are spiritually one. Again thanks to composition, another facet of the main idea of the tragedy is disclosed. If the previous example of repetition showed the spectator the deathlessness of man's kingly *I*, this one should convey the *necessity of the union of the kingly* I, *the masculine* I, *with its counterpart – the feminine* I *which softens his masculine crudeness and aggressiveness.* Here it is Lear's union with qualities of the soul, which he lacked in the beginning and thrust away when he banished Cordelia.

3. This third example of repetition appears as a kind of *parallelism*. The spectator simultaneously follows the tragedy of Lear and the drama of Gloucester. Drama repeats the tragedy. Gloucester suffers no less than Lear, but the results of his suffering are different. Both commit errors; both lose their beloved and faithful children; both also have evil children; both lose their earthly possessions; both meet their lost children again; both die in banishment. Here end the similarities of these two destinies, and the differences of contrasts begin. Let us explore where and how.

Gloucester repeats Lear's destiny, but on a lower level; he does not cross the boundaries of the earthly mind and he does not go mad. He meets the same elemental powers, but they do not widen his consciousness or awaken a higher one; he does not become an integral part of that storm, as does Lear. Gloucester stops there, where Lear's spiritual ascension begins; both say that they will wait patiently, but for Gloucester it is his earthbound limit. Lear goes further; he finds Cordelia again, and for him that is the impulse toward a new and higher life beyond this world. Gloucester meets Edgar again and dies; he is only mortal and cannot penetrate the hidden mysteries lying beyond earthly consciousness. Similar is the path of life, but different are they who travel it! Lear's difference is that the strength of his kingly *I* enables him to create and mold his own destiny; he fights the destiny which circumscribes him and refuses to submit to it like Gloucester. This repetition-parallelism also reveals, first through similarity and then through contrast, still another of the facets of the main idea of the tragedy: *The power of the unbending* I *and striving toward an ideal (Cordelia) make mortal man immortal.*

4. Three times Lear appears in a welter of tragedy, and three times he *leaves* it. A tense atmosphere of expectation fills the stage at the rise of the curtain. The whispering, muted dialogue between Kent and Gloucester, resembling a "pause," forecasts the monarch's appearance. Not until Lear's entrance does the tragedy actually begin. The eventful destiny slowly begins to unfold before the fascinated spectator. Step by step there follows the destruction of the mighty monarch. Lear fights, suffers and loses, momentarily yielding to the long struggle only after the "trial" of his daughters, when, exhausted, he falls into a deep sleep resembling death (Act III, Scene 6). He seems to be defeated. The destiny has completed its first round, and for the first time since his initial appearance Lear departs the world of tragedy. Once more a long, significant "pause" embraces a series of scenes.

Lear's second appearance is unreal and fantastic. He seems a phantom sprung from nowhere into the fields near Dover. If he seems unreal, it is because, as we know, he is already an empty, spiritless shell. He has had his past and he shall have his future, but he has no present. He is a wanderer in suspension. Like a comet, he streaks across the sky of a tragic world and disappears again.

In Cordelia's tent Lear *appears* for the third time. Again a "pause," this time of music and an atmosphere of love and expectation, foretells his dormant presence. Lear awakens: "You do me wrong to take me out o' the grave." How far away was he until this moment? What change did he undergo while hovering beyond the threshold of his tragic world? Unwittingly the spectator compares Lear's first appearance in the Room of State with this third appearance, and grasps the full significance of the ruler's tragic destiny, his inner growth and transformation as a wanderer. And at the end of the play the spectator parts from Lear for the third and last time. Lear again leaves in a majestic atmosphere. Majestic also is the "pause" which follows his physical death. The spectator feelingly watches this slow departure into the other world. This time the repetition convinces us of *Lear's inner growth and of the boundary between two worlds, which only a Lear and not a Gloucester can cross.*

5. Now let us try a similar breakdown of the short scene where Goneril and Regan swear their love to Lear (Act I, Scene 1). The outer form of this repetition is simple: (*a*) Lear's question to Goneril; (*b*) Goneril's answer; (*c*) Cordelia's cue; (*d*) Lear's decision. The same figure repeats with Regan's answer. In the third repetition the figure breaks with Cordelia's answer, and the following scene develops as a result of this threefold repetition. To demonstrate this better let us play the whole scene in our imagination.

Lear appears in the Room of State with all eyes turned upon him. The awe, the veneration and the fear surrounding him are as great as his contempt for these surroundings. Lear's wandering gaze stops nowhere. He is obsessed with himself and his great longing for peace and rest. He abdicates his throne and gives up his power. Goneril, Regan and Cordelia, he hopes, will give him his desired peace; they will carry him lovingly to the hour of his death. And in death, he thinks, he will meet a friend who will offer him his rest.

His first question Lear addresses to Goneril. Now all eyes are turned upon her, with the exception of Lear's, who knows her answer in advance. But the answer is dangerous and difficult. One false note in her voice can throw the spark of suspicion into the heart of the King and awaken his sleeping consciousness. But fear and dark inspiration help Goneril to find the right words and behavior. She penetrates Lear's sleepy consciousness without stirring it. She begins her speech. Her tone, tempo, timbre of voice and even manner of speaking resemble those of Lear himself when he put the question to her. Thus merged with him, her words sound as though they might he Lear's own. Lear is silent and motionless. Goneril's words become more and more hushed, begin to sound like a lullaby which rocks him into an even deeper sleep. Cordelia's interlocutory aside – "What shall Cordelia do?" – sounds like a muted sob. Lear pronounces his decision. The first gesture of this repetition is concluded.

Now, with his consciousness still more enveloped in sleep, Lear puts his question to Regan. The gesture of the composition begins to repeat itself. Regan's task is simpler. Goneril has paved the way and has shown how to achieve the gain that lies ahead. Regan, as always, imitates Goneril. Again Cordelia's heavyhearted aside – "Then poor Cordelia!" – punctuates a sister's speech. Lear pronounces his decision and puts the last question to Cordelia. The repetition starts its third round.

Cordelia's whole being is filled with love for her father, filled with compassion for him and with protest against her sisters' lies. Clear, fiery, awakening, and in contrast to her sisters' voices, sounds her answer: "Nothing, my lord." She wants to free her father from the spell thrown upon him by Goneril and Regan. A heavy, tense pause ensues. For the first time Lear fixes his gaze, upon Cordelia. It is a long, dark stare. Here the figure of repetition breaks. Cordelia has awakened Lear, but – like the weary, sleeping lion disturbed – his wakefulness is an angry roar. His powerful will lashes at the tender, helpless cub who meant only to warn him of impending danger. He takes an arbitrary direction, and catastrophe is inevitable. One after the other Lear commits his three wrongs. Again the repetition discloses a part of the main idea of the tragedy: *The power of an awakened* I *does not yet guarantee the good, the true and the beautiful. All depends on the direction in which the awakened* I *chooses to go.*

Let us proceed to the next law of composition.

Life in its manifestations does not always follow a straight line. It undulates like waves, it breathes rhythmically. Thus *rhythmical waves* assume various characters with different phenomena; they flourish and fade, appear and disappear, expand and contract, circumfuse and centralize, ad infinitum. In application to dramatic art we can consider these waves as expressing only *inner* and *outer* action.

Imagine a meaningful stage pause radiant with power, inwardly active, creating a strong atmosphere and holding the audience in suspense. It is not unusual to find a pause so pregnant, for a pause is never a complete vacuum, gap or a psychologically void space. Empty pauses do not, and should not, exist on the stage. Every pause must have a purpose. A real, well-prepared and perfectly executed pause (long or short) is what we might call *inner action*, since its significance is implied by silence. Its antithesis is *outer action*, which we can define as a moment when all visible and audible means of expression are used to the fullest extent; when speech, voices, gestures, business, and even lighting and sound effects, ascend to their climactic point. Between these two extremes there is a spectrum of outer action in that it increases or decreases in varying degrees. A veiled, muted, almost imperceptible action often resembles a "pause." The very beginning of the tragedy, before Lear's entrance, may be described as such a muted-action pause, and so may the pause after his death at the end of the performance. Ebb and flow of inner and outer action, these are the rhythmical waves of a performance's composition.

Many such rhythmical waves can be found in *King Lear*.

They begin with the pauselike opening scene among Kent, Gloucester and Edmund, when an atmosphere of tense expectation fills the stage, foretelling Lear's appearance and forecasting the events to follow. At the curtain's rise the action has an inner character. Lear enters, the action gradually begins to lose its "innerness." It loses still more as catastrophe approaches. And during Lear's impassioned wrath the action becomes entirely outer in character. When the climax is over, the wave of outer action recedes. The plotting of the two sisters and Edmund's treacherous thoughts again create an inner action. A new, strong wave of outer action hits a peak in the heath scene, where Lear fights the storm. It is followed by torturous longing, solitude and quiet when Lear falls into a deathlike sleep. Thus another big rhythmic wave has ended. This period of inner action is once again followed by a strong wave of outer action in the unbridled scene when Gloucester is blinded. In Cordelia's tent the action is inner once more. In the scene where Lear and Cordelia go to prison, the outer action temporarily resumes the crest. The tragedy ends, as it began, with a deep, inner, majestic pause.

Smaller rhythmical waves can be found within the larger. They must he defined by the actors' and director's taste, by their interpretation of the whole play and of separate scenes. Rhythmical waves make the performance pulsatingly beautiful and expressive; they give it life and kill its monotony.

Some directors incline to the error of imagining that the performance as a whole must either go crescendo toward the end or reach its only climax somewhere in the middle of the play. Either misconception will force them to restrain the stronger means of expression until the middle or the end, thereby unnecessarily vitiating the performance. On the other hand, if they took into consideration that there are several climaxes and many rhythmical waves, they would have no need to withhold the best until the end, when it is too late, or try to sustain a play's force after an artificially supercharged climax in the middle. They would do much better to take full advantage of each and every climax, and make use of every opportunity between them; to rise to the peak of each rhythmical wave in order to invest their productions with maximal impact, relief and variety.

This chapter would not be complete without consideration of the principle upon which the *composition of the characters* is based.

Each character in the play has its specific psychological traits. These traits must be accepted as a foundation for the composition.

In this respect the task of the director and actors is twofold: to emphasize the *differences* of the characters and yet to see that they *complement* each other as much as possible.

The best way to fulfill this task is to conjecture as to which of the three psychological traits dominates each of the characters – will, feelings, or thoughts – and the nature of each trait.

If more than one character possess the same trait, how do they differ in this trait?

Some of the main characters in *King Lear* represent the theme of Evil. The necessity to perform with a negative, evil psychology might give all of them too much similarity; using the same means of expression will certainly make them alike and monotonous. So we examine each of these evil characters and try to find in which way they can be performed differently.

Edmund represents a type in whom the thought element is prevalent. He is deprived of the ability to feel. His quick, keen mentality, forming different combinations with his will (which is nothing but lust for power), produces lies, cynicism, disdain, extreme egotism, unscrupulousness and heartlessness. He is a virtuoso of immorality. Conversely, his lack of feelings makes him firm and fearless in all his cunning plotting.

Cornwall complements Edmund. He is an outspoken *will type*. His mentality is weak and primitive. His heart is filled with hatred. His overdeveloped, unbridled will, uncontrolled by intellect and clouded by hatred, makes him a representative of destructive power among the other evil characters.

Goneril completes the clear-cut trinity with Edmund and Cornwall. Her whole being is woven of *feelings*, but all her feelings are passions and all her passions sensuality.

The Duke of Albany occupies a singular place in the composition of the characters. His *weakness* complements the strength of Edmund, Goneril and Cornwall, yet makes him so different from them. His function is to show the uselessness of moral tendencies if they cannot be made to combat evil powers. Therefore, in spite of his positive intentions, he must be regarded as a negative character.

Regan can be interpreted in different ways. She can be visualized, for one, as a character who *lacks initiative*. Almost everywhere she is shown playing second-fiddle. When swearing her love for Lear, she speaks after Goneril has spoken, imitating her sister's manner of speech. In the scene where the two sisters begin their plotting, the initiative is taken by Goneril, who almost hypnotizes Regan. In her scenes with Lear we see Regan behaving and speaking almost exactly the way Goneril did before her. Even the idea of plucking out Gloucester's eyes originates with Goneril and not Regan. Again, it is Goneril who outwits Regan by poisoning her. Here and there we find Regan uncertain, worried, and even frightened. As she possesses neither Edmund's intellect nor Goneril's passion nor Cornwall's will, it would be consonant to the composition to play Regan as a character who is constantly being led and influenced.

Heartless intellect (Edmund), impure feelings (Goneril), unenlightened will (Cornwall), powerless morality (Albany) and unimaginative mediocrity (Regan) – these compose the characters. They differ from and yet complement each other, thus painting a fairly full and multifaceted picture of the evil raging within the framework of the tragedy.

Another example is one from *Twelfth Night*. Generally, all the characters can be viewed as being in love. But here also the specific traits of love should be found for each character. From the pure, friendly, unselfish love between Antonio and Sebastian to the egotistical, impure love of Malvolio for Olivia, there are available all possible degrees with which to give shade, nuance and definition to the comedy's composition of the characters.

Summarizing this chapter, the following laws of composition were dealt with: Triplicity, Polarity, Transformation, Subdivisions, Main and Auxiliary Climaxes, Accents, Rhythmical

Repetitions, Rhythmical Waves and, finally, the Composition of the Characters.

Of course, not all plays, whether old or modern, provide such a unique opportunity to apply *all* of the suggested principles as does *King Lear*. Nevertheless, even a partial application of them will give the performance life, relief and aesthetic beauty, will deepen its content and make it more expressive and harmonious. In spite of any play's shortcomings or limitations, much can be done to surmount them if the director, the actors, set and costume designers, and all concerned will make a common effort to observe and implement at least some of these principles by whatever theatrical devices at their command.

9

DIFFERENT TYPES OF PERFORMANCES

Between the extremes of tragedy and clowning lie numerous combinations of human emotions.

– C. L.

You may already have noticed that each principle and every exercise introduced in this book, if properly applied, opens one of the many "secret chambers" in our "inner castle." Indeed, like a fairy-tale character you walk from one room of this castle to the other and discover new treasures awaiting you in each. Your talent grows, new abilities develop and your soul becomes richer and freer. This is especially true if the exercises are done with joy and the principles applied with interest rather than carried out laboriously. So, in this spirit of eagerness and adventure let us open one more door and see what treasures will reward us anew.

Undoubtedly you will agree with me that there are many different *types* of plays, each requiring performance in a different way: tragedy, drama, melodrama, comedy, high comedy, farce, slapstick comedy and even the type of performance which we shall call clowning. Innumerable shades and nuances even increase the various types and classifications within the framework of the two extremes known as tragedy and clowning.

Whether you are a tragedian or a comedian or any other type of actor, it would be equally beneficial for you to explore and exercise the different ways of acting called for by the basic kinds of performances listed above. Do not say, "I am a tragedian (or comedian) and I do not need to develop a technique of acting for any other types of performances." For by saying so you will only be doing yourself a great injustice. It is tantamount to saying, "I wish to be a landscape artist, therefore I refuse to study any other form of painting." Think only of the power of contrasts: if you are a comedian, your humor becomes stronger if you are able to act tragic parts, and vice versa. It is the same as the law of human psychology which increases our sense of beauty if ugliness is known to us, or awakens our longing for goodness if we do not close our eyes to evil and shame around us. Even an appreciation of and desire for wisdom needs the suffering of an encounter with stupidity. We must suffer one to understand and enjoy the other. And, besides, you can be sure that any newly acquired abilities in all types of performances will reveal themselves in many unforeseen ways and moments in your professional work. For as soon as you develop them within you, they themselves will find expression through the labyrinthian corridors of your creative spirit.

We do not need to dwell upon all possible types and combination of plays and performances. Our purpose will be adequately served if we deal with the four outstanding and most diverse types and discuss them briefly.

Let us begin with tragedy.

What happens to a human being when he, for some reason, undergoes tragic (or heroic) experiences? We will stress only one feature of such a state of mind: he feels as if the average boundaries of his ego are broken; he feels that psychologically as well as physically he is exposed to certain forces which are much stronger, much more powerful than he himself. His tragic experience comes, takes possession of him and shakes his entire being. His sensation, reduced to words, can be described as *"Something* powerful is now present side by side with me, and *It* is *independent* of me to the same degree that I am dependent upon *It*." This sensation remains the same whether it is caused by an inner tragic conflict, as in the case of Hamlet's main conflicts, or whether the blow comes from outside and is brought about by destiny, as in the instance of King Lear.

In short, a person may suffer intensely, but intensity of suffering alone is drama and not yet tragedy. The person must also feel this powerful Presence of "Something" beside him before his sufferings can genuinely be called tragic. From this point of view wouldn't you agree that Lear makes a truly tragic impression while Gloucester a rather dramatic one?

Now let us see what practical value such an interpretation of the tragic mood can have for us as actors. The investigation is extremely simple. All an actor has to do when preparing a tragic part is to imagine, all the time he is on the stage (while rehearsing or later acting before an audience), that "Something" or "Somebody" is *following him*, driving his character to fulfill its tragic business and to speak its tragic lines. The actor must imagine, or rather sense, this "Something" or "Somebody' as being much, much more powerful than his character and even himself. It should be a kind of *superhuman Presence*! The actor must allow this "Doubleganger" (literally, double-walker) – this specter, wraith or apparition – to act through the character which inspires it. By doing so the actor will soon make a pleasant discovery, that he does not need to exaggerate either his movements, his business or his speech. Neither does he need to inflate himself psychologically by artificial means nor to resort to empty pathos in order to achieve the greatness, the true dimensions of a tragic mood. *Everything will happen by itself*. His "Doubleganger," being in possession of superhuman powers and feelings, will take care of all that. The actor's performance will remain true without becoming so uncomfortably "natural" that it loses its tragic flavor, and without becoming distressingly unnatural because of strained efforts to "perform" that uplifting style which every true tragedy requires of him.

What kind of superhuman *Presence* the actor senses in a given circumstance must be left entirely to his free, creative imagination. It might be a good or evil genius, vengeful and ugly or heroic and beautiful; it might be threatening, dangerous, pursuing, depressing or comforting. It all depends upon the play and the character. In some plays those *Presences* are even made tangible by the authors themselves, like the Furies in Greek tragedies, witches in Macbeth, the ghost of Hamlet's father, Mephistopheles in Faust, and so on. But whether they are indicated by the author or not, the actor will do well to create them himself in order to attune his psychological makeup to that key which will enable him to play tragic parts. Just try making such an experiment and you will see how soon you will accustom yourself to the sensation of such a *Presence*. In a little while there will not even be any need to think of it. You will feel only that you are able to perform tragedy with perfect freedom and truth. Play freely with the *Presence* you invent; let it follow or precede you, let it walk beside you or even fly above your head, according to the mission you want it to fulfill.

But it is quite different when you are going to perform a character in a simple drama. Here you have to remain entirely within the boundaries of your human ego. You do not need to imagine any kind of "Doubleganger" or apparition. All of us are more or less familiar with this kind of acting. We know perfectly well that so long as we have prepared the character, and remain true within the given circumstances, our actor's task for this type of play is fulfilled.

Comedy, on the other hand, sets up before the actor some definite conditions. Here, as in drama, you are again your own self playing the character – but with one predominant psychological feature which the character requires. That feature might be bravado for a character like Falstaff, or extreme stupidity for Sir Andrew Ague-Cheek, or the feature of conceit or superciliousness for some character like Malvolio or false piety for a Tartufe. It might be light-mindedness, shyness, amorousness, cowardice, an unwarranted gaiety or somberness or any other quality demanded of and by the character. But whatever outstanding quality you choose for your comedy character, it must be performed with utmost inner truth and without even the slightest attempt to be "funny" in order to get big laughs. Humor that is true, humor of good taste, can be achieved only with complete effortlessness, by means of the greatest possible ease and strong radiations. Ease and radiations, therefore, are two further conditions for the actor who wants to develop a special technique for performing comedy.

Ease has already been discussed in full in our first chapter. But concerning radiation I wish to add that in order to get into the mood for comedy it is best to try radiating in all directions, filling more and more space around you (the whole stage and even the auditorium) with rays of happiness and gaiety – like a child does quite naturally when expecting or experiencing some joyous event! Even before you enter upon the stage, start these radiations. It may be too late when you are already on stage because the effort then may distract your attention from the actual performance of the part. Make your entrance with this widespread aura already bubbling all around you. If your partners will help you by doing the same thing, the entire cast will soon find itself enveloped in a strong, sparkling comedy atmosphere which, combined with ease and a *quick tempo*, will rouse your genuine sense of humor as well as that of your spectators. In that way you will be giving the full measure of importance to the humorous lines and situations which the author has provided, and your entire comedic effect will be perfect.

Thus you see that a quick tempo is still another condition required by comedy, and here again it is necessary to elucidate a point. Quick tempo, if it is evenly quick all the time, inevitably becomes monotonous. The spectator's attention is dulled by it, and after a while he begins to get the impression that the tempo of the performance is getting slower and slower, with the result that the spectator involuntarily loses his interest in the actors and listens only to the dialogue. To avoid this unpleasant effect, this diminishing of the actor's significance on the stage, the performer from time to time must suddenly slow up his tempo, if only for one line or one movement, or occasionally introduce a short but expressive pause. These means of breaking the monotony of a quick-tempo'd performance will work instantaneously upon the spectator's attention like pleasant little shocks. The spectator, thus refreshed, will again be able to enjoy the quick tempo of the performance and, inferentially, better appreciate the actor's talent and skill.

And now a few words about clowning.

In a way clowning is similar to and at the same time the complete contrast of tragedy. A really great and talented clown, like a tragedian, is never alone while performing. He also experiences a kind of "possession" by certain fantastic beings. But they are of a different variety. If we called the "Doubleganger" of the tragedian a superhuman being, let us consider the humorous retinue of the clown as consisting of *subhuman* beings. To them he gives access to his body and his psychology. Together with his spectators he enjoys their whimsical, eccentric and odd appearances through himself. He is their instrument for the amusement of himself and others.

There can be one or many of these pixies, gnomes, elves, brownies, trolls, nymphs or other "good folk" of that species who take possession of the clown, who make us feel that he is not quite a human being. But all of them have to be nice, sympathetic, lovable, mischievous, funny (and even risible themselves!), otherwise the clowning might become repulsive. They must enjoy their temporary right to use the clown's human body and psychology for their games and tricks. You will find incalculably rich material for creating such "good folk" in genuine folk-fairy-tale literature. They will stir your imagination.

Also bear in mind the important difference that exists between a comedian and a clown. While a comedy character always reacts naturally, so to speak, no matter how peculiar the character and the situation might be, he is still afraid of things when they are frightening, indignant when the situation requires such an emotion and always obedient to the motivation. His transitions from one psychological state to the other are always justifiable.

But it is quite different with the psychology of a good clown. His reactions to a surrounding circumstance are completely unjustified, "unnatural" and unexpected: he might be frightened by things which do not give the slightest cause for fear; he might cry when we would expect him to laugh, or he might utterly disregard a danger that perils him. His transitions from one emotion to the other do not require any psychological justifications. Sorrow and happiness, extreme agitation and complete poise, laughter and tears – all might follow one another spontaneously and change lightning-like without any visible reasons.

By no means, however, is it to be inferred that the clown is permitted to be inwardly untrue and insincere! Quite the opposite. He has to *believe* in what he feels and does. He has to trust the sincerity of all the "good folk" working within and through him, and he has to love their peculiar games and whimsies with all his heart!

Clowning, extreme though it is, can be an indispensable adjunct to the actor in perfecting all the other types of performances. The more you practice it, the more courage you muster as an actor. Your self-confidence will grow with it and a new, gratifying sensation will slowly emerge from within you. "Oh, how easy it is," you will say, "to play drama and comedy after exercises and experiences in clowning!" Also, your so-called *Sense of Truth* on the stage will grow immensely. If you will learn to be true and sincere (as distinguished from natural in this instance) while performing clownish tricks, you will soon find out whether or not your performances have occasionally sinned against this Sense of Truth. Clowning will teach you to *believe in whatever you wish*. Clowning will awaken within you that eternal *Child* which bespeaks the trust and utter simplicity of all great artists.

These four dominants in the scale of different types of performances are sufficiently strong to vibrate those strings of your creative soul which otherwise would remain muted. If you will try to exercise all of them at your leisure, endeavoring to *experience the differences* of moods and manner of speaking and moving which they inspire in you, you will be astonished at how limitless your artistic abilities can be, and what great use you can make, even unconsciously, of these new capacities of your talent.

Take, for your exercises, small fractions of scenes from the three first-mentioned types of plays, and also a few tricks for clowning which you have seen or choose to invent. Act them several times, one after the other, always comparing your experiences with each type. Then take or invent some small indeterminate scene and act out this scene alternately as a tragedy, drama, comedy and as a bit of clowning, using the technical means previously suggested. Many new doors to the human emotions will be opened to you, and your acting technique will acquire greater variety.

Summary:

1   Tragedy is made easier to play by imagining the Presence of some superhuman being.

2   Drama needs a purely human attitude and artistic truth in given circumstances.

3   Comedy requires of the performer four main conditions: stressing a predominant psychological feature of the character, feeling of ease, strong radiations of gay and happy qualities and quick tempo interspersed with slow moments.

4   Clowning calls for the Presence of gay and humorous sub-human beings.

10

HOW TO APPROACH THE PART

> After all our studies we acquire only that which we put into
> practice.
>
> — Goethe

This point has long been the subject of considerable controversy
in our profession, particularly among the more conscientious
actors. It seems to be of especial concern to the actor who prefers
to approach his part systematically in order to save time and effort
in reaching that happy moment when he is at the very core of the
character he is to portray. For all of us well know that it is mostly
in the *initial* stage of our work that we often suffer from
uncertainty and floundering.

Basing ourselves on what we have discussed thus far, there are
several ways to approach the part. One of them is through the use
of your *imagination*, so let us assume that you have chosen to do it
that way.

Therefore, as soon as you get your part, start reading the play
several times until you are quite familiar with it as a whole.

Then concentrate on your character alone, imagining it at
first in scene after scene. Then dwell on the moments (situations,
business, lines) which attract your attention most.

Continue to do this until you "see" the *inner* life of the character as well as its outer appearance. Wait until it awakens your own feelings.

Try to "hear" the character speak.

Either you might see your character as described by the author, or you might also see *yourself* playing the character in make-up and costume. Both ways are correct.

Begin to co-operate with your character, asking questions and getting its "visible" answers. Ask your questions about *any* moment you choose, regardless of the continuity of scenes given in the play, thus improving something of your acting here and perfecting something there as you skim over the whole area of the character.

Start *incorporating* it bit by bit, with business and lines.

Continue this work even when your real rehearsals begin. Bring home all the impressions you have accumulated during stage rehearsals: your own acting, the acting of your partners, the director's suggestions and business he gave you, approximate settings, etc. Include all this in your *imagination*, and then again, going over your own acting, ask the question: "How can I improve this or that moment?" Answer it by improving it first in your imagination and then by actually trying it out (still working at home between rehearsals).

Using your imagination this way, you will find that it facilitates your work. You will also notice that many inhibitions which hampered your work until now will disappear. Our images are *free from any inhibitions* because they are the direct and spontaneous products of our creative individuality. All that hampers an actor's work comes either from an undeveloped body or from personal psychological peculiarities such as self-consciousness, lack of confidence and fear of making a wrong impression (especially during the first rehearsal). None of these disturbing elements is known to our creative individuality; it is as free from personal psychological limitation as our images are free from material bodies.

Your artistic intuition will tell you when this work with the imagination has served its purpose in helping you to establish the character. Then it might be put aside. Do not lean upon it alone for too long, or too heavily, as though it were your only support in approaching a part. You may use more than one means simultaneously.

You can also start your work on the basis of *atmospheres*.

Imagine your character fulfilling business and speaking the lines within the different atmospheres given or indicated by the play. Then create one of these atmospheres around you (as in Exercise 14) and begin to act under its influence. See that all your movements, the timbre of your voice and the lines you speak are in full harmony with the atmosphere you have chosen; repeat this for the other atmospheres as well.

Stanislavsky used to say that it is good thing if an actor can "fall in love" with his character before starting actual work upon it. To my understanding, in many cases he meant falling in love rather with the *atmospheres* which envelop the character. Many productions in the Moscow Art Theater were conceived and interpreted through atmospheres, by means of which the directors and actors "fell in love" with individual characters as well as the entire play. (Plays by Chekhov, Ibsen, Gorki and Maeterlinck, pregnant with atmospheres, always provided the members of the Moscow Art Theater with such opportunities to lavish their affections.)

It often happens that composers, poets, writers and painters begin to enjoy the atmosphere of their future creations long before they start actual work upon them. Stanislavsky was convinced that if the director or actor for some reason did not go through a period of such infatuation, he might encounter many difficulties later on in his work with a play or a part. Undoubtedly this devotion, this love, could be called the "sixth sense" which enables one to see and feel things that remain obscure to others. (Lovers always see more of each other's admirable points than others do.) Therefore, your approach to the part through atmospheres will give you a great chance to discover in the character many interesting and important features and fine nuances which otherwise might easily escape your attention.

You will also make a good beginning by applying what we called the *sensation of feelings* (as in Chapter 4). Try to define the general and most characteristic quality or qualities for the part you are going to work upon. You might find, for example, that the general qualities of Falstaff's character are mischief and cowardliness; or Don Quixote might possess the quality of ease combined with those of romanticism and courage. You might see Lady Macbeth as possessing the quality of a dark, strong will; Hamlet might seem to you a character whose main, overall qualities can be defined as penetrating, prying and thoughtful. Joan of Arc will, perhaps, appear before your mind's eye as permeated with qualities of inner tranquility, openness and extreme sincerity. Each character has its penetrable and definable qualities.

Having found the general quality for the entire character, and having experienced it as a *sensation* of desirable feeling, try to act your part under its influence. Do it in your imagination first, if you wish, and afterward start rehearsing it in actuality (at home or on the stage).

By doing so you might find that the sensations you use to awaken your genuine feelings are not quite correct. If so, do not hesitate to alter them again and again until you are entirely satisfied.

Having chosen certain general sensations for your character, makes notes on the margin of the script. As the result of this procedure you will have a number of sections or bits into which your entire part will be divided. Do not make too many sections, else they may become rather confusing. The fewer the number of bits and sections, the more helpful will they be for your practical work upon the part. About ten of such sections for a medium-size stage role or movie part will suffice. Rehearse your character again, following faithfully the notes you made.

You will remember that the qualities and sensations, as dealt with in Chapter 4, are nothing but the means of awakening your artistic feelings. Therefore, as soon as such feelings are aroused within you, give yourself up to them entirely. They will lead you to the fulfillment of your part. The notes you make while trying to find the right sensations will serve you as a means of refreshing your feelings should they, for some reason, become torpid or even disappear entirely.

Another approach to the part is by means of the Psychological Gesture (PG).

Try to find the correct PG for the whole character. If you do not succeed in finding the over-all PG for the part immediately, you might reverse the process and start anew by finding minor PG's through which the major will slowly come into view.

Start acting, fulfilling business and speaking lines on the basis of the PG you have worked out. If, when applying a PG practically, you discover that it is not quite correct, you must improve it according to your taste and your interpretation of the character. The strength, type, quality and tempo of the PG must be handled freely and deftly, and altered as many times as you deem necessary. The suggestions of your director during rehearsals, encounters with your stage partners and script changes by the author may all be stimuli for altering your PG. So keep it flexible until you are completely satisfied with it.

Use the PG throughout the whole period of the role, whether rehearsing or acting it. Exercise it before each stage entrance.

Define the *general tempo* in which your character lives, as well as the particular tempos of different scenes and moments, and practice your PG anew, according to these different tempos.

Also explore your part with a view to the interplay of *inner* and *outer* tempos. Use every opportunity to combine the two contrasting tempos (see last pages of Chapter 5).

While using the PG as a means of approaching your part, apply it also to ascertain the different *attitudes* your character has toward the others. Thinking that a character always remains the same while meeting other characters in the play is a crucial mistake that even great and experienced actors often make. It is not true, either on the stage or in everyday life. As you may have observed, only very stiff, inflexible or extremely conceited characters always remain "themselves" while meeting others. To perform stage characters in such a manner is monotonous, unreal and resembles a kind of puppetry. Observe yourself and you will see how differently you instinctively begin to speak, move, think and feel while meeting various people, even if the change others produce in you is only small or barely noticeable. It is always you *plus* somebody else.

On the stage this is even more pronounced. Hamlet plus King Claudius and Hamlet plus Ophelia are two different Hamlets, or rather two different aspects of Hamlet; he loses none of his integrity by showing different facets of his rich nature. And unless it is the author's intention to introduce a character that is stiff and monotonous, you must make every effort to find the differences which other characters produce upon the character you are playing. In this respect the PG's will be of invaluable help.

Go over your whole part and try to define what general feelings (or sensations of feelings) the other characters awaken in yours. Do they make it feel warm, indifferent, cold, suspicious, trusting, enthusiastic, contentious, timid, cowardly, restrained – what? Or what *desires* they engender within your character. Do they give it the urge to overpower, submit, revenge, attract, seduce, make friends, offend, please, frighten, caress, protest – which? And don't overlook instances in the course of the play when your character also *changes* its attitude toward the *same* person.

You will often find that the main PG which expresses your character as a whole will need only a slight alteration to incorporate its general attitude toward the other characters. The application of the PG affords the unique opportunity of painting your part in various colors, thus making your performance rich in tone and fascinating to watch.

Should you wish to start your work by building the *character* and *characterization* for it (as described in Chapter 6), begin your "game" with the imaginary body and the center, looking for characteristic features suitable for your role. At first you might use the imaginary body and center separately, and later on combine them.

In order to adopt and acquire easy mastery over them, it is suggested that your take your script and write out all your character's business, including entrances, exits and every movement, no matter how insignificant they might seem to you. Then, one by one, start carrying out all these happenings, big and small, trying to comply with whatever inspirations your imaginary body or center, or both, happen to give you. Do not exaggerate, do not stress their influence, else your movements will become artificial. The center and the imaginary body are in themselves powerful enough to change your psychology and your way of acting without being "helped" by pushing or forcing of any kind. If a fine and delicate expression of your characterization is what you earnestly want, let your good taste and feeling of truth be your guides in this pleasant "game" with the imaginary body and center.

After a while add to the business some lines connected with it; only a few at first, then more and more until the entire text of your part is rehearsed this way. You will soon learn what kind of speech your character is inclined to adopt – slow, quick, quiet, impulsive, thoughtful, light, heavy, dry, warm, cold, passionate, sarcastic, condescending, friendly, loud, low, aggressive or mild, to name only a few. All such nuances of speech will reveal themselves to you through the same means of the imaginary body and center if you faithfully follow their suggestions without hurrying the result. Enjoy your "game" rather than toil at it impatiently.

Not only will your acting and speech become more and more characteristic, but even your make-up will be clearly visualized for you by this simple approach to the part. The whole width and breadth of the character will unveil before you as a panorama in the *shortest time*. But do not drop your "game" until the character has been so absorbed by you that you no longer need to think of your imaginary body and center.

From the very beginning of your work upon the character you might also utilize some of those Laws of Composition which were detailed in Chapter 8. Further commentaries on the subject would only belabor the point, as the examples and analyses of the characters in *King Lear* are amply illustrative of their applications here.

At this juncture I strongly recommend to your attention the principles of Stanislavsky's suggestions for approaching the part. Stanislavsky called them *Units* and *Objectives*, and you will find full descriptions of them in his book, *An Actor Prepares*. Units and objectives are perhaps his most brilliant inventions, and when properly understood and correctly used they can lead the actor immediately to the very core of the play and the part, revealing to him their construction and giving him a firm ground upon which to perform his character with confidence.

Stanislavsky said, in essence, that in order to study the structure of the play and the part it is necessary to divide them into units (bits or sections). He advised starting with big units first, without going into their details, and to subdivide the large units into medium-size and small ones only if they appear too general to you.

Stanislavsky further said that the objective is what the character (not the actor) wishes, wants, desires; it is its goal, aim. The objectives follow one another in succession (or they might overlap).

All the character's objectives merge into one over-all objective, forming "a logical and coherent stream." This main objective Stanislavsky calls the *superobjective* of the character. That means that all smaller objectives, whatever their number, must serve one aim – to achieve the superobjective (the main desire) of the character.

Still further, Stanislavsky said, "In a play the whole stream of individual, minor objectives (as well as the superobjectives of the character) should converge to carry out the *superobjective of the entire play*, which is the *leitmotif* of the author's literary production, the leading thought which inspired his work."

In order to name the objective, to fix it in words, Stanislavsky suggested the following formula: "I want or I wish to *do* so and so . . ." and then follows the verb expressing the desire, the aim, the goal of the character. I want to *persuade*, I want to *get rid of*, I wish to *understand*, I wish to *dominate*, and the like. Never use feelings and emotions while defining your objectives – such as I want to *love* or I wish to *feel sad* – because feelings or emotions cannot be *done*. Either you love or you feel sad, or you don't.[1] The true objective is based upon your (your character's) *will*. The feelings and emotions, naturally, accompany your objectives, but they themselves cannot be turned into an objective. Thus we have to deal with a number of smaller objectives as well as the superobjectives of each *individual* part on one hand, and with the superobjective of the *entire* play on the other.

Now let us see how the foregoing Stanislavsky concepts are best integrated with what we have discussed in this book.

For the process of dividing the part (as well as the entire play)

[1] The way to awaken your feelings and emotions has already been discussed in previous chapters of this book.

into units, the principles introduced in Chapter 8 are suggested. Start by first dividing the part or play into three big units or sections; then, if necessary, make any number of subdivisions.

In Arthur Miller's play, *Death of a Salesman*, the *First Unit* for the leading character would be encompassed like this: Willy Loman, the Salesman, is tired, burdened with age, disappointed, troubled by business and family affairs. He tries to take inventory of what his long and fruitless life has been. He is lost in reminiscences. But he does not as yet want to abandon the fight with his destiny. He accumulates strength for a new assault. The *Second Unit*: The last battle begins. It is a kaleidoscope of hopes, disappointments, brief skirmishes, small defeats, joyful and painful recollections of the past. But the outcome of this battle is only greater bewilderment and the final destruction of all hope. The *Third Unit*: Willy gives up the fight. He has no more strength, no sense of reality, no mind. Quickly he drives to the fatal end.

The *First Unit* for Lopachin, one of the leading characters in *The Cherry Orchard*, might be this: Lopachin, despite his crude character, carefully and even gently starts his fight with the Ranevskys; slowly and gradually, although still restrained, he becomes more and more aggressive. The *Second Unit*: Lopachin deals his decisive blow – he buys the Cherry Orchard. He is victorious, triumphant, but he does not move against the Ranevskys as yet. The *Third Unit*: Lopachin goes into full, now unrestrained action. Cherry trees fall under the blows of the axes. The Ranevskys are compelled to pack their belongings and leave the estate. Old Firs, the senile and faithful servant, who is almost like a member of the Ranevsky family, dies locked up and forgotten in the deserted house (as if symbolically showing Lopachin's victory).

In *The Inspector General* the Mayor prepares for the battle with the Inspector, giving detailed instructions to the officials. This is the *First Unit* for the Mayor's character. The *Second Unit*: The false Inspector arrives, the battle begins. The Mayor's long, patient, painstaking plotting proves successful. The danger is over, the victory is won. The *Third Unit*: The discovery of the fatal mistake. The arrival of the true Inspector. The Mayor, the officials and the women are defeated, humiliated and annihilated.

Having found your three main units in this fashion, you can proceed with establishing their subdivisions, always following the development of the battle that is going on in the play. Consider every new significant phase of the battle as a smaller unit. (But always try to keep in mind Stanislavsky's warning: "The larger and fewer the divisions, the less you have to deal with, the easier it is for you to handle the whole role.")

So much for the units. Now to the objectives.

My comments on the subject concern themselves principally with the means and the order of finding these objectives. Stanislavsky himself, when speaking of the difficulties in finding the super-objectives for the characters, admitted that long and painstaking work is needed because, he said, one has to make many errors and discard many wrong superobjectives before he is able to discover the right one.

Stanislavsky added that very often it is not until *after* several performances, when the *reaction of the audience* becomes apparent that the true superobjective can be realized and fixed. From this statement by Stanislavsky we are bound to infer that the actor must frequently be content with a number of the character's minor objectives without knowing where they lead to.

But my personal contention is that it is of the utmost import-ance for an actor to know in advance or have some general fore-knowledge about the minor objectives' final goal; that is, to understand the main aim of the character. In other words, the actor should be well aware of the *superobjective* for the entire role at the very outset. For how else can he merge all the objectives into "a logical and coherent stream" without making many errors? It seems to me that this difficulty would be more easily resolved if the actor succeeded in finding the superobjective of his character first. After many years of testing the theory I most respectfully submit that it is more practical that way, and the suggestion that follows is born of this conviction.

You know that each more or less significant character wages a fight thoughout the whole play, is in conflict with someone or something. He either wins or loses his battle. In Willy Loman's case, he fights against the unfortunate destiny which oppresses him, and loses. Lopachin of *The Cherry Orchard* fights with the Ranevskys, and wins. The Mayor in *The Inspector General* carries on his fight against the phantom of the Inspector from Petersburg, and suffers defeat.

Suppose we ponder the following questions: What becomes of the character, what does he do or intend to do after he has achieved his victory? What would he do if he won his fight, what *should* he do? . . . The answer to these and similar questions (often projecting beyond the play itself) can indicate more accurately what the character was fighting for throughout the whole play, or what his *superobjective* was. What, for instance, would Willy, the Salesman, look like and what would he do were he to become victorious over his destiny? He would, in all probability, become the most banal type of salesman, as the trend of the play portends. His ideal would perhaps resemble the life of Dave Singleman in the same play, who at eighty-four years of age still "drummed" his merchandise in thirty-one states: "And old Dave, he'd go up to his room, y' understand, put on his green velvet slippers – I'll never forget – and pick up his phone and call his buyers, and without ever leaving his room, at the age of eighty-four, he made his living. And when I saw that, I realized that selling was the greatest career a man could want." And if in addition to this ideal Willy could have a radio, a small kitchen garden and be "well liked," he would feel entirely happy. So the superobjective for him may be defined as: "*I want to live like that old Dave Singleman.*" You are free, of course, to seek better superobjectives and consider the first one as only an indication of the direction which you have to take in your search for the superobjective that will satisfy you.

Now examine Lopachin with a view to the superobjective. Having been a serf on the Ranevskys' estate, Lopachin raised himself to the position of a "gentleman." He now wears a white waistcoat and yellow shoes. He has money, but he craves more. Yet, he still cannot overcome his inferiority complex in the Ranevskys' presence. They ignore him; he does not feel completely free and at ease with them. Now his time has come at last and the victory is his. He desolates the cherry trees, levels the old estate to the ground, already counts his huge, future income. His superobjective therefore might be: "*I wish to become great, self-assured and 'free' through the power of money.*"

Similarly, we cast a forward glance at the Mayor of *The Inspector General*. He has happily escaped punishment and is triumphant over his false victory. What does he do, what becomes of him? He turns into a crude despot. He has already humiliated his townsfolk and he intends to be as arrogant and imperious in Petersburg. His daydreams are coarse and dangerous. The Mayor's superobjective, therefore, is: "*I want to dominate and trample upon everybody and everything within my reach.*"

Now, if you wish, you may try to find smaller objectives for the character whose superobjective is already disclosed or at least indicated to you. You will no longer flounder, as you would have done had you started seeking the smaller objectives first. The superobjective will thereafter reveal to you all the smaller objectives which are subordinate to it.

But once again I must urge you to postpone the work of finding the smaller objectives. There is a still higher viewpoint to be attained. You can climb still higher, to the very summit, from which you can observe the whole play as a big panorama, with all the events, units and superobjectives of the characters contained within it. This summit is the *superobjective of the entire play*.

You will find the superobjective of the entire play, or at least pave the way for its discovery, if you apply the same method of asking questions. But this time you do not address yourself to the characters. You appeal straight to the *audience*. Of course, you need not and should not wait for a real audience; but you can *imagine* your audience and anticipate its future reactions.

The questions the actor and director can ask of their imaginary spectators when looking for the play's superobjective are numerous and varied. Of cardinal importance is to ask them to reveal the *psychological result* they experience after the last curtain has fallen.

Thus, with your meditative mind, you penetrate into the spectators' hearts. You examine their laughter and tears, indignation and satisfaction, their shaken or confirmed ideals – in fact, everything they take home with them after the performance. These will be their answer to your question; these will tell you better than any erudite speculations why the author had written his play and what inspired his work. In brief, what the *superobjective* of the entire play is.

The curious actor may wonder why it is necessary to consult the imaginary audience. Would it not be simpler to consult the author directly, by studying his play with a view to discovering *his* guiding idea, *his* conception of the *superobjective*? Won't the result be the same?

No, it will *not* be the same! No matter how faithfully an actor or director reads a play, it is still *his* own interpretation of what the author intended. And no matter what the author intended, it is what the audience interprets from his play that is the decisive superobjective. The psychology of the audience differs vastly from that of an actor or director, or even the author himself. It is more than a coincidence that we are often surprised by the audience's unpredictable reactions to new plays. Our expectations, hopes and guesses are frequently overthrown by the spectators' response to the opening-night performance. Why? Because the audience as a *whole* senses the play with its heart and not with its brain; because it cannot be led astray by the actor's, director's or author's personal points of view; because its reaction on opening night is immediate, free of any tendencies and unconditioned by outside influences; because the audience does not analyze, but experiences; because it never remains indifferent to the ethical value of the play (even when the author himself intends to remain impartial); because it never loses itself in details or evasions, but intuitively detects and savors the very marrow of the play. All these potential audience responses will give you a more reliable guarantee that the leading thought, the author's main idea, or what we call the *superobjective of the entire play*, will be found as a *psychological result* within the big and unprejudiced "heart" of the audience.

Vachtangov, the famous Russian director, was once asked, "Why do all the plays you direct, and especially the innumerable details you elaborate for your actors, always get across to the audience with unmistakable success?" Vachtangov's answer was, approximately, "Because I never direct without imagining an audience attending all my rehearsals. I anticipate their reactions and follow their 'suggestions'; and I try to imagine a kind of 'ideal' audience in order to avoid the temptations of tastelessness."

By no means should all I have just said be construed as an invitation to deny the significance and importance of the actor's and director's interpretation of the play, or to become resentfully subservient to the audience. On the contrary, genuine and artistic co-operation is recommended. For, having consulted the imaginary audience's big "heart," the interpretation of the play by actors and directors will be better guided and more inspired by the audience's "voice." The audience is an active co-creator of the performance. It *has* to be consulted before it is too late, and especially when searching for the superobjective of the play.

At first the experiences of your imaginary audience will appear before your mind's eye as a spontaneous, unclarified and general impression. But you must draw all the sharp and specific conclusions from it, formulate all the potential thoughts and define all the emotions. A little practice with this experiment should make you adept at it and secure in the feeling that the imaginary audience will not fail you.

For a deeper insight into the audience's "heart," it is necessary to return to our play examples once more.

How many unsuccessful salesmen scurry across the country every day, in all directions? How many of them does an average American citizen see in his lifetime? Dozens and dozens, even hundreds? Does he shed tears over these salesmen's "unfortunate" lot in life? Isn't he rather inclined to take them for granted or ignore them? Does he ever stop to consider that as a class and a trade they have their personal tribulations and miseries? . . . And yet, on the tenth of February, 1949, on the New York stage, a petty salesman named Willy Loman suddenly stirred the hearts and shook the minds of many people. They wept, they loved, their hearts were filled with compassion, they pronounced their verdict: Willy the Salesman is good. And when at the end the salesman willfully parted with his life, the spectators left the theater worried about "something" and were unable to forget Willy and the play for days.

Where is the explanation for the entire effect? Perhaps your answer will be: "The magic of art." Of course; without artists of such magnitude as Arthur Miller, Elia Kazan and his excellent cast, nothing so startling and significant might have occurred. But what is it they revealed to the audience with their magic? Let us evaluate the performance in retrospect, as it might have mirrored itself in the spectator's mind and "heart." (Remember, we are searching for the possible superobjective of the play.)

The curtain rises and Willy the Salesman enters. The audience smiles pleasantly. Its first and primitive theatrical instinct is satisfied: "How natural, how true to life." But the walls are transparent and a flute is heard. The spotlights shift their rays hither and thither. Gradually and almost unnoticeably the spectator feels himself "tuned" in a somewhat different way, for he looks *through* walls, he listens to music *within* something, he follows the light which leads him *beyond* his usual conceptions of time and space. The magic of art has begun. The spectator's perception is now deepened and changed. He watches the salesman, sees his bewilderment and restlessness, follows his slightly chaotic mind.

Yet somehow everything is *not* entirely "natural"; now it is that evanescent "something" within and beyond that causes Willy's restlessness, tiredness and depression. But what is that "something"? Does he desire something strongly and passionately and can't achieve it? Of course he wants to be "well liked," successful in business, and he needs money to pay his bills. But subconsciously the spectator is no longer satisfied with these simple and obvious explanations; the walls are transparent and the sounds of a flute *still come* from somewhere. Willy is sympathetic, he is good. Then what is concealed *behind* the urge for money, success and to be "well liked"? Whatever it is, it must be also good, to coin a syllogism. Linda, his wife, loves and adores him. For what – his need of money?

The more attentively the spectator watches the scenes following one another, the sharper and more penetrating becomes his mind, the warmer his heart, and clearer and stronger grows the suspicion that this salesman, with his pathetic destiny, is not a real being. Is it perhaps only a mask for somebody else? Linda, Biff and Happy are real; they do not hide anything *within* themselves, they are what they are, there is nothing to surmise *behind* them. In fact, it would be strange and "unnatural" if they, like Willy, whose prerogative it is, broke the boundaries of time and space. But only Willy is allowed to be somebody else, wearing the mask of a salesman. And this mask seems to torture Willy.

Soon the mask begins to torture the spectator himself. He wants to get rid of it, free himself from the "Salesman." He begins to realize that Willy's restlessness stems from the same desire, that he too fights his mask, struggles for freedom, tries to tear it from his face, rip it away from his mind and heart, from his whole being. But Willy is hopelessly blind, unaware and unconscious of his own fight. The more the play progresses the more transparent becomes the mask, and suddenly the spectator realizes that a "Man," a valuable human being, is imprisoned and chained *within* and *behind* the "Salesman." The real tragedy begins to be apparent. The "Salesman" whips the "Man" and drives him nearer and nearer to the fatal end. It is the "Man," not his evil double, who worries the spectator. "Willy, wake up! Stop blaming the destiny outside of you," the spectator's heart longs to cry out. "Blame the worst part of it that's *within* yourself. The 'Salesman' is your dark destiny," it warns. But it is too late. Willy gives up his fight. It is night. With the hoe in his hands, with darkness upon him, Willy plans his kitchen garden. It is the last outcry of the perishing "Man." The roar of the car engine is heard . . . Willy kills both the "Salesman" and the "Man."

The performance is over. The *psychological result* of the last battle begins to ripen in the spectator's mind. And perhaps he will even say to himself, "Truly, in the whole of human history there never were times when the Salesman's 'mask' was so menacing and powerful as in our own. If we do not scrutinize and remember what is *behind* it, it will grow and develop like a malignant tumor."

It is native American as well as human tragedy. It is a vital warning which the author gives us by means of his creation. The superobjective of the entire play, which became manifest in the spectator's soul in a manner not unlike this delineation, though perhaps not articulated, can be summed up as: *"Learn to discern the 'Salesman' from the 'Man' within yourself and try to free the 'Man.'"*

The Cherry Orchard provides us with a second example and another type of superobjective.

From the very beginning the spectator becomes aware that the principal character of the play is the Cherry Orchard itself. It is old, beautiful, immensely large, famous and, according to the play, is even mentioned in the Encyclopedia. The battle is centered around it, but it is a peculiar kind of battle in that nobody actually defends the Cherry Orchard. Lopachin fights with its existence. The Ranevskys – will-less, useless and degenerate scraps of intelligentsia – hide their heads in the sand; their resistance is weak and ineffective. Ania, their daughter, dreaming of some dazzling and gorgeous future, soars among the clouds. Their employees and servants are either indifferent or hostile to the Cherry Orchard with its old beauty. And still, it is there; it stands and blossoms though undefended.

The spectator's full sympathy is with it. He loves it as one can love the beauty of an ancient monument; he himself wants to defend it, to awaken the sleeping people, shake off their indifference. The feeling of utter helplessness slowly takes possession of him. He watches Lopachin approaching closer and closer to possession of the Orchard. Tears fill the spectator's eyes, and the sensations of weariness and weakness become almost unbearable. Distant strokes of the axes upon trees are heard. This is the end. The curtain falls. The audience leaves the theater quite moved by the "death" of an inanimate character that had taken on living qualities – the white Cherry Orchard. The audience wants to voice its protest: *"Preserve the best part of the past, lest it fall prey to the ax of powers which stand ever ready to build their ugly future."* This might be the superobjective of *The Cherry Orchard*.

Take the third example.

From the moment the curtain rises, the audience watching *The Inspector General* has many reasons to be happy and gay. The much hated officials make one blunder after another. Being driven into a corner, blinded by fear, they wage their battle against the fake enemy. Evil fights evil, wasting time, wit and money. Good does not participate in this fight till the very end of the play, but the audience knows it is coming and eagerly awaits its crushing blow upon an evil that has outtricked and spent itself. The more the

Mayor bursts with undeserved pride over his spurious victory, the stronger the spectator craves a righteous vengeance. And when Good finally appears, and in two successive blows (the letter by the fake Inspector and the arrival of the true Inspector) wipes out Evil, the audience feels recompensed, grateful and triumphant. For the inhabitants of the small town, lost and oppressed in a vast nation, are rescued at last. But for the spectator this town is only a microcosm, a symbol. The whole nation is hopelessly enmeshed in spidery webs spun by all kinds of "Mayors." The excited audience, whose will has been stirred and its sense of decency rubbed raw, echoes the aim of the author: *"The country must be saved from the crude despotism and absolute power of the hordes of paltry officials! They are often more evil and heartless than the big ones!"*

Incidentally, at the premiere performance of *The Inspector General* this audience sentiment was, in an unguarded moment, admirably summed up by one of the spectators, when he was moved to exclaim, "Everybody got his punishment, and most of all – I!" That was the voice of the biggest "Mayor" of them all – the voice of Nicholas I. In spite of his cold and cruel nature, the Czar had understood the superobjective of the play no less than his subjects.

And that is the way the actor and director can use the device of the imaginary audience for gaining the superobjective of the play, long before the real audience fills the house.

Again the reader is asked to remember that the interpretations given in all my examples are never intended to impose artistic arbitraries. My only aim always is to illustrate the method, and by no means to restrict the creative freedom of any talented actor or director. On the contrary, for the good of his art he is urged to be as original and inventive as his talent and intuitions can possibly make him.

Having found, if only approximately, the superobjectives of the entire play and the individual characters, you might proceed to the medium-sized and smaller objectives. But never try to discern any objective with your reasoning mind. It may leave you cold. You may *know* it, but may not *wish* or *want* it. It may remain in your mind like a headline without rousing your will. The objective must have its roots in your whole being and not in the head alone. Your emotions, your will and even your body must be entirely "filled" with the objective.

Try to realize what actually happens in your everyday life when you get a certain desire, aim or objective that cannot be achieved immediately. What goes on within you while you are compelled to wait until circumstances permit you to satisfy your desire or fulfill your objective? Are you not inwardly *constantly fulfilling it* with your whole being? From the very moment the objective forms itself in your soul, you are "possessed" by a certain inner activity.

Take the illustration of wanting to comfort somebody in distress and, being unable to do it simply by saying, "Don't worry, calm yourself," you need days and days to really accomplish your aim. Are you static in the interim? Not very likely. You will discover that in *all that time* intervening you experience a sensation of constantly comforting the person in distress, whether you are in his presence or not. More than that, you "see," as it were, this person as already having been comforted by you (even in spite of any doubts you may have as to whether the person can be comforted at all). The same is true for the stage. If you do not feel yourself "possessed" by the objective, you can be sure that, to a lesser or greater degree, it still remains within your mind and not within your whole being, that you are still *thinking* and not truly *wishing* it That is the reason so many actors make the mistake of waiting, inwardly passive, for the moment in the play when the author permits them to fulfill it. Let us say the objective starts on page two of the script and its fulfillment does not take place before page twenty. The actor who does not absorb the objective entirely, who does not let it permeate his whole psychology and his body, is compelled to wait passively until page twenty is performed. More conscientious actors, feeling that the objective is not working properly, try to repeat mentally, "I want to comfort . . . I want to comfort. . . ." But that does not help either because such mental repetition is only a kind of head activity which is unable to arouse one's will.

The objective, turned into a PG that stirs the whole being and makes it active, can help you overcome this difficulty. Another way would be to *imagine* your character (from that hypothetical page two to page twenty) as being "possessed" by the objective. Peer attentively into its inner life (see Exercise 10 in Chapter 2) until it awakens a similar psychological state within yourself; or use the *sensations* we discussed to arouse your feelings.

A final summing up of the main suggestions for Approaching the Part in the initial stage of your work:

No matter how conscientious you or your director may be, it is not necessary to use *all* the available means at one and the same time. You can choose those which appeal to you most, or those which give you the best and quickest results. You will soon notice that some are more suitable for one part and some for another. Make your choice freely. In time you will be able to try out all of them and perhaps use them with equal facility and success; but do not overload yourself with more than is necessary for the optimum performance of your part. The method must, above all, *help* you and make your work pleasant, and if properly used will not under any circumstances make it hard and depressing. For acting should ever be a joyous art and never enforced labor.

11

CONCLUDING NOTES

It is inevitable that everyone who attempts to organize and co-ordinate a series of histrionic concepts should be asked why a *talented* actor needs a method at all. It is one of those questions that can be answered only with other questions: Why does a civilized man need a culture? Why does an intelligent child need an education?

At the risk of driving the point home with a sledgehammer, it should be reiterated that *every* art, even the actor's, must have its principles and aspirations, and its professional techniques.

In rebuttal you will often hear actors protest, "But I have *my own* technique." The statement would be more correct if rephrased to mean: "I have my own *interpretation*, my own application of the general technique." But it goes without saying that neither musicians, architects, painters, poets nor any other craftsmen can have their own techniques alone without first studying the basic laws of their respective arts. Inescapable are the rules upon which they ultimately must build those "own" techniques that are to make them individual if not outstanding in their professions.

No matter how naturally talented the actor may be, he will never evolve much for his art or bequeath his own gifts to theatrical posterity if he isolates himself in that small cell of his "own technique" and devices. The art of acting can grow and develop only if it is based upon an *objective* method with fundamental principles. The great number of precious memoirs and observations handed down to us by yesteryear's names in the art of acting are not here minimized as valuable materials for creating a method. But they are, nevertheless, subjective, hence limited in scope. The ideal method of any art must be a well-integrated whole, complete in itself; and, above all, it must be objective.

Those of our colleagues who resolutely refuse to acknowledge any method just because they are talented perhaps may need one more than anybody else. Because talent, the so-called "inspiration," is the most capricious of our endowments. The talented actor is likelier prey to all kinds of professional mischances. He has no firm ground under his feet. The slightest psychological irritation of a moment, an unhappy mood or any physical disturbance, may render his talent inaccessible and block the channel to real inspiration. A method with a well-based technique is the best guarantee against such mishaps. The method, when sufficiently exercised and properly assimilated, becomes the talented actor's "second nature" and as such gives him full control over his own creative abilities, come what may. The technique is his infallible means of calling forth his talent and making it work any time he wishes to invoke it; it is the "Open sesame!" to real inspiration regardless of physical or psychological barriers.

At different times inspiration, if it comes, shows different degrees of power. It may be present, but weak and ineffective. Here again, the technique can strengthen the actor's will power, awaken his emotions and stir his imagination to such an extent that the barely smoldering spark of inspiration will suddenly flare up and burn brightly for as long as the actor desires.

Let us suppose that for some reason an actor feels that his talent is dimmed as a performance approaches. He need have no such qualms if his technique is mastered. For once a part is prepared and elaborated in all its details according to the method, the actor will always play it *correctly* even if he does not feel as "inspired" as he would like to be. For he will always have at his command a kind of "blueprint" of his role and so will not flounder helplessly or be compelled to resort to clichés and bad theatrical habits. He will be able at any moment to survey the whole part and each of its details as though with a bird's-eye view, and with inner calm and assurance proceed from one section to the other and from one objective to the other. It was Stanislavsky who remarked that a part *correctly* played has the best chance of luring back an elusive inspiration.

There is still another reason for a talented actor to recognize the value of an objective technique.

Creative or positive powers in an artist's nature must always combat and thwart those negative influences which, though obscure and sometimes entirely unknown to him, constantly hamper his best efforts. These numerous negative obstacles would include a suppressed inferiority complex or megalomania, selfish and egotistical desires unconsciously intermingled with artistic aims, fear of making mistakes, unrecognized fear of the audience (and often even a hatred of it), nervousness, concealed jealousy or envy, bad and seemingly forgotten examples, and an unrestrained habit of finding fault with others. These are only a few of the things which in time can accumulate in an actor's subconscious like so much "psychological garbage" and swell into noxious evils for his own destruction.

By using the *objective* method and technique the actor will amass within himself a great number of sound and liberating qualities which are certain to displace all destructive influences that lurk obscurely in the dark recesses of his subconscious. What we usually call "developing one's talent" is often nothing more than *freeing* it from the influences that hamper, occlude and frequently destroy it entirely.

The method, when understood and applied, will inculcate in the actor a most gratifying habit of professional *thinking*, whether he is evaluating the creative work of his colleagues or his own. He will then no longer be satisfied with such general terms as "natural," "conversational," "arty," "good," "bad"; or with such expressions as "underacting," "overacting," etc. Instead, he will develop a more indicative professional language and become conversant with more professional terms like Units, Objectives, Atmospheres, Radiating and Receiving, Imagination, Imaginary Body, Imaginary Center, Inner and Outer Tempos, Climaxes, Accents, Rhythmical Waves and Repetitions, Composition of the Characters, Psychological Gestures, Ensemble, Qualities, Sensations, and so forth. Such concrete terminology will not only replace his present vague and inadequate vocabulary, but will sharpen the actor's ability to perceive theatrical impressions, will train his mind to penetrate these impressions deeply enough to know at once exactly what is wrong or right, why, and by what means to perfect his own performances and those of his colleagues. Criticism will then become truly objective and constructive; personal sympathy or antipathy will cease to play the decisive parts they do now in evaluating histrionic art, and players will feel freer to help one another and be helped in return instead of merely praising wanly or blaming viciously.

The actor, especially the talented one, also must not overlook the fact that the suggested professional technique will in every instance facilitate and hasten his good work. Time spent in acquiring it is certain to be turned into a most lucrative investment by the final result! Whenever I am asked if there are any short cuts to the method, I cannot restrain cautioning that a shorter short cut is to do all the prescribed exercises diligently and patiently until they become the actor's second nature.

A simple way to woo the reluctant or impatient urge within you might be to create a vision based on the method, a vision of yourself as *already* having acquired all the techniques, as already in possession of all the new abilities promised by the exercises. Such a vision will set to work within you of its own accord; it will beckon to you and lure you on and on, provided you don't tire or discourage the vision by projecting it too far into the future. If properly exercised and invoked this way, the method will imbue you with the feeling that you have known it all along and practiced always, but perhaps were not as aware of it as you are now. Your reason for thinking that the goal is so remote and difficult to attain, if think it you do, is then bound to vanish. The suggested vision will facilitate and speed the absorption of the technique, which in turn will facilitate and speed your professional work.

I would like to cite still another valid reason for the method's acceptance.

In the process of grasping all its principles through practice, you will soon discover that they are designed to make your creative intuition work more and more freely and create an ever-widening scope for its activities. For that is precisely how the method came into existence – not as a mathematical or mechanical formula graphed and computed on paper for future testing, but as an organized and systematized "catalogue" of physical and psychological conditions required by the *creative intuition* itself. The chief aim of my explorations was to find those conditions which could best and invariably call forth that elusive will-o'-the-wisp known as inspiration.

Furthermore, in an age such as ours, when the trend of life, thought and desires is to become more and more materialistic and dull, the emphasis unfortunately is on physical conveniences and standardization. In such an age humanity is inclined to forget that to progress culturally, life, and especially the arts, must be permeated with all kinds of *intangible* powers and qualities; that that which is tangible, visible and audible is but a small part of our optimum existence and has little claim upon posterity. Afraid to leave the firm ground under our feet, we forever echo, "Let's be practical!" Afraid to adventure and soar artistically, we sink deeper and faster into the ground we hold to. And then, whether we notice it or not, and perhaps too late, we get tired of being "practical"; we suffer breakdowns, rush to psychoanalysts, search for mental panaceas and stimuli or periodically seek escape in cheap thrills, superficial sensations, swiftly changing fads and amusements, and even drugs. In short, we pay dearly for our refusal to recognize the necessity of sanely balancing the practical tangibles with the artistic intangibles. And art is a sphere which suffers most easily and acutely from such an imbalance. Nobody can exhale without inhaling. Nobody can be truly "practical" merely by clinging to the ground and refusing to be strengthened and uplifted by the seemingly "impractical" intangibles which are basic to the creative spirit, which are a kind of psychological "inhaling."

Considering our principles of artistic development from this point of view, do they not provide us with the means of standing firmly upon the ground and yet rising above it to something more durable? You can easily prove this to yourself with a few examples. Take, for instance, the Ensemble feeling. Can you touch it, see or hear it? And yet it is one of the strong *intangible powers* which can be made to exist on the stage as concretely as the actors' bodies or their visible movements and audible voices, as realistically as the settings and their forms and colors. What are Atmosphere, Radiations, and all the Laws of Composition but tangible intangibles? What is the subtle ability of the actor to improvise, to appreciate the *how* of acting more than the *what*? What is the extrasensory power which he consciously generates and uses while acting, and upon which he can rely when he fulfills his Objective correctly, or by which he can embody his *psychological presence* on the stage, that valuable and indisputable presence which never can be so forcefully materialized by any known tangible means?

Add a few more items to your recapitulation. What is the aura of artistic fantasy that surrounds an actor who, while working upon his character, goes through the period of imagining it before prematurely giving it tangible form and appearance? What super-induces such qualities as Ease, Form, Beauty or the sense of Entirety? What underlies the amusing "game" of the Imaginary Centers and Bodies? Or the search for all sorts of contrasts with which to bring relief and variety to his part and the entire per-formance? What is the Psychological Gesture, this friend, guide or, if you wish, the "invisible director" who never leaves and never betrays the actor but follows and inspires him constantly? Does not the spectator *feel* the existence of these things, even though he does not know what they are, if the actor successfully brings them into being from within himself?

There is not a single exercise in this method which does not serve two purposes at once: to put the actor even more firmly on a *practical* ground and at the same time give him a sound balance between tangible and intangible, between exhaling and inhaling. and thus rescue him from banalities and from artistic suffocation.

To the best of my knowledge, theatrical history records the exist-ence of only one method expressly postulated for the actor – that created by Konstantin Stanislavsky (and, unfortunately, much misunderstood and often misinterpreted). Let this book, then, be another effort in the direction of a better theater through better acting. I proffer it as a humble but nevertheless eager attempt to place at the disposal of my colleagues a few systematically arranged ideas and experiences for bringing some order and inspiration to our professional work. "Organize and write down your thoughts concerning the technique of acting," Stanislavsky said to me. "It is your duty and the duty of everyone who loves the theater and looks devotedly into its future." I feel obliged to convey these inspiring words to all my colleagues, in the hope that at least some of them also will, humbly but courageously, formulate and organize their thoughts while trying to find objective principles and laws for furthering our professional technique.

12

EXAMPLES FOR IMPROVISATION

Included in this chapter are several types of little stories, plots, situations and incidents designed to utilize and test what the actor or director has gleaned from the method both at various stages of his progress and at the end of his studies. They can be used to equal advantage for exercises in Atmospheres, Objectives, Characterization, Qualities or any of the other components previously dealt with.

Not all of them are original, but they need not be; the group may select material from any existing literature and adapt it to its specific needs, or it may even invent new ideas for improvisation. Neither, of course, are they intended for public performance save perhaps as demonstrations of the method's efficacy or to illustrate the progressive differences in its application as the group advances step by step.

The cast or number of characters in each of these improvisations naturally depends on the size of the group participating in the exercise.

Finally, in all improvisations *avoid the use of unnecessary words*.

1. THE ROBBERS

On a deserted border between two foreign countries there stands a bleak little inn. It is winter, and the night is stormy and bitter cold.

The dimly lit, smoke-filled main room of the inn is dirty and untidy; the floor is strewn with cigarette butts and the long naked dining table is littered with the stale remains of food and drink.

Scattered about and engaged in divers pastimes are several men and women of varying ages. In face, attitude and attire most of them are as gloomy and unfriendly as their surroundings. Some lie around bored, some walk about aimlessly, some play cards, some engage in lazy taunts and petty quarrels which they never trouble to finish, while others display their ennui by humming softly or whistling mutedly.

And yet it is apparent that they are restless and waiting for something. From time to time one or another steals a surreptitious glance out the window or, signaling silence to the raised voices, opens the door a crack to listen.

The atmosphere of expectation grows tenser by the minute, for the characters thus discovered are a band of robbers staked out by a vast international syndicate. These are specialists in victimizing the prosperous merchants who transport their precious goods across the near-by frontier. They have been alerted that tonight a rich haul will cross the border and, because of the impassable storm and the great distance to the next village, the merchants will no doubt be compelled to seek a haven till daybreak.

Suddenly the leader of the group, who looks less ominous than the rest, emits a long characteristic whistle. Everyone freezes and listens intently as the leader goes to the door and confirms the sound of an approaching caravan.

Then, at his signal, everyone and everything changes as if by magic: a broom sweeps the floor litter into the fireplace; the table is cleared of its refuse and covered with a cloth; the furniture is shifted and the room tidied; more candles are lit and one placed invitingly in the window; a friendly fire is kindled. The slovenly men don coats and other apparel peculiar to the local peasantry; the disheveled women comb their hair, primp and respectably drape shawls over their naked shoulders. The eldest of the women seats herself in a wheelchair by the fireplace and covers her legs with an afghan. And, as a final touch, a big family Bible is materialized for the head of the table by the leader, who now wears dark glasses and a visored cap.

Voices approaching from the distance are soon heard off stage, and three less evil-looking males of the gang are signed to go out and steer the travelers into the inn. The others quietly busy themselves with the normal chores of preparing the family supper.

Presently the three robber emissaries return, ushering in a heavily laden, heavily garbed and muffled group of merchants. The travelers are snow-covered and indicate that they are painfully cold. The comelier of the girls advance to greet them; they help the wayfarers divest themselves of their weighty garments, while the three steerers assist them with piling up their luggage and bundles of merchandise.

Next, the elderly leader bids the merchants welcome and invites them to the table, saying that while his is but a humble inn-keeping family with an invalided wife, there is ample food and wine for all who wish to partake.

The guests eagerly find seats at the table. Platters of food and flasks of wine begin to appear, and a tray is even brought to the "invalided" woman at the fireplace. But before anything is permitted to pass their lips, the host reverently opens the Bible and reads a passage of grace therefrom.

Immediately the travelers fall to, and the girls serving them urge more wine upon them, hastily refilling their glasses even before they are half-empty. This solicitude does not go unnoticed by the merchants. It is evident that the wine served to the members of the household is not poured from the same bottles, and from the seemingly quick-acting effect it has on the guests it is obvious that the wine offered them has been drugged.

Slowly, almost imperceptibly, the atmosphere changes from piety, warmth, friendliness and coziness to one of jovial contentment, then to gaiety, and eventually to abandon. The guests now appear lordly drunk and rollicking, with the members of the band encouraging their recklessness. The girls, having singled out the men most responsive to their charms, tease and flirt with them, and gradually the male robbers retire to the background or appear passive and indifferent. But one of the men produces an accordion and begins to fan the flames with titillating tunes.

In hardly any time there is dancing-and-singing revelry, with the girls spurring the music to greater speed and their partners to greater excitement. The tactic obviously is to stupefy and exhaust the merchants, and it succeeds, for soon the atmosphere bursts into a wild, orgiastic bacchanalia. When the men seem to tire, the girls fling themselves lewdly at them, lure them on with violent lovemaking and ply them with wine and more wine, which the merchants attempt to drink and spill with feigned drunkenness, just as they slyly managed to dispose of the potent wine at the table. And according to plan, one by one the merchants pass out, drop off to sleep or stagger insensibly around the room. The music fades to a pianissimo.

As soon as all the merchants appear to be helpless, that characteristic whistle sounds again from the leader. At once every member of the robber band springs into action again, including the leader and the invalided woman by the fireside. This time they are feline and stealthy in their movements, amazingly artful as they dip into the merchants' pockets for wallets, watches and jewels, as they rummage through the luggage and bundles of merchandise and extract the most precious of valuables. The loot, passed to the leader and stuffed into a sack, is considerable.

Suddenly there is another whistle, unlike the two that preceded it. This one has the shrillness and authority of a police command. The robber band is startled. Instantly the merchants miraculously come to life and each, as though by prearrangement, hurls himself upon the thief nearest to him. A riotous melee ensues, with chairs crashing and dishes and bottles flying . . . The male robbers are finally subdued and handcuffed, their women cowed into submission.

The smallest of the merchants then opens the door and shrills his police whistle into the black night. In response a motor lorry is heard starting up in the distance and rumbling toward the inn. The merchant-detective then faces the culprits and announces that they are under arrest; he orders them led out.

The lorry has pulled up outside the door and its motor is heard idling as the various merchant-detectives wander back and retrieve their clothes and luggage. The small detective is last to leave, ostentatiously taking with him the sack of swag from under the table, where the robber leader had thrown it.

After a pause, the off-stage motor is heard being thrown into gear, then the lorry roaring off and fading out into utter silence. Only the deserted and disordered stage is the mute remaining atmosphere of the little drama just enacted. So it is held for a few moments, until the stillness is broken by the fall of the curtain.

2. THE OPERATING ROOM

It is three o'clock in the morning at the hospital.

The evening before, a distinguished foreign statesman visiting the country met with an automobile accident while returning from an important banquet given in his honor.

What was at first believed to be a minor head injury turned out to be a serious skull fracture as the night progressed. The diplomat's aides as well as officials of the government he is visiting are gravely concerned. Tomorrow the news will be flashed across the world. The people of both nations will voice their alarm. Hence the country's most celebrated brain surgeon has been summoned out of bed and the statesman hastily conveyed to the hospital.

The improvisation begins with the dark operating room. An apprentice nurse enters and switches on the lights. The hospital superintendent enters behind her; nurses soon follow him and he orders them to prepare the room for the great emergency operation. In fairly quick succession enter the diagnostician, X-ray specialist and anesthetist. All engage in their respective tasks with worried mien and professional dispatch.

The atmosphere is one of great expectation and extraordinarily weighty responsibility. The reputation of the hospital and the fate of future relations between the two countries depend on the success of the operation.

Soon the great brain surgeon himself enters. He examines the diagnostician's case-history chart and the X-ray plates, checks equipment and personnel, gives further instructions. Then the nurses help him and his assistants to wash up and don surgical garb.

When all is in readiness, the patient (imaginary rather than real) is wheeled in and transferred to the operating table. He is anesthetized, given blood transfusions.

Eventually the operation begins in this tense atmosphere, with the celebrated surgeon and his two assistants hovering over the patient's head. Most of this action is in pantomime and instruments and other paraphernalia are passed and removed chiefly by hand signals.

But during the operation a crisis develops. The anesthetist warns that the patient's pulse is getting dangerously low and his breathing more labored and spasmodic. The indications and reactions are that the patient is slipping away fast. It is a moment of high tension.

Whereupon the brain surgeon is compelled to make a drastic decision – to inject a new drug which the patient may not be able to withstand in his present condition, or which will prolong his life until the surgery is completed and his normal functions are restored. It is a fifty-fifty chance. The surgeon orders the injection of the new drug.

The operation continues. After a while the anesthetist, now the center of attention, renders reports that the pulsebeat is getting stronger, the breathing better. The patient is gaining and holding on firmly. The tension relaxes somewhat.

Finally the operation is over – and successful.

The patient is wheeled out. Assistants and staff congratulate the great surgeon on his skill and daring. The atmosphere is one of great satisfaction as the nurses help the doctors doff their surgical dress and wash up.

As some of the assistant doctors are ready to depart, they pause to repeat their congratulations to the great man and bid farewell to the others. Meanwhile the nurses are tidying up the room, and one by one they leave as they finish.

All but the surgeon and the apprentice nurse have dispersed. She helps him on with his overcoat and accompanies him to the door. He takes a final look around the room in which a great historical event has just been enacted. His contentment is apparent. The young nurse switches off the lights and the curtain falls, as it rose, on the dark operating room.

3. CIRCUS TRIANGLE

The characters are members of a renowned international circus Their acts are top-flight, and they are so conscientious and have gotten along so amicably for many years that they are virtually one big family sharing in the fame and fortune of the enterprise.

The scene is the area of small dressing tents behind the big top. It is intermission time, and the performers are resting or making preparations before the second half of the show. In front of one tent are the Clown and his wife, who is the Bareback Rider; he is helping her hook up the back of her costume. On a bench near the

next tent sit the Ringmaster, smoking, and the handsome Trapeze
Artist, who is lacing on a pair of trick shoes and testing with a
crossbar whether they will snap on properly for the thrilling climax of his act. At another tent male and female acrobats are
limbering up. Near and around still other tents similar little
vignettes of circus-folk life are going on. There are no animals or
trainers. though; they are elsewhere on the grounds.

The banter, directed mostly at the traditionally pessimistic
Ringmaster, concerns how well the show is going over and the
biggest crowds ever drawn in this town. It is an atmosphere of
good feeling, mutual respect and tolerance so common to families
who are welded together by a long-established and successful
business.

When the scene has been sufficiently under way, the Ringmaster consults his watch and announces that it's time to get the
last half of the show started. He exits, and soon his whistle is
heard off stage and the band strikes up. Then, on hearing their
cues, some of the actors run off to perform, returning after suitable
intervals. There is a steady flow of this routined activity.

The Clown, Bareback Rider and Trapeze Artist remain, seemingly awaiting their own cues. The latter appears to be having
trouble with his shoes, unlacing, relacing and retesting them
impatiently as his entrance approaches; he is still fiddling with
them when he hears himself announced from the ring and his
impatience only increases; he barely completes his preparations
when the agitated Ringmaster rushes on to summon him. The
Ringmaster signals for the act's entrance music to start up again
and the Trapeze Artist follows him into the ring.

The behind-the-scenes movements and costume changes of the
various acts continue as before, with the Clown and Bareback
Rider now helping the others wherever they are needed.

Suddenly there is a chorus of off-stage shrieks followed by a
deafening, ominous roar from the crowd. The cast freezes. That
thunder of voices can mean only one thing – an accident, the

dread terror that plagues all circus people. Then, as though released by the ensuing silence, the performers surge toward the entrance, crowding and craning for a glimpse of the tragedy. Slowly the knot of performers melts apart to form an alley, through which the Ringmaster and a couple of acrobats carry out the limp form of the Trapeze Artist and place him near his tent.

Then a startling thing happens. With a cry of anguish the Bareback Rider breaks away from the group of performers and hurls herself upon the prostrate Trapeze Artist, moaning and sobbing, cradling his head in her arms and kissing his pallid, deathlike face!

The implications are obvious. The performers are at first shocked by this uncontrollable revelation of her love for the injured man, then embarrassed for the Clown, her husband. No such blemish has ever marred the family life of the circus before. The Clown is equally embarrassed by her outburst, and stunned speechless by the discovery of the illicit love affair.

For several moments the performers stand there as though immobilized by their discomfort, gazing pathetically at the Clown, trading glances with one another to confirm their own reactions. Only the Ringmaster has the presence of mind to order them to go about their business and carry on with the show. The Doctor has been called, he says, and will see to the victim.

The performers scatter and resume their movements as before, trying politely to ignore the uncomfortable scene of the hapless woman and her lover, and the Clown, motionless and stupefied, staring down at his betrayers.

Presently the Doctor hurries on and, releasing the unconscious man from the distracted woman's embrace, begins to minister to him. Then, as though by a hasty decision, the Ringmaster orders the Clown to go out and do his act, to get the crowd settled back to normal with a few laughs. He leads the gloomy Clown out toward the ring and is soon heard announcing him.

While the Clown is doing his act off stage, the Doctor is

working on his patient. His examination discloses no serious injuries, so he begins to administer drugs to revive him. Soon there are signs of movement, and as the Trapeze Artist slowly returns to consciousness the Bareback Rider begins to regain her composure.

By the time the Clown returns from the ring, the Doctor has the Trapeze Artist sitting up, reassuring him that he suffered no great damage and congratulating him on his miraculous luck. After instructing him to rest up for a couple of days, the Doctor departs, leaving the trio of cuckolded Clown and exposed lovers.

The comings and goings of the other performers are now carried on at a distance. They skirt the scene, hastily remove themselves, and those who are not required in the ring retreat to the privacy of their dressing tents, lowering the flaps. The Trapeze Artist, unaware of what had transpired while he lay unconscious, is puzzled by their unconcern and even coldness, by their deliberate efforts to avoid him after so near-fatal a fall, and by the generally strange atmosphere. And he is completely baffled by the fidgety distress of the Bareback Rider and the tense, silent stares of the Clown.

There is no curtain yet – not until the group can supply a satisfactory conclusion to this improvisation. How can it end, how should it end, without being banal or unduly melodramatic?

4. SUNDAY AFTERNOON

The locale is the home of a low-bourgeois family in a provincial town somewhere in the south of France. The family is one of those prolific clans with numerous aunts, uncles, cousins and in-laws.

The time is a dull Sunday afternoon, and the weather is oppressively hot. Everybody is lazing and lolling through the day and trying not to be too miserable in starched Sunday attire.

The men would rather be off napping under a shady tree, or telling stories in the cool wine cellar, were it not for the women; and the women would no doubt be in dishabille in their darkened boudoirs were it not for the fact that they could no longer avoid inviting M. Pichaud, the aged local apothecary, over for his periodic visit – and they all know what an unconscionable bore he is going to be.

They hear the gate creak, and one of them bestirs himself long enough to remark that M. Pichaud is arriving quite early. Perhaps he will leave early, too, another says hopefully.

But instead of M. Pichaud, it is M. Labatte who raps on the door and enters when bidden. The family's surprise is doubled when it is discerned that M. Labatte is not making a purely social call. For the lawyer, as good a friend as he is an advocate, is carrying his ancient briefcase.

However, the M. Labatte is a cute one. He does not at once, nor for some time, reveal the purpose of his mission; instead, he is coy, he intrigues them to speculate on his important reason for troubling them on the Sabbath and for exerting himself on such a hot day, he teases them with reminders of what a good friend he has always been to the family, and drops hints that he is about to become their greatest benefactor.

Bursting with curiosity, the family coax and cajole him to come to the point. Tantalizingly, painfully, the lawyer approaches the great moment of his disclosure.

Do they remember one black sheep named Pierre Louis, their bachelor cousin twice removed, with whom they would have nothing to do?

There are mixed reactions from the family: some frown, some wince, some scowl, some sense trouble, some wrinkle their noses in disdain; all indicate that they are terribly let down.

M. Labatte begs them all to be charitable, for one must show mercy in death if not in life, especially when the bachelor cousin has made amends upon his demise. Had he not turned his back on the assorted children he fathered and left his entire fortune of almost a million francs to – whom? *Ah, mais oui!* Of course! To none others than the family M. Labatte is now calling upon.

There is a stunned silence, then a few gasps – and words better not uttered, so choked off. Thereafter the family members are more careful to contain their joy, and for the sake of appearances they even try to maintain the dignity of grieving gentlefolk.

But the effort proves much too great for all of them. Gradually, unable to suppress their true feelings for long, they relax their manners. Soon their masks are completely discarded; they are in a celebrative mood and bursting with gaiety. To commemorate the occasion, the head of the family brings up from the cellar a rare bottle of cognac he has been saving for a special event, and the women fetch glasses and cakes.

Then, just as the cork is popped, there is a slow, methodical rapping on the door. *Mon Dieu!* it must be M. Pichaud, the old apothecary. They had forgotten all about him. Now he will surely stay and stay, and talk and talk, and they will never be rid of him!

Instantly the head of the family leaps to the door and directs the others while he stands against it. With a conspiratorial flurry the bottle is hidden from sight, the cakes removed, the glasses taken from the room, the legal document replaced in the briefcase and the briefcase slipped under the sofa. Then, when all have settled into a peaceful Sunday afternoon tableau, M. Pichaud's knock is answered and he is admitted.

After the perfunctory exchange of greetings, the family finds little to say to the ancient pill-roller, but he manages pretty well on his own. He elaborates on the heat, discourses on modern medicants and how they are making a mockery out of the noble profession of pharmacy; he complains of his aches and pains and renders an account of the town's latest vital statistics. His is practically a monologue and his listeners are tortured almost to death and desperately eager to get back to their celebration. The question of how to get rid of the old codger is written on all their faces. After a while some of the family pretend to nod, others rudely carry on side conversations, and a couple of the women giggle disrespectfully and leave the room.

Finally, M. Pichaud indicates that he is not too old to sense something strange in their attitudes, that he is unwelcome for some reason, that they are trying to conceal something from him. And since no effort to entertain or refresh him appears likely, he soon finds an excuse to make his departure.

When M. Pichaud has gone, silence is maintained only until the gate is heard creaking shut. Then they burst their bounds. The cakes and glasses reappear, the bottle of cognac materializes and several more with it. They drink to each other's health, and to the illness that took poor Cousin Pierre Louis off to a better world; they drink to all the francs awaiting them, and M. Labatte drinks to his fee. They drink to anything anybody suggests in their orgy of unrestrained glee.

Just before the curtain they are deciding to leave for Paris immediately and start spending some of the money before anybody else can lay claim to it.

5. SEASCAPE

For two days a storm has been raging at sea with unremitting violence. The fate of the four fishing boats that had set out almost a week ago for the seasonal catch, and should have returned by now, is unknown.

On the shore of the ancient fishing village are gathered the fishermen's families and the townfolk, waiting glumly in the merciless downpour, hopefully scanning the forbidding horizon for a sign of the long-overdue craft and the missing men.

The atmosphere is one of hope yet fear, commingled with despair yet stoical patience born of long tradition.

In due time someone seems to sight a distant object – it might be a vessel, perhaps two – battling the storm on the sea's furious vastness. Stronger telescopes reveal it to be only one boat, its broken mast creating the impression of another alongside it.

Which of the vessels it might be cannot at once be determined, but as the ship heaves and tosses into better view its deck appears to be packed with fishermen. That can mean only one thing to those on the shore, that the other ships have foundered and some of their crews have been rescued.

But which ships have been lost – and who among the crews? The suspense is maddening as some of the braver townspeople put out to sea in lifeboats to help bring in the crippled craft and its exhausted cargo.

As each lifeboat finally beaches its load of rescued fishermen, it becomes clearer and clearer which families are suffering losses and which are having their loved ones restored. For example, a little girl thinks she recognizes her daddy and runs to embrace him – only to shrink back when he turns out to be somebody else's father.

It is also perceivable that there are psychological barriers as well as psychological differences in the reactions of both sides. The lucky ones cannot express their full measure of happiness too openly in the presence of the others' misery, and the unlucky ones cannot be so inhuman as to begrudge or ignore the joy of those more fortunate, even in the face of their own tragedies.

What happens, then? Do the mourners draw apart from the rejoicers and form separate groups, or what? How do they react in a situation such as this?

6. THE CONFLICT

In the vast farming country in which he has taken up practice, Dr. Starke is the only physician within a two-hundred-mile radius.

But the dedicated doctor has not been able to make his calls for several days and is praying that he will not be summoned away from his small hospital-home. For at the moment his little girl and only child lies critically ill with a dangerous infection.

He, his wife and a nurse have been taking turns doing everything that human skill and medical science are capable of in an effort to save her life. Now, at last, the child is in the final stages of the crisis she has been undergoing. Her life hangs delicately in the balance; one moment of neglect might prove fatal. And although he is more exhausted than the women, the doctor insists on maintaining this last vigil himself so that there will be no possibility of error.

Then, what the doctor had prayed to avert, happens. Mr. Blohm, his nearest farming neighbor, comes to call him out on an emergency case. Mrs. Blohm has suffered a heart attack!

The doctor's wife will not let him go; the doctor explains why he cannot answer the call right now. A fine psychological conflict predominates: if the doctor leaves the baby – and if he refuses to go to the stricken wife – ? The two men understand each other.

But how would the group resolve this situation without acting it angrily, without rudeness or rancor?

7. DIRECTORIAL DEBUT

Julian Wells is a very young, terribly sincere and still unspoiled stage director. His enthusiasm and a boundless passion for work have won him quick success – and Hollywood has snapped him up early in his career.

Thus we find him on a studio set, rehearsing the first big scene of his first picture. His energy is infectious; he encourages even the smallest bit player and is considerate of everyone down to the lowliest "grip." The set is a little island of kindness, harmony and *élan vital*.

The ecstasy of the cast increases as they rehearse again and again, and when they go through the scene for the last time it is so perfectly executed that everyone is deliriously happy.

The mood of artistic inspiration still prevails as preparations for shooting begin; it seems to flow from the young fountainhead and drench them all. Eventually the scene is shot. It is so sparkling a gem, so flawless in every detail, that only one "take" is necessary.

At the cry of "Cut!" there is that tense moment of sustained awe, then everybody on the set bursts into expressions of joy. They congratulate the director, the female players throw their arms around him, and they lavish compliments upon one another. Never, in their opinion, has anything so brilliant been immortalized by the camera before. And as a sort of punctuation to the joyous occasion, a smattering of applause comes from the dark recesses of the sound stage.

Everyone turns toward the applauders to see the producer and a flunky emerging from the darkness, where they had quietly observed the proceedings. Everything was excellent, super – and good, too – the producer assures them, and his flunky nods agreement. But –

Thereupon the producer begins making suggestions – "only suggestions, y'understand" – for bettering this and improving that. The flunky's head snaps in total accord.

Gradually the atmosphere and everybody's high mood change. As the producer tears apart the whole perfect structure of the scene bit by bit, the spirits of the director, cast and staff sink lower and lower.

Disagreeing with the "suggestions," humiliated in front of his company, the director begins to defend himself and the others, getting angrier by the minute. The embarrassed actors slowly disappear from the set, as though they know the futility of the director's gesture and what the outcome will be. The crew recedes and vanishes in their wake.

Alone with his flunky, and the director, the producer gives his ultimatum: either the director will do that scene over the producer's way, or another director will.

At the end of the improvisation the young director, deserted, his soul scorched from his first baptism of Hollywood fire, is holding his head in his hands, debating the things that many a young man before him has debated in the same way and for the same reasons.

8. STOP LAUGHING!

Tortolino is a famous old clown. His grown daughter thinks there is none funnier. So does Sasso, his protégé, a talented lad whom the clown has trained to follow in his footsteps. With this bond strengthening their affection, Sasso and the girl fell in love and recently married. Thereupon the old clown revised his act in order to form a partnership with his son-in-law.

But so superior does Sasso prove to be that he steals the show from the old man at each performance. It is not long before the youngster becomes the star of the act and the old clown just barely hangs on as the lesser of the team.

The old man would like to be happy but cannot help feeling terribly hurt. He is proud of his creation, pleased with the young couple's new-found bliss, yet irked by the loss of prestige which he must bear in silence.

On this night of the improvisation, as is the custom every night after the show, the three of them are preparing to have supper together. The newlyweds are overjoyed with their marriage and the success that is beginning to attend it, but they must suppress their gaiety because the old clown is feeling his decline so keenly. Worse, that night the girl had discovered her father drinking secretly, a thing he had never done before. They converse haltingly throughout the meal but manage to convey the situation and the impasse it has reached.

It is a most embarrassing atmosphere. They try to avoid talking shop and find little else to talk about that will not reflect on the old man's ignominious situation. What can they say? Whatever any of them says will sound false. What can they do? There seems to be no solution. The happiness they all had hoped for and gained has turned into bitterness.

During the meal the old clown excuses himself from the table several times. His daughter knows that he is tippling and hesitates to tell Sasso for fear of adding to his dilemma. But Sasso soon guesses what is going on. The old clown gets drunker and drunker each time he returns to the table, and he begins to look and react suspiciously at their silence; their strained looks and whatever else they do. He excuses himself again and says good night.

As Tortolino leaves, he is drunk for the first time in his career, and the somber youngsters know that it won't be the last time. For as the old clown reaches the door, he turns on them and, with all the agony of his pent-up feelings and his frustration, shouts, "Stop laughing!"

9. THE TUTOR

To earn some extra money, a poor college student is tutoring a well-to-do, freckle-faced teenager in mathematics. To her father the girl is a minx; to the tutor she is an imp, a scheming little brat.

The lesson is going tolerably well until the tutor gives his pupil a problem she can't solve. Vengefully, she challenges the tutor to do the problem himself. He can't find the solution either! He hems and hews, renews his explanations, lapses into double-talk – but he still can't come up with the correct answer. The pupil derives a sadistic pleasure from his befuddlement; she rides him like an old hand.

To add to the tutor's discomfort, Papa, the paymaster, enters at this juncture to sit in and listen to his daughter's progress. The tutor attempts to retreat into a new problem, but the mean little girl goads him back into the difficult one. He has another try at it, several tries, but to no avail. Then Papa, realizing the tutor is stumped, shows them both how to solve it.

Now the student is painfully embarrassed and fully expects that momentarily his services will be terminated. But Papa reveals himself as a good Joe, tries to gloss over the incident, explains that he had flunked the same problem several times himself as a youth, and as a consolation finally invites the young man to stay for dinner.

The tutor accepts, and Papa leaves them to resume the lesson. But as they start again, the little brat has a triumphant, knowing glint in her eye, and it is plain from her snickers that she will have the upper hand in the future, as she always has in everything.

10. TRAPPED

A party of tourists is being conducted through a famous copper mine in Montana, a mile below the earth's surface. They are a heterogeneous lot, a conglomeration of types and characters who would scarcely find themselves thrown together under any other circumstance.

In addition to the guide, the party includes (among others perhaps) a stockbroker and an embezzler who is awaiting his chance to defraud him, the financier's wife, two women teachers, a prostitute, a honeymooning couple, a murderer and a detective on his trail, an incurable alcoholic, and a young girl who knows her days are numbered by a fatal disease and is therefore crowding perhaps a last vacation into her life.

The elevator has just disgorged them and retreated up the shaft, leaving the tourists to accustom themselves to the dim light and cavernous atmosphere. Then, just as the guide instructs them to snap on their flashlights and is about to lead them farther into the mine, there is the deafening roar of a tremendous explosion. The party is hurled to the ground by the impact. Tons upon tons of rocks and dirt cascade down the elevator shaft and overflow into the mine entrance. Incalculable pressures pack the debris tight. The tourists are completely sealed in!

When they recover from the shock of the blast and the cave-in, they suffer still another shock upon realizing that they are all seriously trapped. Their hidden natures come to the fore in these minutes of panic. The young bride screams her terror, the broker demands that the guide do something; his wife faints and the prostitute works over her; the murderer and detective snatch at shovels and desperately start tunneling; the alcoholic reaches for his flask for a much-needed drink, only to find it smashed in his pocket – and so on for the rest of the characters.

In short, in these first reactions to their entombment the egotism of each is seen to assert itself. Then, as further developments indicate that they are slowly being cut off from all contact with possible rescuers, as their hunger and thirst increase, as their flashlight batteries begin to weaken and fade their lights, as they become aware that through failure of the ventilating system their oxygen is being depleted by the poisonous underground gasses – then egotism turns to hatred and is manifested in every word and deed.

Condemned to die, they fight against it like vicious, predatory animals, blaming the others for their own shortcomings, shifting responsibility for their plight, berating each other for their inability to escape. Those who have vengeance in them wreak it, those who have cowardice display it, and those who have mercy and forbearance withhold it.

Yet there is a deep, abiding sense of fellowship in all of us that springs to life when the imminence of death is final and conclusive. Such a moment comes for these victims, when they acknowledge that all hope is gone and they face the inevitable; that they must all die together and may as well accept it.

From that moment on there begins a reversal, a sloughing off of all the mortal frailties and abominations. By various acts, gestures and sacrifices they reveal of themselves that which is more desirably human and true, all that is basically good and sincerely unselfish.

What they do or how they signify that they are converting these last minutes of life into a Utopia heretofore unattainable, is the improvisational challenge to the group, as were the earlier opportunities in this exercise for the development of incidents germane to each character. But the resulting impression must be so convincing that it justifies the remark of one of them, to the effect that he has never seen such peace and harmony among humans before. Moreover, he knows that it will end, that they will all revert to their old selves if ever they are rescued – and he prays that they will not be!

Whether they finally should be rescued, and how they will react if they are – those are still further improvisational latitudes which the group may accept or decline, depending on the particular purpose for which the exercise has been selected.

APPENDIX

A practical guide to the application of the Michael Chekhov Psychological Gesture (PG) Technique

Translation and commentary by
Andrei Malaev-Babel

The concept of Psychological Gesture remains one of the most popular aspects of Michael Chekhov's creative heritage. The goal of this appendix is to provide every actor and reader with a detailed guide to the practical application of the Psychological Gesture (PG) Technique. In Chapter 5 of *To the Actor*, Michael Chekhov concentrates on the PG technique in application to the character as a whole. At the same time, Chekhov mentions that the Gesture can also be used "for any segment of the role, for separate scenes or speeches, . . . or even separate sentences". However, while presenting the reader with six vivid examples of PGs for different characters, the book offers no explanations on multiple uses of the PG. In the other classical work by Chekhov, *On the Technique of Acting* (1942 English-language version), the chapter on Psychological Gesture appears in rather expanded format; it offers unique materials that substantially complement and develop our knowledge of the PG technique as presented in *To the Actor*. But even this definitive text does not provide a complete explanation of all the aspects of the Psychological Gesture Technique. For a detailed guide on the multiple use of the PG Technique, we ought to address the Russian-language version of *On the Technique of Acting* (*O Tekhnike Aktyora*), issued by Chekhov in 1946. This volume, originally published and distributed by Chekhov at his own expense, despite popular belief, isn't a mere Russian translation of his English-language version. The Russian version is different from English editions not only in content, but most importantly – in structure. Throughout the book, the student-reader is being carefully guided through the sequence of steps that lead to mastering the elements of the Chekhov Method. The chapter on the Psychological Gesture from *O Tekhnike Aktyora* serves as a foundation for this Guide. It contains the most complete reference on different aspects of the PG Technique, arranged in a logical, harmonious structure. Since many of the PG materials in the Russian-language chapter appear somewhat scattered in different English-language Chekhov editions, this Guide concentrates only on materials previously unavailable to English-speaking students and theater practitioners.

FANTASTIC PG

Michael Chekhov is widely known not only as a great theatrical master-teacher and theoretician, but also as one of Russia's greatest twentieth-century actors. As an actor, Chekhov followed a unique trend in theatrical art, one described by the Russian director Evgeny Vakhtangov as "fantastic realism". All of the characters created by Chekhov at the Moscow Art Theater (MXAT) and MXAT II, had a tendency to appear larger than life, or even exaggerated. At the same time, they never became flat or psychologically shallow, and never turned into caricatures. In other words, the actor always realistically justified his characters, both emotionally and psychologically. His characters remained complex human beings, but perhaps the kind of human beings one might see in a dream or imagine in their fantasies. That is why, in the eyes of the audience, these characters often manifested universal ideas, such as life and death, love and hate, beauty and ugliness. They had a power to resonate with such universal issues; they could also stir the most intimate, the most sacred feelings and thoughts in the audiences' hearts and minds. The Chekhov Method does not directly explain the unique creative individuality of Michael Chekhov the actor. That's why the nature of his supernatural talent still remains a mystery that many contemporary actors are striving to unveil.

In the PG chapter of *O Tekhnike Aktyora* the author offers a term that never appears in any other Chekhov edition – the "Fantastic PG". He calls his student-readers to observe the forms of plants and flowers, architectural forms, different landscapes, fantastic characters from myths, legends and fairy tales. He teaches them to discover PGs and qualities for such objects and creatures, and by doing so, to make them alive, to breathe soul into them, to discover and master their imaginary "will forces and feelings". He calls such PGs fantastic. By introducing the actor's body and psychology to working with abstract, inanimate objects and fantastic characters, Chekhov helps them discover certain hidden resources within themselves. Developing such resources will not only make your acting rich, unpredictable and inspired, it will help you lift it above an everyday, primitive, naturalistic plane. Through working with fantastic PGs actors will discover that they too can approach universal issues and ideas, no matter what kind of character or play they are performing: a realistic or a fantastic one.

You can make your PG resemble more or less everyday naturalistic gestures. You can also create a *fantastic* PG. Through it you will be able to convey the most intimate, the most original artistic concepts.

These Chekhov words as well as the very term of the Fantastic PG provide us with an invaluable insight into the hidden goal of the Chekhov Method. It also brings us a bit closer to the essence of the incomparable creative individuality of Michael Chekhov the actor.

THE PRACTICAL APPLICATION OF THE PG

Several original illustrations used in this appendix have never appeared in any of the English-language Chekhov editions. The outstanding theater designer and book illustrator Nicolai Remisoff prepared these for the Russian-language *O Tekhnike Aktyora*. Several similar drawings appear earlier in *To the Actor*, accompanied, however, by very different captions and explanations. (To compare texts and drawings from the appendix with the ones in this and other English-language Chekhov editions is by itself quite an intriguing exploration.) Notice how in the following passage Chekhov demonstrates the process of discovery and development of the PG, and compare it with the description of drawing 4 in Chapter 5.

There are five possibilities for application of the PG in the practical work.

(1) For the role as a whole

You can use the PG to master *the character as a whole*.

For example, while working upon the part of The Mayor from Gogol's "The Inspector General", you might discover that his will has a tendency to strive forward (gesture) in a cowardly manner (quality). You create a simple PG, corresponding with your first impression. Let us assume that this gesture will be the following

Drawing 1

one (see drawing 1). Having fulfilled and concretely experienced it, you will now feel an urge for its further development. Your intuition might prompt you: *down to the earth* (gesture), *heavily and slowly* (quality) (see drawing 2). The new experience of the PG will lead you to new movements. Now it might become, perhaps, like this: the gesture receives an inclination to the side (canniness), hands clench into fists (intense will), shoulders lift up, the entire body slightly bows towards the earth, knees bend (cowardliness), feet are slightly turned inside (secretiveness) (see drawing 3).

Drawing 2

(2) For separate moments of the role

While working upon a role as a whole, you can also search for PG's for its separate moments. The nature of this process is similar to the previous one. The only difference is that you are now fixing your attention upon one single moment, examining it as a finished and complete whole.

Let us suppose that you already have a PG for the entire role and now are seeking a series of gestures for its separate moments. They

Drawing 3

all differ from each other to a degree. What should you do in that case? Should you try to connect them into one? *No.* Keep them in the same state as you discovered them, and use each of them separately, allowing them to influence you freely. By doing so, you will soon discover that despite the differences between the gestures, they are still serving the same goal, complementing and enriching one another. You will also notice how they start changing gradually and *independently* in their details and nuances. You will follow their will, rather than imposing your own will upon them. Unless you destroy their lives with your impatient intellectual interference, the PG's will grow and develop like living, animate beings. Through them you will be speaking directly with your creative subconscious.

(3) For separate scenes

With the help of the PG you can also penetrate, regardless of the role you perform, into the essence of each *separate scene*.

The essence of the scene is determined by characters' actions, their relationships, characterizations, atmosphere and the style of the scene, as well as its place within the composition of the entire play. While gradually creating the PG for the scene, always appeal to your creative intuition. The scene will appear before you as an *entirety*, despite all the variety and complexity of its elements. With the help of the PG, you will be able to see the predominate will and emotion of the scene clearly.

Let us take an example from "The Marriage" by Gogol (grooms and Agafya, act I, scene 19).

Here is the short synopsis of the scene from *The Marriage* that will help you understand Chekhov's example. One of the main characters of the play, Agafya the bride, is faced with an awkward situation, one where she is being forced to choose her future husband from a group of six (!) grooms. Thanks to the efforts of her overly-energetic matchmaker, all six men arrive at the bride's house almost simultaneously. By the beginning of scene 19, we find all six of them in the room, highly suspicious of each other, the matchmaker and the bride, and feeling quite competitive.

Gradually all six grooms begin attacking the bride with direct questions, demanding that she make her final choice. Feeling totally scared, ashamed and confused, the poor woman finally bursts out of the room, leaving the six grooms in a state of complete amazement.

With the arrival of the last groom, following the moment of awkward silence, the gesture of the scene looms before you. The waves of hope and fear ascend and descend heavily and awkwardly within the space that seems huge and empty. From the very beginning the characters in the scene are surrounded by an atmosphere of tension. While seeking a gesture for a scene, you might experience a desire to embrace as much space around you as possible. Your arms sway slightly, as if they were holding a large sphere, filled with air (see drawing 4). Your arms, shoulders and chest contract slightly. The quality of hope and fear permeates your gesture. The destiny of all the participants in the scene should be decided within the period of five to ten minutes. Emptiness and uncertainty become unbearable. The grooms initiate a conversation on the subject of the weather. The tension grows, and the space contracts further: your hands press the sphere and grow steadier. The increasing tension is now fraught with explosive energy. The grooms, as if throwing themselves into the fire, approach the awkward subject closely. The space around you, that used to be huge and empty, becomes extremely contracted and tense: your arms lower and press the space surrounding you with the utmost force (see drawing 5). The bride, being unable to tolerate this tension and shame, runs away – the atmosphere explodes (see drawing 6)!

In this example, it is important to note that we are dealing with the gesture, expressing the overall objective dynamic of the scene or, in Stanislavsky's terminology, the scene's "through-line of action". This gesture embodies the scene from the perspective of the author, the director, or, perhaps the theatre, and not from the

Drawing 4

Drawing 5

Drawing 6

point of view of any particular character in the scene. This or a similar gesture, in the rehearsal process, would have to be first rehearsed and then fulfilled (inwardly) by the entire group of actors participating in the scene. Remisoff's pictures, illustrating the gesture, never show it in its entirety. They represent separate stages or phases of the growing gesture. One priceless element of the Russian-language version of *O Tekhnike Aktyora* is that it is the only Chekhov work that clearly illustrates that the so-called Psychological Gesture is, in fact, a continuous movement, not a frozen position.

Another important component of the PG Technique that clearly appears in both Chekhov's example and Remisoff's illustrations is the category of the imaginary space. Chekhov first describes the space as a large sphere, huge and empty. (This sphere is almost visible in drawing 5.) What follows is the transformation of the space under the influence of the gesture. The sphere is first being gradually contracted, its quality changing from emptiness to tension, and finally the sphere explodes.[1]

(4) For the score of atmospheres

You can use the PG in order to master the score of atmospheres.

As I already mentioned, the atmosphere has its predominant will (dynamics) and feeling and, according to these elements, the atmosphere can be easily realized by means of their inherent gesture and quality. Let's take another example. The final scene from Gorky's play "The Lower Depths" gives us a characteristic example of a strong atmosphere that appears unexpectedly. The tenants of a shelter are preparing for their nightly debauchery. They strike up a song, but . . .

> (*The door opens quickly.*)
> BARON (*standing on the threshold, shouts*): Hey! . . . you there! Come . . . come in a hurry! In the lot . . . out there . . . the Actor . . . has hung himself!
>
> (*Silence. All look at the* BARON. NASTYA *makes her appearance from behind him, and slowly, with wide-open, staring eyes, goes to the table.*)

---

[1] The category of the imaginary space will be further discussed at the end of this work. For now, however, let us notice an apparent connection between the PG and the imaginary space.

SATIN (*in a low voice*): Ugh! . . . He's spoiled the song . . . The foo-ool!
Curtain.

With the arrival of the Baron the atmosphere changes abruptly. It starts with a shock, and its tension in the beginning is at a maximum. Its strength gradually weakens by the end. Its predominant initial quality can be experienced as sharp pain and amazement. It changes into melancholic despondency by the end. You are making your first attempt to discover the PG. It might be, for example, like this (see drawing 7): your hands are thrown up (amazement) quickly (power, force), your fists are clenched (pain and force). Perhaps you will discover that the quality of pain from the first shock can be more strongly realized through a different gesture; having thrown up your arms, you cross them above your head (see drawing 8). After a pause, you will slowly lower your arms with an increasing quality of melancholy, and hold them close to your body (depression). The ending phase of the atmosphere is associated with helplessness – you will gradually unclench your fists, lower your shoulders, stretch your neck and straighten your legs while pressing them tightly against each other (see drawing 9).

Having executed these kinds of PG's, you and your partners will get the feeling of the scene's atmosphere. It will radiate into the audience through any blocking suggested to you by the director and any lines given to you by the author. It will unite you with both your partners and the audience; it will inspire your acting and free you from clichés and bad stage habits.

With the character of the Mayor from *The Inspector General* (drawings 1, 2, and 3) Chekhov demonstrates the process of discovering the PG; here he reminds us that there is no limitation for perfecting the gesture. He teaches us not to be afraid to discard the first gesture in a constant attempt to discover a better one. While the first variant of the beginning phase of the PG in *The*

Drawing 7

Drawing 8

Drawing 9

Lower Depths is strong (drawing 7), the second variant (drawing 8) speaks truer to the essence of the moment. It also shows how a small variation can entirely change qualities and the psychological content of the gesture: hands thrown up, fists clenched – quality of pain and a strong "protesting" will-power; hands crossed above the head – quality of pain and a weak "protecting" will-power. The latter is much truer to the psychology of the tenants of the shelter in *The Lower Depths*. These "former people" do not *protest*, they try to *protect* themselves from the harsh reality of the outside world. The actor's suicide shocks them as a reminder of that inevitable reality. At the beginning of the scene all characters live with the warm feeling of anticipation of the nightly debauchery – a regular attempt to drown in wine the reminder of their destined reality. This pathetic attempt is the kind of a "song" that the actor has "spoiled" with his tragic and desperate deed.

(5) For the speech

I will attempt, by example, to demonstrate to you the practical application of the PG in your work upon the role.

Let us suppose, that you are preparing Horatio's monologue in the scene where the Ghost first appears to him (Shakespeare's *Hamlet*).

HORATIO
But soft, behold! lo where it comes again!
I'll cross it, though it blast me.
Stay, illusion!
If thou hast any sound, or use of voice,
Speak to me:
If there be any good thing to be done,
That may to thee do ease, and grace to me,
Speak to me:
If thou art privy to thy country's fate,

Which happily foreknowing may avoid,
O! speak;
Or if thou hast uphoarded in thy life
Extorted treasure in the womb of earth,
For which, they say, you spirits oft walk in death,
Speak of it: stay and speak! Stop it, Marcellus.

As before, you are appealing to your imagination. While listening carefully to Horatio's speech and looking closely at his movements, you make the first attempt to create a PG for his speech. It appears to you as an ardent, violent *thrust forward*, as a desire to detain the Ghost and *penetrate* its mystery. Suppose the first "draft" of your PG was like this: a strong thrust forward with your entire body, your right arm also striving forward and upward (see drawing 10). You rehearse the gesture many times and then try to say the lines of the monologue (this time without a gesture), until you can hear the general character of your gesture with its qualities affecting the lines that you say.

Now step-by-step you start searching for the details of the monologue. Perhaps the first moment, prompted by your creative intuition, will be the contrast distinguishing the beginning of the monologue from its ending. Horatio starts addressing the Ghost *firmly*, and yet with a feeling of *awe. A plea* can be heard in his words. Yet the Ghost starts to leave without giving an answer. Horatio's efforts are useless. He's growing impatient. His confidence is now turning into *bewilderment*, his awe is replaced with *offensive insistence*, his plea becomes *an order*, and instead of solemnity it is *harsh irritability* that can now be heard in his words. You already have two gestures: one mirrors the will and the quality of the beginning, the other – the will and the quality of the end (see drawings 10 and 11). They are based upon the principle of polarity.

Having mastered and exercised these gestures, you now say the lines of the beginning and the end of the monologue. Do it until the polarity that you've built into the gesture starts permeating your lines.

Drawing 10

Drawing 11

Michael Chekhov continues by applying the Law of Triplicity to Horatio's monologue. He goes on to show how the middle part serves as a gradual transition from the beginning of the monologue to its conclusion. He later breaks the middle part into several sections, suggesting his students discover appropriate PGs for each part, as well as transitions between. The Russian-language version *O Tekhnike Aktyora* contains the following important passage, where Chekhov demonstrates that there is truly no limit to perfecting the gesture. Each section of the monologue, however small, can be explored even further. Chekhov uses one of the key elements of his technique, namely the Principle of Preparation, to show that even more elaborate details can be found within the small section of the monologue.

Now let's take a look at the first part of the monologue: Imagine the vague expectation accumulating in Horatio's heart as he is waiting for the meeting with the mysterious Ghost. The tension between belief and disbelief has been agitating his soul! What hidden force has already lived within him *before* he ever pronounced his first line in the presence of the mysterious Ghost! Do you now feel that the beginning of the monologue has its own prelude – a preparation? Express it in a gesture: before your arm thrusts forward, it makes a wide, strong yet soft movement, as though drawing a circle within the space above your head. Your body, following the movement of your arm, also sways forward (see drawing 12). Everything that accumulated in Horatio's soul in anticipation of the meeting, as if *preceding* the speech, comes out in this prelude. ("But soft, behold! lo where it comes again!"). Following the prelude come Horatio's lines: "I'll cross it, though it blast me! . . .". You now look closely at the last, concluding part of the monologue. Horatio lost his dignity, self-control and peace. His soul is empty. What precedes his last words? Nothing! There is no "prelude". The words burst out abruptly, swiftly, without any preparation.

You also might encounter a case where what's taking place on

Drawing 12

the stage happens to be one of the important moments of the play, where not only every movement, but every sound and quality of your voice play a crucial part in the development of the action. At the same time, the lines provided by the author are insignificant, inexpressive and even weak in their content. In this case, all the responsibility lies upon you as an actor. *You* should fill the insignificant lines with the power and depth of the moment. Here the PG might do you an invaluable service. You will create it based on the psychological content of the given situation, and you will use it as a foundation for both your acting and the author's text. Let's take as an example, the "mousetrap scene" from *Hamlet* (act III, scene 2). Hamlet presents a play at court. Actors perform the scene of poisoning the King. Hamlet observes King Claudius, and his reaction to the scene will tell Hamlet if Claudius has truly committed the murder. The tense atmosphere foreshadows a catastrophe. The wounded conscience of the king arouses chaotic powers within his soul. The crucial moment is approaching; the murderer on the stage pours poison into the ear of the sleeping "king". Claudius loses his self-control. The pregnant atmosphere explodes:

> OPHELIA. The King rises.
> HAMLET. What, frightened with false fire?
> QUEEN. How fares my lord?
> POLONIUS. Give o'er the play.
> KING. Give me some light. Away!
> POLONIUS. Lights, lights, lights!

You notice that except for Hamlet's line, all the other lines are deprived of deep meaning. If you are playing the role of Claudius, and decide to say the line simply the way that it's given by the author, you weaken the strength of the climactic moment in your performance as well as in the tragedy as a whole. Horror, hatred, the tortured conscience and longing for revenge – the King is running – and, perhaps, is still trying to maintain his royal dignity. Images of possible revenge and escape flicker inside the King's mind, but his thoughts are tangled, confused, they slip away from him, as though a thick fog is clouding his sight. He has no support; he is entrapped like a wild, hunted beast ... There is so much to convey to the audience at this moment, yet the lines fail to express the significance of the moment. You are searching for the PG. Despite the complexity of the moment, your gesture should always remain simple and clear. Perhaps your creative intuition prompts you to *a wide gesture of falling backward, flat on your back*, into the realm of the unconsciousness and uncertainty, into the darkness ... Your hands and arms are powerfully thrust upward and thrown back along with the entire body and head. Your palms and fingers open in self-defense, in *pain, fear and coldness* (the gesture's qualities). Having thrust backwards up to the bodily limits, you continue to fall deeper and deeper in your imagination (drawing 13). Rehearse the gesture, perfecting and developing it, and when all its forces and qualities start resonating in your lines, they will fill your phrase with the previously lacking significance of the moment.

The following passage does not seem to apply to the PG concept directly, nevertheless in the Russian book it is included by Chekhov as part of the PG chapter.

Remembering what serious attention Chekhov paid to the issue of composition, we include here this invaluable passage. It offers

Drawing 13

an actor yet another technique for making their artistic speech live.

Every element of the Chekhov Technique is deeply connected with all others; the gesture, for instance, is inseparable from the image. The Chekhov concept of "many-leveled acting" shows how many inner activities take place simultaneously within the actor's psychology. One inner activity often draws the other, and that creates the kind of complexity and richness of the actor's presence on stage that distinguished Chekhov himself in every role.

AN IMAGE BEHIND THE LINE

A few words about the role of the imagination in artistic speech.

Rational content or the abstract thought that stands behind the lines of our everyday speech do not allow it to rise to the higher degree of artistic expressiveness. On the stage, however, we often reduce our speech to an even lower level by depriving it of even a mere rational content. Lines turn into shallow forms of sound. Such lines quickly bore the actor and become an obstacle in his work upon the role. The actor starts forcing his feelings, resorting to vocal clichés, inventing "intonations", stressing single words and finally weakening his/her creative impulses.

One of the best means to enliven the speech and to lift it above the level of everyday speech is to resort to the power of our imagination. The line that has an image behind it gains force and expressiveness, and remains fresh, no matter how often you repeat it. If a certain scene strikes you as essential for the play as a whole and for your role in particular, try to discover its main phrases and the important words in the phrases, and then turn these into images. By doing so you will enliven your speech. Its expressiveness will gradually spread beyond the boundaries of the chosen lines, evoking more and more within you the creative joy that comes from speaking the lines of your role. How else would you, without having well developed images behind the lines, speak from the stage King

Lear's monologues, such as "Hear, Nature, hear, dear goddess, hear!" (Act I, Scene IV), "Blow, winds, and crack your cheeks!" (Act III, Scene 2), "You do me wrong to take me out o' the' grave . . ." (Act III, Scene 7) etc. You can also take the lines that apply only to one certain theme in the play, and create images for each of these lines. You can, for example, accentuate all the lines where Lear speaks about his children. Upon a more in-depth approach toward the work, you will discover that nowhere in the entire tragedy does he put the same meaning into the words "Cordelia", "Regan" and "Goneril" or address his daughters as "you", "thou" etc., with the very same connotation.

Behind these words different images appear in Lear's mind. You, as the actor playing the part of Lear, should evoke these images in your imagination. You will see how these images will fill with great expressiveness the words, phrases and scenes. Another example: in "The Twelfth Night" you can stress all the words connected with the theme of love (all the characters in "The Twelfth Night" are either attracted to somebody or in love with someone). As you find different images for your speech, they will inject freshness and spontaneity, while also contributing to the main theme of the play. And it's not only the important words that you must imagine and refresh in your role – behind every word that "does not turn out well" you can create an image that will make it come alive. "What a cute little nose does your master have", says the Mayor's daughter to Osip (Gogol's *The Inspector General*). How often does the actress stress this line, aiming to make the audience laugh. Wouldn't it be easier to imagine this "cute little nose" and let the image make the line funny, alive and easy?

Rehearse the images you create, day after day – perfect and strengthen them.

Let us go back to the PG.

THE PG GOES BEYOND THE LIMITS OF THE PHYSICAL BODY

Exercise. Start with simple movements: lift up your arm and lower it, stretch it forward, sideways etc. Do these movements avoiding unnecessary physical tension. *Imagine* energy radiating in the direction of the movement.

Then produce the same movement with greater physical strength and in a faster tempo, imagining, as before, the radiating force.

Now do the same movements with the excessive tension. Gradually decrease your muscular tension, at the same time imagining that the physical force is being replaced by the growing mental strength. Get up and sit down, walk around the room, kneel down on your knees, lie down etc., trying to do these movements using only your *inner* strength. After completing the movements outwardly, continue them inwardly.

Produce the PG with different qualities, trying to forget about your physical body and concentrate exclusively upon the inner strength of the gesture. Your radiation will independently assume the qualities of the PG.

Do a simple exercise (clean up the room, set the table, arrange books in your library, water flowers, etc.). Try to perceive the inner strength and radiation connected with the movements.

Again do a series of simple movements, but solely in your imagination. In this case you will be dealing with the pure form of inner strength and radiation. Do a similar exercise with the PG.

Through such exercises you will introduce yourself to the power that is conveyed to the audience from the stage, attracting their interest and attention.

An imaginary space and time

Exercise. Start with simple gestures: lift up your arm in a moderate tempo, while imagining that *a long period of time* is passing. Do the same gesture, accompanying it in your imagination by the notion of *a very short period of time.*

Continue with such simple exercises until you feel that your imagination has gained a certain convincing power.

Do the gesture of opening in a moderate tempo (see drawing 14). Continue it in your imagination for an indefinite period of time, spreading it upon an endless distance. Imagine the same gesture produced instantly within a confined space, while actually doing it in the same moderate tempo.

Do the same with the gesture of closing.

Start with an opened gesture and then close it, contracting a formerly endless space to the size of a tiny dot (see drawing 15). Do this gesture first in a long period of time, then, in a short period of time. The same gesture – first in a long period of time, in a confined space, and by the end quickly, in an endless space.

Discover for yourself several variations with the PG.

Now proceed with simple improvisations. For example, a shy person enters a store. He is choosing and purchasing something he needs. Let the shyness emerge as a result of the space around you *contracting* in your imagination throughout the course of the improvisation. Then, a boorish, overly familiar person enters the store. Try to achieve boorishness by mentally *expanding* the space during the improvisation. Finally, improvise a bored, lazy person before a bookshelf, choosing a book to read. Laziness and boredom come by means of an "expanded time". Repeat the same action, as a very curious person, searching for a particular book, would do. Experience the mentality of a curious person as a result of "contracted time". Outwardly try to keep your improvisations approximately the same length every time. Do the same with the characters from plays and literature.

Notice your "fantastic" experiences of time and space in your everyday life. Observe people you meet, trying to guess how they experience space and time.

Drawing 14

Drawing 15

Chekhov's advice is born of personal practice and experience. As with every natural born actor, he was constantly involved in such observations. In the following passage from his 1927 memoir, *The Path of an Actor*, Chekhov recalls one of the most personal moments of his life: the death of his dearly loved father. With tremendous courage and sincerity, Chekhov goes on to confess that while being present at the death bed and not being able to help, he, nevertheless, could not tear himself away from the "sight of horrible human suffering". What Chekhov takes out of this experience is so much deeper than any kind of "emotional memory", and it serves as a great lesson for every actor.

How wrong we actors can be when it comes to portraying death on stage! We pay too much attention to the physiological processes, which we think, represent the picture of death. It is not an artistic choice, simply because the naturalistic portrayal of physical suffering that occurs just before a person's death cannot be art. We must not torture audiences, suffocating and writhing in the cramp of agony before them. Nothing except pain and disgust can be aroused within the audience through this means. And the more truthful our portrayal of the physical sufferings of a dying man, the further will we deviate from the picture of death, as it should be presented in art. Death on the stage must be portrayed as a slowing down and disappearance of the feeling of *time*. The actor, portraying death, in that moment should design his rhythmical patterns in such a way that the audience, following his acting would feel the slowing down of time and would imperceptibly arrive at a pause, as though the slowed down rhythm stops for a second. This very pause will create the impression of death. At the same time the audience should be free from having to watch vulgar and inartistic means of portraying the physiological processes of a dying man. Of course, for such an artistic task, one needs to master a high level of acting technique. It is important that the actor learns not only to feel time on the stage, but also gain command of that feeling. . . .

The body within the space, and rhythms within the time – those are the means of expression for the actor.

Michael Chekhov calls on the contemporary actor to master concepts of imaginary time and space. For an actor, just becoming aware of these categories, it can bring new depth and complexity to their work on stage. However, it is the trained ability to transform time and space on stage with the power of the actor's imagination, which helps actors to convey the inner life of their characters and gives them true power over their audience. The technique of creating imaginary time and space can be applied directly in rehearsal and performance. It can also be used in the actor's work upon the Psychological Gesture. The PG can gain a completely new meaning for the actor when exercised in conjunction with these two categories. Imagine the space around you as having some definite quality: contracting or expanding, dark or bright, wide or narrow. Perform the Gesture within this imaginary space. Discover certain inner rhythms that belong both to the Gesture and to the space. Imagine that the Gesture transforms the space around you. Create numerous combinations with the PG, imaginary time and imaginary space. Constantly change their qualities, and discover numerous psychological nuances and combinations.

The concept of the PG would not be complete without these two categories. The deep inner connection that exists in between imaginary time, imaginary space and Psychological Gesture should be explored and exercised by every actor interested in mastering the principles of the Michael Chekhov Technique.

Index